Edward Mussey Hartwell

Physical Training in American Colleges And Universities

Edward Mussey Hartwell

Physical Training In American Colleges And Universities

ISBN/EAN: 9783744725101

Printed in Europe, USA, Canada, Australia, Japan

Cover: Foto ©Andreas Hilbeck / pixelio.de

More available books at **www.hansebooks.com**

CIRCULARS OF INFORMATION

OF THE

BUREAU OF EDUCATION.

No. 5–1885.

PHYSICAL TRAINING IN AMERICAN COLLEGES AND UNIVERSITIES.
BY EDWARD MUSSEY HARTWELL, Ph.D., M.D.,
OF JOHNS HOPKINS UNIVERSITY.

WASHINGTON:
GOVERNMENT PRINTING OFFICE.
1886.

CONTENTS.

	PAGE.
Letter of the Commissioner of Education to the Secretary of the Interior	5
Ideals of manly excellence	7
Systems of physical training	9
Introduction of gymnastics into America	21
Condition of physical training in America prior to the introduction of the "new gymnastics"	25
The new gymnastics	26
Opening of the era of building gymnasia in colleges	29
Department of physical training at Amherst College	30
College gymnasia built since 1860	39
Dr. Sargent's developing appliances	44
Number and cost of college gymnasia buildings in the United States	59
Descriptions of the principal gymnasia	68
Young Men's Christian Association gymnasia	87
Architects and furnishers of gymnasia	92
Military drill and discipline a physical training	92
Athletic sports in the United States	106
Concerning play-grounds	112
The Yale system of athletics	115
Professionalism and intercollegiate contests	124
Physical education for scholastic women	132
Instruction in hygiene	135
Concluding remarks and suggestions	152
APPENDIX.	
Physical training in Germany	157

LETTER.

DEPARTMENT OF THE INTERIOR,
BUREAU OF EDUCATION,
Washington, D. C., October 24, 1885.

SIR: In spite of the frequent reference among educators and in educational literature to the fact that all education should aim at producing a sound mind in a healthy body, it is well known that this important truth is too often forgotten by school officers, teachers, and parents. Generally in American rural schools, and too often in our city schools, the conditions requisite to health are ignored. Too frequently schoolhouses are unhealthy in their location, their surroundings, or internal arrangements.

Beyond the instruction in hygiene the main attempts to conserve health in the public schools have consisted in introducing German gymnastics, or in paying a more careful attention to the laws of heating and lighting and the supply of pure air and water. Sometimes the introduction of manual labor has been looked upon as the sure prevention of all disease; athletic sports have been tried; and recently more careful attention has been given to the whole subject, especially in connection with our colleges. The Ling system of gymnastics is received with increasing favor. More and more believe that the best physical training will not aim to make either acrobats or athletes, but to promote health of body and mind. The efforts of Prof. Edward Hitchcock at Amherst College and of Dr. D. A. Sargent at Harvard have been attended with most beneficial results, and serve to greatly increase the care of the health of college students.

The number of gymnasia of merit has greatly increased. Calls for a report upon this new development in physical training have been urgent and frequent. I have therefore employed E. M. Hartwell, M.D., Ph.D., to collect the information accessible and prepare a report upon the subject. His report is contained in the following pages, which are recommended for publication. If our colleges and universities can lead the way in devising and establishing the best hygienic training, their example will soon affect favorably all other grades of instruction.

I have the honor to be, very respectfully, your obedient servant,
JOHN EATON,
Commissioner.

The Hon. SECRETARY OF THE INTERIOR.

Publication authorized.

H. L. MULDROW,
Acting Secretary.

PHYSICAL TRAINING IN AMERICAN COLLEGES AND UNIVERSITIES.

IDEALS OF MANLY EXCELLENCE.

Philosophical speculations regarding the nature and future of man's body and soul underlie and determine all our schemes and endeavors for the nurture and training of youth. There appear to be four principal ideals of manly excellence, which, singly or in combination, have dominated the minds of the promoters and governors of educational foundations, and in accordance with which physical training has been favored, tolerated, neglected, or contemned. We may characterize these ideals broadly as the Greek or æsthetic, the monkish or ascetic, the military or knightly, and the medical or scientific.

The first three have been influential in varying degrees from very early times. The fourth, although compounded of ancient elements, is so strongly tinged with utilitarian and psycho-physical ideas that it is best described as modern. All of these ideals are traceable to conceptions of human nature and destiny which may be roughly classed under the two heads of lugubrious and cheerful.

THE GREEK IDEAL.

The Greek ideal, it is needless to say, was not lugubrious. "Everything that is good," says Plato in the "Timæus," "is fair, and the fair is not without measure, and the animal who is fair may be supposed to have measure. Now we perceive lesser symmetries and comprehend them, but about the highest and greatest we have no understanding; for there is no symmetry greater than that of the soul to the body. This, however, we do not perceive, nor do we allow ourselves to reflect that when a weaker or lesser frame is the vehicle of a great and mighty soul, or, conversely, when a little soul is encased in a large body, then the whole animal is not fair, for it is defective in the most important of all symmetries; but the fair mind in the fair body will be the fairest and loveliest of all sights to him who has the seeing eye."

Well might Charles Kingsley say of the Greeks, "To produce health, that is, harmony and sympathy and grace, in every faculty of mind and body, was their notion of education."

The antithesis between the Greek and the ascetic ideals is clearly indicated in a remark of Apuleius concerning Egyptian and Greek modes of worship. "The Egyptian deities," he says, "were chiefly honored by lamentations, and the Greek divinities by dances."

THE MONKISH IDEAL.

The ideal of the monk, which, after the first few centuries of the Christian Church, exercised such a profound influence upon European thought and life, was of Asiatic and, to a considerable extent, of Egyptian origin. "The duty of a monk," said St. Jerome, "is not to teach, but to weep." Weeping and self-torture might well absorb the energies of men who conceived that all flesh was the creation of Satan, and championed the belief that soul and body are independent and mutually antagonistic entities.

When it was held that "the greatest of all evils was pleasure, because by it the soul is nailed or riveted to the body," and that mental and spiritual health were best subserved by bodily weakness, we cannot wonder that "a hideous, sordid, and emaciated maniac," to borrow the words of Lecky, "without knowledge, without patriotism, without natural affection, passing his life in a long routine of useless and atrocious self-torture, and quailing before the ghastly phantoms of his delirious brain, became the ideal of the nations which had known the writings of Plato and Cicero and the lives of Socrates and Cato."

Such views as these, although they were treated as heretical by the earlier Fathers of the Christian Church, became accepted dogmas of the Church of Rome in the Middle Ages; and one may hear similar doctrines far from faintly echoed, if he will attend to the sermons of many of the Scotch, English, and American divines who have within the last three centuries striven to establish or perpetuate religious terrorism.

THE MILITARY IDEAL.

The military ideal of manliness, now existing side by side with the monkish ideal, now confronting and challenging it, has played a most important and conspicuous part in the education of the sons of noblemen and of gentlefolk. Herodotus tells us that the sons of the Persians, from their fifth year to their twentieth, were carefully taught three things only,—to ride, to draw the bow, and to speak the truth. Physical training was predominant in the education of free-born youth among the Spartans, Romans, and ancient Germans: it consisted chiefly of martial exercises and the chase, and its aim was the formation of an agile and enduring soldiery. "Plaienge att weapons" formed a necessary part of every gentleman's education in Britain as well as on the Continent, even later than the sixteenth century.

"I swear I'd rather that my son should hang than learn letters. For it becomes the sons of gentlemen to blow a horn nicely, to hunt skillfully, and elegantly carry and train a hawk. But the study of letters should be left to the sons of rustics." These are the words of an English gentleman, of the time of Henry VIII, who, on hearing letters praised, " was roused to sudden anger and burst out furiously."

The ideal of the Greeks sprang from a passion for beauty and harmony, and a joyous sense of well-being; that of the theologian and the monk was conditioned on and determined by a profound ignorance of, and a bitter contempt for, the body; while that of the soldier and the knight owed its peculiar features to a rude appreciation of bodily force and skill, gained from experience in camp and field.

THE MODERN IDEAL.

It is not to the generative vigor of any or all of these ideals that we owe our modern doctrine of the interdependence of body and mind; which doctrine is but vaguely, if at all, apprehended by the majority of those who quote with generous unction the time-worn *mens sana in corpore sano* line of Juvenal, who exhorts men not only to "pray for a healthy mind in a healthy body," but also to "ask for a brave soul unscared by death." No: the belief " that to work the mind is also to work a number of the bodily organs; that not a feeling can arise, not a thought pass, without a set of concurring bodily processes," is the child of the scientific spirit embodied in the new physiology and the new psychology, and was engendered, as we know, through the labors of Harvey and Haller, Du Bois-Reymond, Müller, and Weber, Helmholtz and Wundt.

Mr. Huxley, it may be fairly said, voices the views of a large and increasing number of scientific thinkers when he says:

That man, I think, has had a liberal education who has been so trained in youth that his body is the ready servant of his will, and does with ease and pleasure all the work it is capable of; whose intellect is a clear, cold logic engine, with all its parts of equal strength and in smooth working order, ready, like a steam-engine, to be turned to any work, and spin the gossamers as well as forge the anchors of the mind; whose mind is stored with a knowledge of the great and fundamental truths of Nature and of the laws of her operations; one who, no stunted ascetic, is full of life and fire, but whose passions are trained to come to heel by a vigorous will, the servant of a tender conscience; who has learned to love all beauty, whether of nature or of art, to hate all vileness, and to respect others as himself.

SYSTEMS OF PHYSICAL TRAINING.

It would be interesting, did the scope and limits of this paper permit it, to discuss fully and in detail the means adopted, at different times and in various countries, to realize the ideals of which we have spoken. Some statements of a suggestive rather than of a descriptive nature must suffice.

THE GREEK SYSTEM.

In Guhl and Koner's "The Life of the Greeks and Romans" we find the gymnasia mentioned first among the public buildings of Greece because they were "center-points of Greek life." The authors go on to say:

Games and competitions in various kinds of bodily skill formed a chief feature of their religions festivals. This circumstance reacted on both sculpture and architecture, in supplying the former with models of ideal beauty, and in setting the task to the latter of providing suitable places for these games to be celebrated.

THE PALÆSTRA.

For purposes of this kind, as far as public exhibition was not concerned, the palæstræ and gymnasia served. In earlier times these two must be distinguished. In the palæstra young men practiced wrestling and boxing. As these arts were gradually developed, larger establishments, with separate compartments, became necessary. Originally such places were kept by private persons; sometimes they consisted only of open spaces, near a brook, if possible, and surrounded by trees.

THE GYMNASIUM.

Soon, however, regular buildings, gymnasia, became necessary. At first they consisted of an uncovered court surrounded by colonnades, adjoining which lay covered spaces, the former being used for running and jumping, the latter for wrestling. In the same degree as these exercises became more developed and as grown-up men began to take an interest in these youthful sports, these institutions grew in size and splendor.

Minute descriptions of these establishments by Greek authors we do not possess, but the important parts are known to us from occasional remarks, particularly in the Platonic dialogues. There we find mentioned the *ephebeion*, where the youth used to practice; further, the bath, to which belonged a dry sweating bath for the use of both wrestlers and visitors. The *apoduterion* was the room for undressing. In another room, the *elaiothesion*, the oil was kept for rubbing the wrestlers, and there possibly this rubbing itself took place. In the *konisterion* the wrestlers were sprinkled with sand, so as to give them a firmer hold on each other. The *sphairisterion* was destined for games of ball, while other passages, open or covered (collectively called *dromos*), were used for practice in running, or simply for walking. A particular kind of covered passage were the *xustoi*, which had raised platforms on both sides for the walkers, the lower space between being used by the wrestlers.

Among the Doric tribes, but chiefly in Sparta, physical education consisted principally in hardening the body of the young citizen-warrior against the influence of pain and exertion; among the Ionian tribes, and chiefly at Athens, the harmonious development of body and soul, *i. e.*, grace and ease of bearing and demeanor, were the objects chiefly aimed at. At Athens the gymnasia were public institutions, supported by public or private means, at which *epheboi* (youths old enough for military service) and men spent a part of their day in athletic exercise and in instructive and social intercourse. These were the *Lukeion*, the *Kunosarges*, the *Akademia*, the *Ptolemaion*, the splendid gymnasium of Hadrianus, and the small gymnasium of Hermes. The number of palæstræ at Athens was still greater. They were all private institutes kept by single *paidotribai*, and destined for the athletic education of boys only. In smaller cities the joint practice of youths and grown-up men in the same locality was frequently inevitable. But it is erroneous to suppose that the palæstra was exclusively the resort of the *athletai*. The separation of youths and men from the boys was desirable, both for moral and educational reasons; for the difficulties of the task increased in proportion to the age of the aspirant.

THE GAMES.

Before entering upon the single exercises we must try to define the three general appellations, *gymnastic, agonistic,* and *athletic.* The first term comprises all kinds of regulated bodily exercise for the purpose of strengthening the body or single limbs. The *agonistic* comprises the gymnastic exercises tending to prepare the *athletai* for the wrestling matches, which formed an important feature of the national festivities, particularly of the games of Olympia. Here assembled, invited by the peace messengers of Zeus, the delegates of empires and cities, not to speak of crowds of enthusiastic spectators from the most distant shores. The flower of Greek youth came up to test their skill in the noble competition for the crown of Zeus. Only he whose untainted character and pure Hellenic descent had been certified was allowed to approach the silver urn which contained the lots. A previous training of at least ten months at a Greek gymnasium was further required for obtaining the permission of taking part in the holy contest.

The ethic purpose of gymnastic art came to be more neglected, when artificiality and affectation began to prevail. It was then that the noble art deteriorated into a mechanical profession; the *athletic* is the later signification of the term.

THE TEACHERS.

The teachers of gymnastics among the Athenians were known as *gumnastai* and *paidotribai;* the former having to superintend the general development and training of the body, while the latter directed the single exercises. The *sophronistai* were responsible for the good behavior of the boys. The whole gymnasium and all its teachers were under the charge of a superintendent, termed the *gumnasiarchos.* His position was highly honorable and responsible. The principal exercises taught in the palæstra and the gymnasium were running, leaping, wrestling, throwing the discus, throwing the spear, boxing, and the *pagkration*, a combination of boxing and wrestling. Various ball games were also in vogue, and much attention was given to bathing.

It resulted from the best Greek training that Sparta needed no walls of defense save the bodies of her sons, and that Athens furnished models of manly vigor and beauty which have been alike the admiration and despair of sculptors since the days of Phidias.

SYSTEMS OF THE MIDDLE AGES.

In comparison with the comprehensive and well directed methods of the Greeks, the means employed for the bodily training of the would-be priest or soldier seem crude and primitive in the extreme. In the better days of monachism it was held that a laboring monk had but one devil to fear, while one who had idle hands must needs contend against a legion. Accordingly labor in the field, the garden, and the vineyard became a well recognized factor in the course of training laid down for many of the religious orders, and especially of the Benedictines, the champions and saviors of classical learning in the west. Although the ghostly enemies of the young gentleman, or noble, were far from being ignored, yet his training was mainly directed toward rendering him fit to encounter savage beasts and men-at-arms. The exercises and pastimes of the tilt-yard, the village-green, and the bear-pit, differed widely indeed from the exercises of the palæstra, the gymnasium, and the stadium, though not so widely as from the feats achieved by scholastic and religious youth with mattock, spade, and pruning-hook.

BRITISH USAGES.

In view of the kinship of American and British schools and scholars, our purpose will be best served if, in the present connection, we confine our attention chiefly to British usages as regards scholastic and knightly training in mediæval and early modern times.

MEDIÆVAL STUDENT-LIFE.

Asceticism [says Mullinger, the historian of the University of Cambridge, in his chapter on mediæval student-life], as it was then the professed rule of life with the monk, the friar, and the secular, was also the prevailing theory in the discipline of those whom they taught and trained for their several professions. The man fasted, voluntarily bared his back to the scourge, kept long and painful vigils; the boy was starved, flogged, and sent to seek repose where he might find it if he were able. * * * Lever, the master of St. John's, in an oft-quoted passage, describes the scholars of his college, then (in 1550) the poorest in proportion to its number in the whole University, as going to dinner at ten o'clock, content with a penny piece of beef, among four, having a little "porage" made of the broth of the same beef, with salt and oatmeal, "and nothing else." After this slender dinner, he continues, "they be either teaching or learning until five of the clock in the evening, when they have a supper not much better than their dinner. Immediately after the which they go either to reasoning in problems or unto some other study, until it be nine or ten of the clock, and then, being without fire, are fain to walk or run up and down half an hour to get a heat in their feet when they go to bed."

SPORTS AND PASTIMES.

Of the sports and pastimes of those days we have little record; but we know the use of the cross-bow to have been a favorite accomplishment; cock-fighting, that "last infirmity" of the good Ascham, was also a common amusement; while, from certain college statutes requiring that "no fierce birds" should be introduced within the precincts of the college, we may infer that many of the students were emulous of the falconer's art. It is not uninteresting to note that a custom of the present day, the daily walk with a single companion, was originally inculcated by college statute, while this in turn is said to have derived its precedent from apostolic example.

The statute referred to, dates from the year 1336, which was a little more than sixty years before the founding of Winchester College by William of Wykeham, who strenuously and particularly forbade—in the statutes which he drew up for the government of his scholars—pretty much every kind of sport, whether it were gentlemanly or loutish.

TRAINING UNDER HENRY VIII.

From the letters of young Gregory Cromwell's tutor to his pupil's father, the Earl of Essex and the King's chief secretary, we derive some insight as to the education of a young nobleman of the time of Henry VIII, at which time it was said that "gentlemen strive more to bring up good hounds than wise heirs." It appears from the letters alluded to that young Cromwell had " hours limited for the French tongue, writing, playing at weapons, casting of accounts, pastimes of instruments," and that for his recreation he used "to hawk and hunt and shoot in his long bow."

Henry VIII strove to foster the practice of martial exercises throughout the realm. We are told of his " continuing daily to amuse himself in archery, casting of the bar, wrestling, or dancing, and frequently in tilting, tourneying, fighting at the barriers with swords and battle-axes, and such like martial recreations, in most of which there were very few who could excel him."

LAWS REGARDING ARCHERY.

He caused Parliament to enact, in 1511, that " every man being the King's subject, not lame, decrepit, or maimed; being within the age of sixty years, except spiritual men, justices of the one bench and of the other, justices of the assize, and barons of the exchequer, do use and exercise shooting in long bows, and also do have a bow and arrows ready continually in his house, to use himself in shooting; and that every man having a man child or men children in his house shall provide for all such, being of the age of seven years and above, a bow and two shafts, to learn them and bring them up in shooting." Each village was, in 1541, required to maintain a pair of archery butts. It would seem that this statute was held to apply to school-boys and collegians; for, while it is provided in the ordinances of Shrewsbury school, made by the authorities of the town in 1578, that the " schollers shall plaie upon thursdaies ones there be a holidaye in the weeke and no day els but the thursdaie," it is prescribed that the " schollers plaie shal be shootinge in the long bowe and chesse plaie and no other games except it be runninge, wrastlinge, or leapinge." It is also noteworthy that certain playgrounds, at Eton and Harrow respectively, are still termed " The Shooting Fields " and " The Butts."

It is not safe, however, to infer from enactments like the above that systematic physical training, even in the single particular of archery, was ever generally enforced in English schools and colleges. System and compulsion in such matters have ever been contemned both by teachers and pupils.

Roger Ascham, in his "Toxophilus, the Schole of Shootinge," published in 1545, declares that "if shooting could speak, she would accuse England of unkindness and slothfulness," and further states that " very many play with the King's acts, * * * many buy bows, because of the act, but yet shoot not."

VIEWS OF CARDINAL POLE.

Very few men in England, during the middle third of the sixteenth century, were so well qualified to set forth and criticise the educational methods of his time as Reginald Pole, legate under Pope Paul III, archbishop of Canterbury in the time of Queen Mary, and chancellor both of Oxford and Cambridge. Pole, who had been educated at the Universities of Oxford, Paris, and Padua, and was on familiar terms with the most renowned scholars of his day, was a man of eminent ability and great independence of character. There can be little doubt that in "England in the Reign of Henry VIII. A Dialogue between Cardinal Pole and Thomas Lupset, Lecturer in Rhetoric in Oxford. By Thomas Starkey, Chaplain to the King," the opinions of Pole regarding the educational needs of England are set forth with substantial accuracy.

Pole favors the opinion of those who say that "the weal of man resteth not only in the mind and the virtues thereof, but in the body also, and in the prosperous state of the same," as being "very truth."

"First and most principal of all ill customs used in our country is that which toucheth the education of the nobility," says Pole, " whom we see customably brought up in hunting and hawking, dicing and carding, eating and drinking, and in all vain pleasure, pastime, and vanity." Pole is equally severe on the education of the "men of the church," who he declares "are not brought up in virtue and learning, as they should be, nor well approved therein before they be admitted to such high dignity, * * * for commonly you shall find that they can nothing do but patter up their matins and mass, mumbling up a certain number of words nothing understood."

ON COMPULSORY EDUCATION OF THE NOBILITY.

Pole distinctly favors compulsory education and public schools, in order to remedy the "ill customs" noted above, as may be seen from the following quotation:

But here is, Master Lupset, not only in our country, but also in all other which ever yet I knew, a great lack and negligence of them which rule in common policy, and that is this: that in no country there is any regard of the bringing up of the youth in common discipline and public exercise. But every man privately in his own house hath his master to instruct his children in letters, without any respect of other exercise in other feats pertaining to nobility no less than learning and letters, as in all feats of chivalry. Therefore there would some ordinance be devised for the joining of these both together, which might be done after this manner, likewise as we have in our universities, colleges, and common places to nourish the children of poor men in letters; whereby, as you see, cometh no small profit to the common weal.

So much more we should have, as it were, certain places appointed for the bringing up together of the nobility, to the which I would the nobles should be compelled to set forward their children and heirs, that in a number together they might the better profit. And to this company I would have appointed rulers certain of the most virtuous and wise men of the realm, the which should instruct this youth to whom should come the governance after, of this our common weal. Here they should be instruct, not only in learning and virtue, but also in all feats of war pertaining to such as should be hereafter in time of war captains and governors of the common sort. This should be the most noble institution that ever was yet devised in any common weal. Of this should spring the fountain of all civility and politic rule; yea, and without such a thing I can not tell whether all the rest of our device will little avail. I think it will never be possible to institute our common weal without this ordinance brought to pass and put into effect.

Pole's ideas, we need hardly say, were too novel and theoretical to be adopted in his day; and it would be extremely difficult to realize them in England even in our day. Milton and Bacon, Fuller and Locke, and Herbert Spencer, have all argued in favor of physical training, in a strain more or less similar to that of Pole. But the realization of their generous theories has never been widely and systematically undertaken by the teachers of British youth.

Athletic sports, such as boating, cricket, and foot-ball, have come to be highly prized and lauded. We are far from denying their great educational value, but it is clear that they owe their essential features chiefly to the beliefs and customs of that most uncritical and prejudiced class of conservatives, the British undergraduate, rather than to the schemes and endeavors of innovating thinkers and reformers. It is equally clear that innovators and dreamers have been largely influential in quickening and determining the development of modern methods, both of physical and mental training, on the Continent of Europe. As we shall have occasion to point out further on, physical training in America owes more to German than to British models.

AMERICAN IDEAS AND CUSTOMS.

When we recall the fact that our oldest American colleges, like their early English models, were established primarily to recruit with learned men the ranks of the clergy, there is left no ground for wonder that physical training has so slowly won its way to recognition as a necessary part of a sound education. American educators were long ruled by British notions as to curriculum and discipline; the American public was mainly animated by narrowly "practical" and utilitarian ideals; and American collegians, who were not too serious to play at all, disported themselves after inherited British fashions in their intervals of study.

HARVARD AND DARTMOUTH CUSTOMS.

The means afforded students for recreation a hundred and fifty years ago were decidedly scanty, if we may judge from the only mention of them in the "Ancient Customs of Harvard College, Established by the Government of It." "Custom 16" runs as follows: "The Freshmen shall furnish bats, balls, and foot-balls for the use of students, to be kept in the buttery." Dartmouth College, in New Hampshire, was founded in 1769. In a statement made two years later by its first president, Rev. Dr. Wheelock, concerning its aims and methods, we find a recommendation, on which the changes were rung by college officers and trustees for more than fifty years in the east, and whose echoes are still ringing in the west. President Wheelock recommended the students to "turn the course of their diversions and exercises for their health to the practice of some manual arts, or cultivation of gardens and other lands, at the proper hours of leisure and intermissions from study and vacancies [vacations]".

VIEWS OF DR. RUSH.

Dr. Benjamin Rush, of Philadelphia, who was a signer of the Declaration of Independence, was long the foremost teacher in the foremost American medical college of his day, that of the University of Pennsylvania. Dr. Oliver Wendell Holmes inclines to believe that Dr. Rush not only gave direction to the medical mind of the country more than any other one man, but that he "typifies it better than any other." Dr. Rush urged his students "to turn nature out of doors and appeal to art," and published abroad his belief that "the time must and would come when the general use of calomel, jalap, and the lancet should be considered among the most essential articles of knowledge and the rights of man." One has but to turn to Dr. Rush's "Essays, Literary, Moral, and Philosophical", to find that his notions as to artificial and heroic practice were not confined to medical matters. Among these essays is one published in 1790, on the "Amusements and Punishments Proper for Schools." Dr. Rush voiced the prevailing sentiment of his time, and of many of our time as well, in proposing that "the amusements of our youth shall consist of such exercises as will be most subservient to their future employments in life." He favors agricultural and mechanical employments as means of diversion and training, and notes with approval that "in the Methodist College, in Maryland, a large lot is divided between the scholars, and premiums adjudged to those who produce the most vegetables from their grounds, or who keep them in the best order." "The Methodists," he adds, "have wisely banished every species of play from their college." Again he says:

All the amusements of the children of the Moravians at Bethlehem, Penn., are derived from their performing the subordinate parts of several of the mechanical arts; and a considerable portion of the wealth of that worthy and happy society is the product of the labor of their little hands.

MANUAL LABOR SCHOOLS AND TRAINING.

It was in accordance with such notions as those of President Wheelock and Dr. Rush that farm, manual labor, and Fellenberg schools were founded, and societies for promoting manual labor in literary institutions were organized somewhat extensively in the United States during the first third of the present century.

In South Carolina.

The first of these farm-schools was that established in 1797 at Lethe, in Abbeville District, S. C., in accordance with the terms of the will of Dr. John de la Howe, a native of Hanover, in Germany, who left the bulk of his estate, comprising a farm of 500 acres and 1,000 acres of forest, for the educating, boarding, and clothing of twelve poor boys and twelve poor girls of Abbeville District. The school did not go into actual operation till twenty years later.

In Massachusetts.

When Amherst College was founded at Amherst, Mass., in 1821, it possessed at the start "an advantage over all other colleges," according to the Boston *Recorder* published in September of that year, which notes the purchase of "a large field for the express purpose of affording each charity student an opportunity of cultivating a quarter or half acre in that manner which his taste and judgment should dictate." While preparing this paper we have been assured that "ecclesiastical students find plenty of recreation and amusement, either walking, working in flower gardens, or riding."

Tyler's "History of Amherst College" states that "all the earlier terraces on College Hill were the work of the officers and students of Amherst College. And every spring, for many years, the students were in the habit of devoting one day to raking off the chips and clearing up the grounds." "Chip-day" at Amherst, it is to be remembered, was probably imported from Williams College, whence came Amherst's first president and students. At Williams College, years before and for years after the foundation of Amherst, the students had, in addition to a "chip-day," a "mountain-day" and a "gravel-day," the former being devoted to tramping, and the latter to regraveling the college walks. The Faculty granted these holidays for the purpose of "fostering in the students the habits of physical labor and exercise so essential to vigorous mental exertion."

GERMAN CUSTOMS AND THEIR INFLUENCE.

Prior to 1825, physical training, in its proper sense, had no recognition or standing in the curriculum of school or college, if we except the United States Military Academy at West Point, and one or two institutions modeled on it. The germ of such physical training as exists at present in many of our colleges came from abroad, and was planted by German exiles in New England soil.

Among the ancient Germans, bodily exercises were generally and strenuously cultivated for the sake of training men for war, the chase, and the sacred games. In the Middle Ages, bodily training was restricted to military gymnastics, and these were largely monopolized by the feudal aristocracy, none but knights being allowed to take part in the tournaments, whose origin is attributed to the German King, Henry I. The opposition of the Church and the introduction of firearms finally brought about the downfall of the chivalric games.

VIEWS OF THE REFORMERS.

Although the reformers, Luther, Melancthon, and Zwingli, urged the revival of gymnastics as a part of the education of all classes of youth, it was not until the last decades of the last century that any considerable attempt was made to systematize and enforce gymnastic training in Germany.

THE PHILANTHROPISTS.

The philanthropists, who, as regards the physical side of education, were the precursors of Jahn, the father of German Turning, made such an attempt in the reformed courses of instruction, by means of which they strove to supplant the "old education" and follow "the method of nature." Basedow, Campe, Salzmann, Guts Muths, Pestalozzi, and Fellenberg, all gave physical training a prominent place in the schools which they instituted or controlled. In so doing, however, they were only following, and that for the most part consciously, the suggestions contained in Rousseau's Émile, which was published in 1762, and contained much that seems but an echo from the essays of Montaigne, "On the Education of Children" and "On Pedantry," which appeared some eighty years before the Émile. Rousseau's main thesis is found in his claim that his "system is nature's course of development," and that "the great secret of education is to manage it so that the training of the mind and body shall serve to assist each other."

BASEDOW AND THE PHILANTHROPINUM.

Basedow, who was born at Hamburg in 1723 and was by nature an innovator, first attracted attention by his controversial writings on theological subjects. He was incited to devote himself to educational reforms by reading Émile, which a recent writer characterizes as "perhaps the most influential book ever written on the subject of education." In 1774, Basedow founded at Dessau his famous school, the Philanthropinum, "in which," says Von Raumer, "the views of Rousseau were strictly followed, and where these views were by every means sought to be introduced into actual life." Basedow's division of the day was as follows: eight hours for sleep; eight hours for food and amusement; and, for the children of the rich, six hours for school work and two for manual labor, while the children of the poor were to have two hours of school work and six of manual labor. His pupils in the Philanthropinum were taught wrestling, running, riding, dancing, besides carpentry and wood-turning, and were regularly taken on long walks into the country. They were also instructed as to the structure and functions of the human body by the private physician of Prince Dietrich, Basedow's patron. With Basedow philanthropy was indeed a passion to the last. With his dying breath he said, "I wish my body to be dissected for the good of my fellow-creatures."

It is noteworthy that Basedow and his immediate disciples and imitators employed both gymnastic and industrial exercises in their efforts to secure physical training to their pupils.

Fellenberg, at his schools in Hofwyl, near Berne, in Switzerland, added military drill to instruction in gymnastics and handicrafts.

GUTS MUTHS.

The influence of the Greek ideal is clearly traceable in the writings of Montaigne, Rousseau, Basedow, Guts Muths, and Jahn. "In the year 1785," says Guts Muths, "I entered, when still a youth, the school of Schnepfenthal, near Gotha, and thereupon Salzmann, its head, conducted me to a place saying, 'Here are our gymnastics; within this little space we amuse ourselves daily with five exercises, though they are still only in their rudiments.' These exercises had been first tried at Dessau where Salzmann had previously been. He soon intrusted me with the direction of this first beginning of exercises. All that I found out from ancient usages, from the historical remains of earlier and later antiquity, all that reflection and sometimes chance offered to me, was brought forward for the sake of amusing experiments. Thus the chief exercises increased, were subdivided into new forms and tasks, and were subjected to rules often laid down with great difficulty. Thus originated, after seven years' experiments, in the first edition of my 'Gymnastics for the Young' (1793), my first attempt to call attention to a subject that had been quite forgotten and only existed in history." Under Rector Vieth, at Dessau, gymnastics gained great popularity during the very time that Guts Muths was experimenting at Schnepfenthal. Guts Muths' efforts met with hearty recognition in Germany. Nachtigall in Denmark, and Ling in Sweden, made systematic gymnastics popular and general among their countrymen. To Ling was due the development of the system of medical gymnastics known as the Swedish Movement Cure, and also a system of general bodily training still much prized in Sweden and Norway.

JAHN AND THE TURNERS.

The extraordinary progress made by gymnastics in Germany during the first quarter of the present century was mainly due to the quickening and organizing genius of Friedrich Ludwig Jahn, known to all German Turners as "Father Jahn." "His idea," says Schaible in his "Essay on the Systematic Training of the Body,"

was to unite the people of Germany into one nation, intellectually, morally, and physically strong against the threatening enemy of the west. Boldly and vigorously, a real reformer, he advanced toward his high ideal, the realization of which was attained with a surprising rapidity, notwithstanding the many impediments that stood in his way. The number of his pupils increased daily. His ideas of a revived national education were in this work ["Deutsche Turnkunst"] offered to the nation, and were enthusiastically received. Soon gymnastics took a national character. Boys, youths, and men of all classes of society took part in the exercises, and gymnasia sprang up in all parts. Nor was it long before from their gymnasia [in 1813] thousands of Turners of all ages rushed forth on a given signal as volunteers to the unfurled standard of their Fatherland, to prove, in a deadly struggle for freedom and country, the strength and self-reliance which they had acquired in the gymnasium.

After the German war of independence the effect of gymnastic training was fully recognized. On their return from the battle-fields the gymnasts went again to their work with vigorous zeal. Gymnastics had gained a considerable importance through the valor and endurance shown by the Turners during the war. Gymnasia were established throughout Germany, from the primary school to the university [sic].

In the troublous times that followed the war of independence, Jahn and the Turners were denounced as liberals and enemies to the state, and in 1819 the gymnasia throughout Prussia, and in all Germany with the exception of Würtemberg, were closed. Jahn was thrown into prison and kept there until 1825. He lived to see gymnastics introduced into the schools in 1842, and Turners' societies flourishing all over Germany. He died in 1852 at the age of seventy-four.

Gymnastics for the sake of securing a symmetrical development of the bodily powers were not introduced into America before 1825. Military drill was up to that time employed in only a few institutions, and in them mostly for professional purposes. Educators in the United States, so far as they made any effort to provide for physical training, did so mainly with the view of providing an outlet for what were then termed "animal spirits," or for the purpose of decreasing the cost of an education by such means as had been advocated by President Wheelock and Dr. Rush.

FELLENBERG AND THE HOFWYL SCHOOLS.

The attempts of Pestalozzi and Fellenberg to unite industrial and intellectual training excited much more interest than did their efforts to bring about the harmonious development of every human faculty.

Pestalozzi's attempts at Neuhof, Stanz, and Yverdun, in the period from 1780 to 1809, were practical failures. What he was unable to accomplish was largely realized by Fellenberg and his successors at his schools in Hofwyl, near Berne, in the years 1807–'48. The Hofwyl establishment, to which Fellenberg devoted his time and fortune, included the literary institution, which dated from 1807, the agricultural or poor school, begun in 1808, the normal school, established a little later, and the intermediate or practical institution, which was started in 1827. Fellenberg's ideas on physical education are of especial interest, since they are so much more liberal and enlightened than those of the majority of his American imitators. The Hofwyl schools were organized and managed in accordance with the ideas expressed in the following extract from Fellenberg's writings:

Pure air, a suitable diet, regular exercise and repose, and a proper distribution of time, are the principal means of physical education. It is as essential that a pupil leave his studies during the time appropriated to relaxation, as that he study during the hours devoted to that purpose. Voluntary exercise is to be encouraged by providing suitable games, by affording opportunities for gardening, and by excursions and bathing. Regular gymnastic exercises should be insisted on as a means of developing the body; a healthy action of the bodily frame has an important influence on both mind and morals. Music is to be considered as a branch of physical education having powerful moral influences. The succession of study, labor, musical instruction, and play, should be carefully attended to. The hours of sleep should be regulated by the age of the pupil.

At Hofwyl the gymnasium was a high-ceiled room, 100 feet long and 50 feet wide, with a floor of earth. It was well furnished with apparatus. Besides fencing and dancing, military drill was taught. Riding-horses, saddlery and carpentry shops, gardens, and a swimming pool, were provided for the scholars' use.

INTRODUCTION OF GYMNASTICS INTO AMERICA.

FELLENBERG SCHOOLS IN AMERICA.

Fellenberg's demonstration of the fact that "a poor boy, taken in his ninth year and staying till his eighteenth year was completed, paid by his labor during the last half for the expenses of maintaining him over his earnings during the first half," seems to have made a deep impression on "practical educators" in the United States sixty years ago. In Volume XV of *Barnard's Journal of Education* the following statement occurs:

The Gardiner Lyceum in Maine was established in 1823, for instruction in the scientific principles of mechanics and agriculture, and in 1824 a Fellenberg school was opened at Windsor, Conn., by Messrs. Stebbins & Sill. But the desire to afford means by which poor students might defray the expenses of their education while at the same time pursuing their studies, was more influential than any other motive in the introduction of the manual labor system. The first institution founded upon this system was the Maine Wesleyan Seminary, planned in 1820 by Elihu Robinson of Augusta, Me., and put into operation in the spring of 1825. The Oneida Institute of Science and Industry was founded at Whitesboro', N. Y., in 1825-'26, and became one of the most successful manual labor schools in the country. In 1826 was also formed the Andover Mechanical Association at Andover Theological Seminary, Massachusetts, solely for the purpose of invigorating and preserving health, without any reference to pecuniary profit; but the success of the system of mechanical labor instituted by them made it a model which was followed in many similar institutions. Theological seminaries, colleges, and minor schools, in almost every State of the Union, were established with manual labor as an essential principle in their constitution.

In 1831 the Society for Promoting Manual Labor in Literary Institutions was formed in New York City, "for the purpose of collecting and diffusing information calculated to promote the establishment and prosperity of manual labor schools and seminaries in the United States, and for introducing the system of manual labor into institutions now established, without diminishing the standard of literary and scientific attainment." Theodore D. Weld was the general agent of the society, of which Zecariah Lewis was president. Mr. Weld made a report based on an extended tour among the "leading literary institutions in Ohio, Indiana, Illinois, Kentucky, Missouri, Tennessee, and Alabama." After his report was published the society ceased to labor for the accomplishment of its objects. The manual labor of which the mass of college students are capable is far too rude to afford profitable educational or pecuniary results, and far too onerous to be attractive for its gamesomeness. Students so poverty-stricken as to resort to the menial drudgery of scullions and waiters and field-hands may be commended for their pluck and assiduity, but it is time that a protest was entered against such practices except in cases of the direst necessity. The spectacle of college students seeking tips and drink-money is not a pleasant one.

THE FIRST GYMNASIA IN AMERICA.

The first gymnasia in this country were erected out of doors, in bald imitation of Græco-German models. It is possible that as early as 1821 the Latin School at Salem, Mass., had some sort of a gymnasium, without instructors being provided for its users; but it seems clear that the Round Hill School, established at Northampton, Mass., in 1823, for the liberal education of boys, by Messrs. George Bancroft and Joseph Green Cogswell, was the first institution in this country to make gymnastic exercise a part of the regular course of instruction. This was done in 1825, when the Round Hill Gymnasium was erected under the supervision of Dr. Charles Beck, who had been a pupil and friend of Father Jahn, in Germany.

GYMNASTICS AT ROUND HILL SCHOOL IN 1825.

I am greatly indebted to the venerable Dr. George C. Shattuck, of Boston, who was a pupil at Round Hill, for the following account of the physical training pursued there:

> Dr. Beck, the teacher of Latin, afterward the professor of Latin in Harvard University, was the teacher of gymnastics. A large piece of ground was devoted to the purpose and furnished with all the apparatus used in the German gymnasia. The whole school was divided into classes, and each class had an hour three times a week for instruction by Dr. Beck. At the same time there were a dozen riding horses and classes for riding three times a week. Gardens were assigned the boys, in which they raised plants and vegetables. A piece of land was set apart for building huts. Baseball, hockey, and foot-ball were the games. I remember playing in a match game at the time of the Presidential election in which Adams and Jackson were candidates. The Jackson boys beat. You notice how much was done for physical training. I remember Mr. Edward Everett speaking at an annual exhibition and telling us how much better a school, how much greater advantages we enjoyed than Mr. Cogswell and himself had at Exeter. Though the school had only an existence of twenty years or less, and failed from want of pecuniary support, I believe that its influence has survived, and a great stimulus was given by it to the cause of education. Developing the bodily powers and strengthening the constitution were there first recognized as of great importance in the education of boys. The boys were very healthy. I only recall one death, from typhoid fever.

In 1828 Dr. Beck published at Northampton a translation of Jahn's "Deutsche Turnkunst". Jahn's enthusiastic idealizing spirit seems to have been caught by his pupil, for Dr. Beck, in his preface, alludes to the advantages to be "derived by a republic from gymnastick exercises, uniting in one occupation all the different classes of the people, and thus forming a new tie for those who, for the most part, are widely separated by their different education and pursuits of life." In the republic of letters Dr. Beck did, indeed, as a professor of Latin, exert a genuine influence; but gymnastics have as yet achieved very little in the way of shaping the affairs of the American Republic, at least in the direction indicated in the preface above cited.

The Round Hill School, in other features than those instanced in Dr. Shattuck's letter, reminds one of Fellenberg's schools at Hofwyl. This is far from surprising when we consider that both Mr. Bancroft and Mr. Cogswell had studied and traveled in Germany, and that Mr. Cogswell's published letters show that he had visited Fellenberg at Hofwyl, and Pestalozzi at Yverdun.

GYMNASTICS AT OTHER SCHOOLS.

It is stated by Barnard, in his *Journal of Education*, that

Dr. Griscom, who had become acquainted with the gymnastic system from personal observation in the schools of Pestalozzi and Fellenberg in 1818 and 1819, introduced it to some extent into the High School in New York, established by him under the auspices of the New York High School Society in 1825, in imitation of the Public High School of Edinburgh.

Dr. Shattuck himself has, as is well known, done much to perpetuate the ideas inculcated by his masters at Round Hill, by endowing St. Paul's School at Concord, N. H., which enjoys a wide and deservedly high reputation for training boys. It is enough to say that the school has won its success largely because it has been managed in accordance with the designs of its founder, whose views are thus stated in his deed of gift made about 1856:

The founder is desirous of endowing a school of the highest class for boys, in which they may obtain an education which shall fit them either for college or business: including thorough intellectual training in the various branches of learning; gymnastic and manly exercises adapted to preserve health and strengthen the physical condition; such æsthetic culture and accomplishments as shall tend to refine the manners and elevate the taste, together with careful moral and religious instruction.

THE FIRST GYMNASIUM AT HARVARD COLLEGE.

Dr. Follen, another German exile, was for a time a teacher at Round Hill; like Dr. Beck, he later became a Harvard professor. It was due to Dr. Follen's efforts, backed by an appeal, from the medical professors of the college, strongly recommending the practice of gymnastics, that a gymnasium was organized at Harvard College in May, 1826. Says Rev. Dr. Cazneau Palfrey, in the *Harvard Register*:

A meeting of all classes was held in the college chapel, such a meeting as I do not remember hearing of on any other occasion, at which a response was made to this appeal, and resolutions passed expressing our readiness to follow the suggestions made in it. One of the unoccupied commons halls was fitted up with various gymnastic appliances, and other fixtures were erected on the Delta [*i. e.*, the college playground]. But Dr. Follen did not confine his operations to these two localities. One day he was to be seen issuing from the college yard at a dog-trot, with all college at his heels, in single file and arms akimbo, making a train a mile long, bound for the top of Prospect Hill. My impression is that the procession was stopped by a farmer who threatened prosecution for damages.

GYMNASTICS AT YALE AND OTHER COLLEGES.

In September, 1826, the corporation of Yale College voted an appropriation of $300, to be expended under the direction of the faculty for the "clearing and preparing of the grounds [on the college green] for a gymnasium and for the erection of apparatus for gymnastic exercises, with a view to the promotion of the health of the students." In 1826 the Dwight Brothers established a school, known as the New Haven Gymnasium, in whose course of instruction a prominent part was assigned to gymnastics.

In 1828, at Amherst College, a petition of the students for a bowling-alley was denied by the faculty on the ground that it would cause too much noise, but chiefly because "public sentiment would not justify the countenancing of such a game." We may remark in passing, that the new gymnasium at Amherst is provided not only with bowling-alleys but also with billiard tables. The example of Harvard and Yale as to gymnasia, not to speak of that of Round Hill, less than ten miles distant from their college, must have had weight with the Amherst Faculty, at least to the extent of allowing an out-of-door gymnasium. One who entered Amherst as a student in 1829 describes a gymnasium which consisted of "a few horses and parallel bars, with one or two swings in the grove, but even these belonged to a society of students who guarded their property with jealous care."

VIEWS AND EFFORTS OF DR. J. C. WARREN, OF BOSTON.

Dr. John Collins Warren, in his day the foremost surgeon in Boston, was for many years Professor of Anatomy and Surgery in the Harvard Medical School. For some years prior to 1825 he lectured to the students of the college on the laws of health. He was prominent in establishing the Tremont Gymnasium, in 1825, in Boston, being its first president, and also in forwarding Dr. Follen's enterprise at Cambridge in 1826. Dr. Warren endeavored to secure "the distinguished philosopher and gymnasiarch, Professor Jahn," for the head of the Tremont Gymnasium. But "Mr. Jahn was so situated," says Dr. Warren in his "Biographical Notes", "that we could not, without obtaining more means than were at our disposition, lead him to abandon his own country and establish himself for life in ours. The idea of obtaining his aid was therefore relinquished, and I afterward addressed Dr. Lieber, a gentleman of education and in other respects well fitted to take the superintendence of a public gymnasium." The Dr. Lieber referred to was Dr. Francis Lieber, the distinguished publicist, who later became Professor of Law in Columbia College, New York.

Dr. Warren goes on to say that the establishment of the Tremont Gymnasium, "as is apt to be the case in this country in regard to novelties, acted contagiously on city and country. Small gymnasia were established in connection with most of the schools and academies and colleges, male and female." In 1830 Dr. Warren delivered an address "On the Importance of Physical Education," before the American Institute of Instruction, at Boston. This paper was republished in England, and formed the basis of a small volume on "The Preservation of Health", published by Dr. Warren in 1846. The lecture contains many sound suggestions and criticisms regarding certain abuses, which have by no means disappeared as yet, in female education. How short-lived was the interest evoked by Jahn's pupils, in gymnastics for educational purposes, may be seen from the following extract from Dr. Warren's address:

> The establishment of gymnasia throughout the country promised at one period the opening of a new era in physical education. The exercises were pursued with ardor, so long as their novelty lasted; but, owing to not understanding their importance, or some defect in the institutions which adopted them, they have gradually been neglected and forgotten, at least in our vicinity. The benefits which resulted from these institutions, within my personal knowledge and experience, far transcended the most sanguine expectations. * * * The diversions of the gymnasium should constitute a regular part of the duties of all our colleges and seminaries of learning; and * * * the system of rewards, so dangerous when mismanaged in literary education, might be introduced without any ill effect.

Dr. Warren was very tenacious of his high opinion concerning gymnastics, for we find mention in his Journal, under the date of January 8, 1853, that he "Had much conversation with President Walker [of Harvard College]. Recommended to make gymnastic exercises a part of the duty of the student."

CONDITION OF PHYSICAL TRAINING PRIOR TO THE INTRODUCTION OF THE "NEW GYMNASTICS".

Teachers as a body fifty years ago had neither the training nor the inclination for achieving success in the domain of physical education. What might have been the result if Drs. Beck, Follen, and Lieber had not quit the field it is vain to surmise, since even they were governed more by theoretical and æsthetic notions than by scientific knowledge of the laws of bodily health and development. The late Dr. E. Jarvis, in his "Practical Physiology", notes that when the gymnasium was established at Harvard University in 1826, "the students were invited to go to the play-ground at 12 and engage in the gymnastic exercises till 1 o'clock: These were very active, and some of them violent, for men and boys of their strength, so that when they left the field for dinner they were generally fatigued, and some were almost exhausted. Those who were most fatigued ate their dinner with less than their usual relish, and felt neither refreshed nor comfortable afterward."

When we consider that in the case of the early gymnasia the appliances were rarely protected from the weather; that competent native teachers did not exist; that funds were not forthcoming to attract such from abroad; and that the prepossessions of the teaching class, and of boards of trust, were in general such as to render them indifferent, if not positively averse, to the maintenance of a genuine and thoroughgoing system of bodily training, the reasons are not far to seek for the slow and often retarded development of physical training as a branch of American education.

Here and there a handful of enthusiastic and athletically inclined students, as at Princeton College in 1857, would attempt to furnish and maintain a gymnasium, or would patronize some private venture of an athlete or pugilist; but there appears to have been no well-considered and sustained attempt by the authorities of any American college to provide its students, either with instruction in gymnastics or adequate facilities for athletic sports, during the period extending from 1826 to 1860.

THE GYMNASIUM AT THE UNIVERSITY OF VIRGINIA.

Possibly the University of Virginia presents an exception to this statement, inasmuch as there was a large out-of-doors gymnasium maintained on the grounds of that institution from 1852 till the outbreak of the war. A competent gymnast and sword-master, a Frenchman, had it in charge; but in order to support himself he had to eke out the small sum received from the students by cultivating a kitchen-garden and keeping a Russian bath-house.

REVIVAL OF INTEREST IN PHYSICAL TRAINING.

Just before and just after the outbreak of the war in 1861, a great interest sprang up, especially among students, in regard to gymnastics, feats of strength, and athletic sports. During this period Dr. Windship appeared in Boston as the champion and exemplar of the severest form of gymnastics, that of lifting heavy weights. The Tom Brown books by Thomas Hughes, which were published about this time, served to fire the imagination of school-boys and collegians, and to enhance the interest of their elders in athletics and gymnastics. The Doctors Taylor in New York and Dr. Lewis in Boston attained considerable success as exponents of Ling's Medical Gymnastics, or the Swedish Movement Cure.

THE NEW GYMNASTICS.

DR. DIO LEWIS AND HIS INFLUENCE.

Dr. Dio Lewis labored strenuously for the introduction of his "new gymnastics for men, women, and children," and succeeded in organizing in 1861 his Normal Institute for Physical Education in the city of Boston. President Felton, of Harvard University, was its active and earnest presiding officer up to the time of his death. The Institute embraced the departments of anatomy, physiology, and hygiene, that of vocal culture, and that of gymnastics. The full course of instruction was ten weeks. At Boston, and later at Lexington, a large number of teachers of the "new profession" were graduated. The first class, graduated in September, 1861, numbered fourteen.

Dr. Lewis's book, "New Gymnastics for Men, Women, and Children, with a Translation of Prof. Kloss's Dumb-bell Instructor and Prof. Schreber's Pangymnastikon," was widely read, and reached its eighth edition in the course of two years. It was believed that an era had begun in which the "new gymnastics" would be universally introduced into the schools throughout the land. The problem of physical education was considered solved, because free gymnastics could be carried out in any school-room without removing the desks.

MISS BEECHER'S EXPERIMENTS IN CALISTHENICS FOR GIRLS.

Prior to 1861 very little had been undertaken in the way of teaching girls gymnastics, though Miss Catherine E. Beecher's efforts in that direction at Hartford, Conn., and later, in 1837, at Cincinnati, O., merit notice. In her "Educational Reminiscences and Suggestions", published in 1874, Miss Beecher says:

In Cincinnati I invented a course of calisthenic exercises, accompanied by music, which was an improvement on the one I adopted at Hartford. The aim was to secure all the advantages supposed to be gained in dancing-schools, with additional advantages for securing graceful movements to the sound of music. These exercises were extensively adopted in schools, both east and west, but finally passed away. One reason was that they demanded a piano or some other instrument, and a large room without furniture; another was the want of appreciation of physical exercise, and of the importance of training young girls to simple *gracefulness*. To meet the first difficulty, I arranged a system of exercises which could be used in a school-room without removing desks and benches, to be performed either with or without music; and this method is found in my work on physiology and calisthenics, which has been extensively adopted. Dr. Dio Lewis's system of gymnastics includes many of my methods, with additions which seem objectionable in this respect: they are so vigorous and *ungraceful* as to be more suitable for boys than for young ladies. When physical education takes the proper place in our schools, young girls will be trained in the class-rooms to move head, hands, and arms gracefully; to sit, to stand, and to walk properly, and to pursue calisthenic exercises for physical development as a regular school duty as much as their studies; and these exercises, set to music, will be sought as the most agreeable of school duties.

Such exercises are not as yet so sought, to any considerable extent, we may remark.

THE GYMNASIA OF THIS PERIOD.

Although the glowing anticipations concerning the immediate and future usefulness of the light gymnastics, as distinguished from the heavy gymnastics, as the Turning exercises were called, were not realized, the era of building gymnasia dates from 1859–'60. Up to 1859 no college in the country possessed a commodious and well furnished building devoted to the purposes of physical training. In the year 1859–'60, however, Amherst, Harvard, and Yale Colleges built gymnasia.

T. W. HIGGINSON ON GYMNASTICS.

An article entitled "Gymnastics," by Thomas Wentworth Higginson, in the *Atlantic Monthly* for March, 1861, admirably reflects the sentiment of that time on the part of those who were anxious to improve educational methods. Mr. Higginson says:

It is one good evidence of the increasing interest in these exercises that the American gymnasia built during the past year or two have far surpassed all their predecessors in size and completeness, and have probably no superiors in the world. The Seventh Regiment gymnasium in New York, just opened by Mr. Abner S. Brady, is 180 by 52 feet in its main hall, and 35 feet in height, with nearly 1,000 pupils. The beautiful hall of the Metropolitan Gymnasium, in Chicago, measures 108 by 80 feet, and is 20 feet high at the sides, with a dome in the center 40 feet high and the same in diameter. Next to these probably rank the new gymnasium at Cincinnati, the Tremont Gymnasium at Boston, and the Bunker Hill Gymnasium at Charlestown, all recently opened. Of college institutions the most complete are probably those at Cambridge and New Haven. The arrangements for instruction are rather more systematic at Harvard. * * *

Gymnastic exercises are as yet but very sparingly introduced into our seminaries, primary or professional, though a great change is already beginning. * * * Until lately all our educational plans have assumed man to be a merely sedentary being; we have employed teachers of music and drawing to go from school to school to teach those elegant arts, but have had none to teach the art of health. * * * It is something to have got beyond the period when active sports were actually prohibited. I remember when there was but one boat owned by a Cambridge student, and that boat was soon reported to have been suppressed by the Faculty, on the plea that there was a college law against a student's keeping domestic animals, and a boat was a domestic animal within the meaning of the statute. * * *

It would be unpardonable, in this connection, not to speak a good word for the favorite hobby of the day—Dr. Lewis and his system of gymnastics; or, more properly, of calisthenics. .* * * Dr. Windship had done all that was needed in apostleship of severe exercises, and there was wanting some man with a milder hobby, perfectly safe for a lady to drive. The Fates provided that man also in Dr. Lewis—so hale and hearty, so profoundly confident in the omnipotence of his own methods and the uselessness of all others, with such a ready invention, and such an inundation of animal spirits, that he could flood any company, no matter how starched or listless, with an unbounded appetite for ball-games and bean-games. How long it will last in the hands of others than the projector remains to be seen, especially as some of his feats are more exhausting than average gymnastics; but in the mean time it is just what is wanted for multitudes of persons who find or fancy the real gymnasium to be unsuited to them. It will especially render service to female pupils so far as they practice it; for the accustomed gymnastic exercises seem never yet to have been rendered attractive to them on any large scale, and with any permanency.

In another connection the same writer says:

Wherever Dr. Lewis's methods have been introduced important advantages have followed. He has invented an astonishing variety of games and well-studied movements, with the lightest and cheapest apparatus, balls, bags, rings, wands, wooden dumb-bells, small clubs, and other instrumentalities, which are all gracefully and effectually used by his classes, to the sound of music and in a way to spare the weakest when lightly administered or to fatigue the strongest when applied in force. Being adapted for united use by both sexes, they make more thorough appeals to the social element than ordinary gymnastics; and evening classes, to meet several evenings in a week, have proved exceedingly popular in some of our towns. These exercises do not require fixed apparatus or a special hall. Dr. Lewis himself is now training regular teachers to carry on the same good work, and his movement is undoubtedly the most important single step yet taken for the physical education of American women.

OUTCOME OF THE "NEW GYMNASTICS."

Further on we shall have occasion to outline the development of military drill and discipline as a feature in school and college training, and to speak of the stimulus given by the War to all forms of bodily training and exercise, and especially to athletic sports and contests. At this point we need only note that, although what we may term the light gymnastic movement was instrumental in causing the erection of a considerable number of school and college gymnasia and the inauguration of a few poorly-endowed and rudely-organized departments of physical culture, the force of the movement was soon spent, and the schemes for physical training assumed a semi-military character.

OPENING OF THE ERA OF BUILDING GYMNASIA IN COLLEGES.

The Amherst, Harvard, and Yale gymnasia, as was stated above, were built in 1859–'60. Their external dimensions were, respectively, 72 by 50 feet, 85 by 50 feet, and 100 by 50 feet. They cost, respectively, in round numbers, $15,000, $10,000, and $13,000, and were, for their time, elaborate and well furnished structures. The Amherst gymnasium was named the Barrett Gymnasium, in honor of Benjamin Barrett, M.D., of Northampton, Mass., who was the largest contributor to the fund for its erection. Dr. Barrett's name does not appear on the roll of the Round Hill School; but it is not unlikely that familiarity with the workings of that institution may have been influential in determining his gifts to the Amherst gymnasium. One gentleman, who declined to give his name, gave $8,000 toward the building of the Harvard gymnasium. These three gymnasia have all been outgrown, and those at Amherst and Cambridge have been replaced by costly and vastly improved edifices.

CHARACTER OF THE TRAINING ADOPTED.

From the outset compulsory exercise has been required of all ablebodied students at Amherst, under the control and direction of an educated physician, whose professorial chair was accorded a place at the faculty table. Gymnastics have never been required at Harvard, where Dr. D. A. Sargent was, in 1879, appointed Assistant Professor of Physical Training, and Director of the Hemenway Gymnasium. His predecessors were a professional teacher of boxing, and a master of military drill. At Yale College no very comprehensive or commendable system of administration has as yet been worked out.

DEPARTMENT OF PHYSICAL EDUCATION AT AMHERST COLLEGE.

The salient facts concerning the beginning, growth, and peculiarities of the department of hygiene and physical education of Amherst College demand our attention at this point; for, as has been well said by President Eliot of Harvard, "It is to Amherst College that the colleges of the country are indebted for a demonstration of the proper mode of organizing the department of physical training."

VIEWS OF PRESIDENT STEARNS.

When the late W. A. Stearns, D.D., was inaugurated as President of Amherst College, in 1854, he devoted a considerable portion of his discourse to enforcing the proposition that no course of education was complete that did not devote special attention to securing the normal development and healthy working of the body. In his first report to the trustees, in 1855, President Stearns said:

> No one thing has demanded more of my anxious attention than *the health of the students*. The waning of the physical energies in the midway of the college course is almost the rule, rather than the exception, among us, and cases of complete breaking down are painfully numerous.

A year later he tells the trustees that the breaking down of the health of the students is, in his opinion, "wholly unnecessary." In his report for 1859, President Stearns again returns to the consideration of the question of students' health, and says:

> Time and experience have convinced me of an imperious demand, in the circumstances of an academic life, for immediate and efficient action on this subject. Many of our students come from farms, mechanic shops, and other active occupations, to the hard study and sedentary habits of college. Physical exercise is neglected, the laws of health are violated, the protests and exhortations of instructors and other friends are unheeded. The once active student soon becomes physically indolent, his mental powers become dulled, his movements and appearance indicate physical deterioration. By the time Junior year is reached many students have broken down in health, and every year some lives are sacrificed. Physical training is not the only means of preventing this result, but it is among the most prominent of them. If it could be regularly conducted, if a moderate amount of physical exercise could be secured as a general thing to every student daily, I have a deep conviction, founded on close observation and experience, that not only would lives and health be preserved, but animation and cheerfulness and a higher order of efficient study and intellectual life would be secured. It will be for the consideration of this Board, whether, for the encouragement of this sort of exercise, the time has not come when efficient measures should be taken for the erection of a gymnasium and the procuring of its proper appointments.

These remarks were rendered emphatic by a statement concerning the death of two seniors who had broken down under college life.

INSTITUTION OF THE DEPARTMENT BY THE TRUSTEES.

The trustees concluded that the time for erecting a gymnasium had come, and set about raising the money for it, with the result before alluded to. It was unanimously voted by the trustees—

To establish a department of physical culture in this college, and that the duties of its professor shall be:

(1) To take charge of the gymnasium and give instruction to the students in gymnastics.

(2) To take a general oversight of the health of the students, and to give such instruction on the subject as may be deemed expedient, and under the direction of the Faculty, like all the other studies.

(3) To teach elocution so far as it is connected with physical training.

(4) He shall give lectures from time to time upon hygiene, physical culture, and other topics pertaining to the laws of life and health, including some general knowledge of anatomy and physiology.

(5) The individual appointed to have charge of this department shall be a thoroughly-educated physician, and, like other teachers and professors, shall be a member of the college Faculty. It is distinctly understood that *the health of the students* shall at all times be an object of his special watch, care, and counsel.

At the suggestion of Dr. Nathan Allen, of Lowell, Mass., the well-known writer on hygiene and sociology, then and now one of the trustees of the college, it was voted to designate the head of the newly created department as the Professor of Hygiene and Physical Education. Dr. Allen was also mainly responsible for the definition of the duties of the professorship as embodied in the vote quoted above.

The plan of the president and Faculty alluded to under the second head of this vote was as follows:

First, The main object shall not be to secure feats of agility and strength, or even powerful muscle, but to keep in good health the whole body. *Second*, That all the students shall be required to attend on its exercises for half an hour, designated for the purpose, at least four days in the week. *Third*, The instructor shall assign to each individual such exercises as may be best adapted to him, taking special care to prevent the ambitious from violent action and all extremes, endeavoring to work the whole body, and not overwork any part of it. *Fourth*, That while it may not be expedient to mark the gradation of attainment, as in the intellectual branches, yet regularity, attention, and docility should be carefully noted, so as to have their proper weight in the deportment column of the student's general position. *Fifth*, That some time shall be allowed out of study hours for those volunteer exercises which different men, according to their tastes, may elect for recreation, and particularly that the bowling alleys be not given up to promiscuous use, but be allotted at regular hours to those who wish to make use of them—all these volunteer exercises, of whatever kind, to be under the supervision of the gymnasium instructor. *Sixth*, That the building shall always be closed before dark, that no light shall be used in it, and no smoking or irregularities of any kind shall be allowed in it. *Seventh*, That the instructor ought to be a member of the Faculty, and give in to it his marks and occasional accounts, and receive directions as other officers of the college are accustomed to do.

The department has been administered from the first without any material deviation from the plan thus outlined.

HISTORY OF THE DEPARTMENT SINCE 1860.

In August, 1860, J. W. Hooker, M.D., a graduate of Yale College, was appointed Professor in this department. It is said of him that he had "given special attention to physical training, and, being himself a skillful gymnast, possessed qualities that eminently fitted him for starting such an enterprise. But before the close of the year his health failed, and he resigned his position, and died in about two years afterward." The attention and coöperation of the students were the more easily enlisted in the new departure, owing to the martial spirit then so rife. During the spring of 1861 Colonel Lyman, a distinguished drill-master, was employed to give instruction and training in military tactics and exercises.

In August, 1861, Edward Hitchcock, M.D., a graduate of Amherst College and of the Harvard Medical School, was appointed Dr. Hooker's successor. Dr. Hitchcock has served continuously in that capacity from then till now.

The best exposition of the Amherst system of training and its results is found in Dr. Hitchcock's "Report of Twenty Years Experience in the Department of Physical Education and Hygiene in Amherst College, to the Board of Trustees, June 27, 1881. Amherst, Mass.: Press of C. A. Bangs & Co., 1881," from which the following extracts are taken:

> Physical culture as expressed to Amherst College students by the experience of the past twenty years, means something besides, something in addition to, muscular exercise. It includes cleanliness of skin, attention to stomach and bowels, relaxation from daily mental work, freedom from certain kinds of petty discipline, but with so much requirement and restraint as will give coherence, respect, and stability to the methods of maintaining health and the men employing them.
>
> The way in which students here are called upon to secure health, and its correct and normal maintenance for college requirements, is to be sure of some active, lively, and vigorous muscular exercise at stated periods; not requiring a rigid military or hardening drill of certain portions of the body, but offering them such exercises as shall, while regularly engaged in, be vigorous, pleasant, recreative, and at the same time, even without a manifest consciousness of it, be calling into exercise their powers in active, vigorous, easy, and graceful movements. Light wooden dumb-bells, weighing about one pound each, are placed in the hand, and then a series of movements are directed and timed by music, occupying in all from 20 to 30 minutes each day, and are simultaneously performed by a whole class under the lead of the captain.
>
> Believers in heavy gymnastics are apt to regard our exercises as perhaps well enough for girls and children, because they are only the swinging of one-pound dumb-bells for less than half an hour. And they would reflect upon the exercise and call it calisthenics, and not dignify it by the term gymnastics. To this we would only say, "What's in a name?" If calisthenics only accomplishes what we need, our wants are satisfied. * * * Certain it is that the young men at the close of one of these exercises, with the temperature at 60°, have ordinarily secured moisture on the skin, are breathing full and deeply, the blood circulates, the abdominal viscera are sufficiently stimulated, and their muscles are limber and elastic; they have gained good exercise, and the whole man has the feeling that he has worked in a physical way, and yet is not exhausted. The whole body in the loose and easy uniform, unconstrained by a rigid piece of apparatus, is given a freedom of action which cannot

PHYSICAL TRAINING IN AMERICAN COLLEGES.

be acquired by the stolid march, or the constraint of either fixed or many kinds of movable gymnastic apparatus; and, lastly, the students generally feel, withal, that they have had a good time. And the mental and social freedom allowed and encouraged in these exercises conduces to the rapid and healthful evaporation of superfluous animal spirits, generated by the physical and mental confinement of study.

And while our methods are not so perfect as might be devised with more complete apparatus and better men to direct, if health of college be the only thing to be considered, they do seem to be good as far as they go; enough for the large majority, and of some service to all. * * *

During the first few years of our work, the simpler and easier forms of heavy gymnastic work were required of *all* the class; every man was expected to practice heavy gymnastics under direction of the leader, one of the class. This became very tedious work, irksome and impossible for some men to do except with such effort, moral and physical, as was injurious to be put on a large part of every class. * * * But it was found out that the men who were sound in all four of their limbs and eyesight could go through movements enough with wooden dumb-bells to secure the necessary muscular waste and development for healthful study, and hence no requirement for heavy gymnastic work has been made of any student for the past fifteen years. At the same time there are a few who take as naturally to heavy gymnastics, and as profitably too, as ducks to water, and these are allowed and encouraged to reasonable efforts in this direction. These at first are guided and watched, but they are at length allowed and expected to go on with their exercise in this direction at their own discretion, save with the aid of one of the older classes who has shown himself the best gymnast in college.

And once during each year a prize exhibition is held, when the individual students may compete with each other in heavy gymnastics, and the classes may show their proficiency in light exercises with dumb-bells and marching. For the first few years the morning hour was secured as the best time for the physical exercises of the college. And while in theory, and perhaps fact, this is the best time for exercise, yet the hour of early evening, between daylight and darkness, has come to be the time which we have of late most largely employed for gymnastics. * * *

STATISTICAL WORK AND RESULTS.

One of the first duties I felt called upon to perform after your appointment to this Professorship, was to prepare blanks for several anthropometric observations of the students of college. This I did partly to enable the students to learn by yearly comparison of themselves how they are getting on as regards the physical man. The ulterior object, however, was to help ascertain what are the data or constants of the typical man, and especially the college man. I have conceived no theory on the subject, and have instituted but very few generalizations; but my desire has been to carefully compile and put on record as many of these observations as possible for comparison and verification of statistical work in this same direction by many other persons in America and Europe.

In many of the final results of these twenty years data, it is interesting to find a general correspondence to the established data of more numerous measurements of the human body, and in the variation from authorities of large experience we find the differences as a whole in favor of the student. These results seem to show that we must expect different physical characteristics in those who pursue the scholarly life, from others whose occupations are unlike them in so many ways, and when properly understood and carried out we believe that the advantages will be found on the side of the scholarly life.

In the fall of 1861 I took measurement of all the college students in seven particulars, and have faithfully made these examinations of almost every sound man since connected with the college up to the present date. The measurements are made of the Freshmen soon after entering, and are repeated upon them near the end of each year of the course. Thus every man who goes through college has been observed five times. These observations during the first year were the age, weight, height, chest girth, arm girth, fore-arm girth, and body lift. The second year the capacity of the lungs was added, and for the last five years the finger reach and the chest expansion, and for the last two years the comparative strength of the two hands.

* * * * * * *

The health of college, so far as figures and statistics can show it, must be represented by data of the sickness of students, and, like the anthropometric observations, those of sickness are made from all the students, and by yearly reckonings. During these twenty years 5,443 different entries, not individuals, have been on the annual catalogues. Of this number 1,365 were entered on the sick list, representing those who during their course have been absent from all college duties on account of sickness for more than two consecutive days in term time. This gives a per cent. of the students by entries, as at one or more times disabled by illness, of 25.26. A noticeable point appears in the record of sickness as possibly showing the healthfulness of college life; it is the decrease of illness from Freshman to Senior year. The data are given in Table No. 4, but the fact of interest is that while the per cent. of Freshmen sick is 20.30, that of the Seniors is 19.05.

It may be thought, however, that as classes decrease in numbers, perhaps the diminution of sickness is only on a par with the numerical falling off of the classes. But while the health increase of the course is 10.18 per cent., the natural dropping out is only 5.95 per cent.

The time lost by sickness, as averaged on every student, is 2.65 days yearly. This of course is constructively applied. Although but 1,375 students are recorded on the sick list, yet the number of cases of sickness recorded is 1,725. This means that some have been on the sick list two or more times, or 25 per cent. of the whole number sick; and the amount of time actually lost from college exercises by each of the sick men has been 10.39 days on the average.

The maladies of college life are those of youth, and not debility or infirmities. As would be expected, colds and slight lung difficulties are the most numerous, constituting nearly one-half of the whole amount; and while physical injuries stand second on the list of causes, it is instructive to learn that no serious or permanent injury has ever happened from the gymnastic exercises, required or voluntary.

A natural inquiry is, if many of the students have left college on account of ill health. * * * Seventy are reported as having left college on account of physical disability, or more than three each year. Of these, however, twenty-two, or less than one-third of the whole number, have re-entered and graduated with the class next to the one which they first entered. Or, to put it numerically, 48 out of 2,106, or 2.27 per cent. of our students, failed in their college course on account of sickness. Do the records of other occupations appear more favorably?

By the laws of viability, or chance of life in males from birth, as established by census returns and life insurance tables, this "chance of life," the world over, decreases from the ages of 15 or 16 on to 25, then rises to 30, and then falls to the end of our existence. Or the curve of viability ascends rapidly from birth to 15 or 16 years, and then slowly descends to old age. But by the Health Records of our students we find a variation from this law, since we learn that sickness diminishes in our life here from 18 to 22 years of age. This fact, with some others already mentioned, discriminates in favor of the healthfulness of student life.

* * * * * * *

Another subject illustrated by this department and its statistics is the amount of growth, and is seen in Table No. 6. This embraces many of the students who have completed the course, or given the data at entering and graduating, with a difference in time of three years and six months, and an age of 19.2 and 22.11. Seven hundred and forty-nine men have been measured, and these have furnished 5,160 items of the seven different points of observation. Of all these men measured, 26.15 per cent. give an increase in all the items during the whole period observed. And 47.39 per cent. of the men show some of the same measurements at Senior as at Freshman year. And it is not the oldest or those least developed in whom this occurs. And 53.40 per cent. give one or more items less at Senior than Freshman year, and 28.17 give one or more items less, and also one or more the same. Of the items measured, however, a different showing is made. The average of the whole 5,160 items shows 76.97 per cent. increased during the course, 13.58 per cent. less at the end of the course, and 9.43 per cent. the same as at entrance to college, and it will be seen that some men give both increased and diminished items: some items may be smaller and some items be larger at the same time. The average increase of the 26 per cent. of these, in weight has been 12.27 pounds, 1.05 inches in height, 1.45 in chest girth, 0.85 inches in arm girth, 0.685 in fore-arm girth, 28.4 cubic inches in lung capacity, and nearly 4.50 times in body lift. This is what the college student may expect to grow from the 19th to the 23d year of his life. The items and points of increase may be found in Table No. 6.

A part of the work in this department is instruction in the general laws of health, and in anatomy and physiology. The lectures in health are given the first term of Freshman year, and the subjects are those which specially pertain to student life, such as exercise, food, use of alcohol and tobacco, care of the eyes, the relation of body to mind, and kindred matters.

The instruction in human anatomy and physiology is given by study of a text-book, a printed abstract, and illustrative lectures. Much of the illustration is aided by the clastic models of Auzoux, nearly $1,000 worth of which have been given to the college within the past few years. This study is taken up early in the Sophomore year. Optional study in comparative vertebrate zoölogy has been carried on in addition to other work, and can be well illustrated by the collections in Appleton Cabinet.

* * * * * * *

In athletic sports, rowing, base and foot ball, and college games generally, this department has ever given encouraging though not inciting words. We have encouraged home sports and games, and not stimulated the young men to enter into the hot and violent contests with professional gamesters. With the example of the oldest and largest colleges, and with the comity, rivalry, and good fellowship so largely existing, it is but natural that our college should desire to compare its muscle and wind with those in similar positions. We have had several trials, and been as successful as we ought to expect with smaller numbers to select from, and some disadvantages incident to our geographical location.

In our home athletic sports we have taken a deeper interest. The annual and semi-annual field days have always been well attended, both by contestants and spectators, and we have a good record. And the preparation and participation in these contests, this department has ever regarded as a full equivalent for the required gymnasium exercises, as they are always undertaken under leaders, or directors, who have carried them through with systematic and thorough drill. And for the training of all the students, it seems clear that there are a certain number who must have these hard and severe tests in developing and maintaining their powers up to their best possibilities.

Besides the regular class exercises as required, and the heavy work as encouraged and allowed, there are always a few who need special exercise and advice. These are attended to as well as our limited apparatus will allow. But in the coming near future, when we can see an enlarged and well equipped health building, we may then hope for advanced hygienic development in the few who require special training to secure the normal and healthful development.

TABLE No. 1.—*Measures of 2,106 different students of Amherst College, showing the averages of each class for twenty years, in age, weight, height, chest girth, arm girth, fore-arm girth, lung capacity, body lift, finger reach, chest expansion, and the comparative right-hand and left-hand strength.*

	Seniors.	Juniors.	Sophomores.	Freshmen.	College average.	College mean.
Number observed	1,113	1,148	1,263	1,489	5,013	....
Age	22.24	21.87	20.57	19.31	21.10	....
Weight	142.19	140.59	139.39	133.19	138.84	131.00
Height	67.94	67.86	67.53	67.33	67.66	67.50
Chest girth	35.97	35.61	35.44	34.76	35.40	35.50
Arm girth	11.77	11.72	11.69	11.23	11.19	11.25
Fore-arm girth	11.21	11.07	11.06	10.80	11.02	....
Lung capacity	251.05	250.07	249.23	233.08	241.79	230.00
Body lift	11.33	11.31	10.58	8.61	10.25	11.00
Finger reach	69.72	69.78	69.70	69.60	69.69	....
Chest expansion	3.18	3.33	3.45	3.00	3.02	....
Right-hand strength	92.02	88.99	90.45	87.83	89.69	....
Left-hand strength	86.48	85.96	86.05	83.34	85.50	....
Per cent. strongest with right hand	98	97	96	96	95	....

TABLE No. 2.—*Maxima and minima of every measurement of the 2,106 students observed.*

	Age, years and months.	Weight in pounds.	Height in inches.	Chest girth in inches.	Arm girth in inches.	Fore-arm girth in inches.	Lung capacity in cubic inches.	Body lift.	Finger reach in inches.	Chest range in inches.
Maxima	35.6	216	76.5	43.00	15.5	15.50	426	65	81.10	5.50
Minima	15.3	84	58.0	27.25	8.0	8.25	115	2	48.00	1.50

TABLE No. 3.—*The mean observations of the measures of Amherst College students for twenty years, from a total of 34,384.*

Weight in pounds.	Number.	Height in inches.	Number.	Chest girth in inches.	Number.	Arm girth in inches.	Number.	Lung capacity in cubic inches.	Number.	No. of times body lifted.	Number.
175	69	72	104	40	61	14.0	44	340	53	21	88
167	105	71	291	39	165	13.5	81	320	94	20	176
159	238	70	385	38	394	13.0	323	300	275	18	372
151	490	69	808	37	704	12.5	602	280	608	16	610
143	798	68	955	36	1,079	12.0	1,117	260	871	14	790
135	1,157	67	986	35	1,164	11.5	1,205	240	1,287	12	940
127	1,198	66	790	34	1,098	11.0	1,245	220	1,275	10	1,075
119	982	65	571	33	682	10.5	658	200	732	8	796
111	487	64	371	32	310	10.0	316	180	379	6	590
103	163	63	208	31	104	9.5	77	160	148	4	302
95	46	62	65	30	41	9.0	17	140	39	2	120
....	5,733	....	5,534	....	5,812	....	5,685	....	5,761	....	5,859

TABLE No. 4.—*Data of student sickness and physical disability for nineteen years and nine months in Amherst College.* (*Students' names on the annual catalogues 1861 to 1881, inclusive, 5,443.*)

	Names on annual catalogues for 20 years.	Names on sick list.	Per cent. of each class to whole college.	Per cent. of sickness in each class to whole college.
Seniors	1,192	260	21.90	19.05
Juniors	1,270	319	23.33	23.37
Sophomores	1,465	386	26.92	28.28
Freshmen	1,516	400	27.85	29.30
Total	5,443	1,365	100.00	100.00

Students on the sick list 1,375
Cases (not individuals) of sickness 1,725
Cases on sick list more than once in the year 350
Per cent. of college on the sick list 25.26

Maladies of the students, and their proportion, when it equals one or more per cent. of the whole. (*This is the number of cases, not students.*)

Maladies.	Per cent.	Maladies.	Per cent.
Colds, pneumonia, bronchitis, &c.	37.4	Liver and bilious	2.3
Physical injury	8.8	Neuralgia	1.8
Febriculæ	4.8	Malaria	1.7
Eyes—weak and sore	4.7	Mumps	1.7
Quinsy and sore throat	4.6	Diphtheritic	1.1
Boils	4.1	Measles	1.1
General inability	3.1	Teeth	1.1
Typhoid fever	3.1	Stomach	1.1
Bowels	2.6	Overwork	1.0

TABLE No. 5.—*The measures of weight, height, chest, arm girth, lung capacity, and body lift of 2,106 different students of Amherst College, arranged by age.*

Age.	Number of observations.	Weight.	Height.	Chest.	Arm.	Lung capacity.	Body lift.
17	330	131.99	66.60	33.87	11.12	224.8	8.58
18	1,172	134.07	66.96	35.10	11.36	238.7	10.35
19	1,511	135.84	67.30	35.38	11.52	240.3	10.82
20	1,358	138.12	67.95	35.52	11.57	248.8	10.97
21	1,171	140.00	68.01	35.58	11.69	250.1	10.84
22	807	141.07	68.11	35.98	11.77	250.8	10.92
23	559	141.21	68.31	36.20	11.71	257.0	10.63
24	362	142.42	68.44	37.23	11.74	261.0	10.62
25	216	145.12	68.68	36.66	11.79	263.6	10.11
26	141	144.91	68.82	37.46	11.81	262.5	10.71
27	71	144.40	68.30	36.95	11.84	268.4	10.37
28	30	140.71	68.52	36.28	11.57	209.8	8.51
29	19	142.68	68.09	36.41	11.51	260.5	9.86
30	18	146.50	69.19	36.70	11.61	279.5	7.50

TABLE No. 6.—*Giving the measure of 749 students of Amherst College at two intervals of three years and six months, and at an average age of nineteen years and two months at the first observation, showing their physical development during this period.*

		Per cent.
Number of men measured	749	.....
" " increased in all items	196	26.15
" " decreased in some items	401	53.40
" " both same and increased items	355	47.39
" " both same and decreased items	211	28.17
Number of items secured	5,160	.....
" " showing increase	3,972	76.97
" " same Freshman and Senior year	487	9.43
" " less on Senior year	701	13.58

	Weight.	Height.	Chest.	Arm.	Fore-arm.	Lung capacity.	Body lift.
Greatest individual gain	56.00	6.00	6.50	4.00	3.50	1.34	25.00
Averages of increased men	12.27	1.05	1.45	0.853	0.685	28.4	4.50
Per cent. of decreased items	11.00	0.00	20.31	13.46	25.27	14.64	20.13

SYSTEM OF REWARDS.

The "system of rewards" advocated by Dr. J. C. Warren in 1830, in connection with his suggestion that "the diversions of the gymnasium should constitute a regular part of the duties of all our colleges and seminaries," has assumed considerable proportions, and is considered valuable at Amherst. There are three scholarships connected with this department, and the following prizes are annually competed for:

The Sawyer prize, given by the late Edmund H. Sawyer, of Easthampton, a gold medal of the value of fifty dollars, for the best work in human anatomy and physiology.

Gymnastic prizes: (1) The Gilbert prize, given by Frederick Gilbert of Cincinnati, O., class of 1877, one hundred dollars to the class which, during the year, shall most faithfully discharge its duties in the gymnasium, and carry out most fully the instruction of the professor of hygiene. (2) The Ladd prize, given by William M. Ladd of Portland, Or., class of 1878, fifty dollars a year for excellence in heavy gymnastic exercises at the annual exhibition.

COLLEGE GYMNASIA BUILT SINCE 1860.

The list of colleges, not to mention numerous high, normal, and private-adventure schools, which provided their students with gymnasia during the period 1860–'81, is a considerable one, and includes such institutions as the following for young men: Beloit, Bowdoin, Dartmouth, Hamilton, Oberlin, Pennsylvania, Princeton, Union, Wabash, Williams, and Yale Colleges; and Brown, California, Cornell, Harvard, Vanderbilt, Wesleyan, and Wisconsin Universities; and the Massachusetts Institute of Technology, Phillips Andover Academy, St. Paul's School, Williston Seminary, and Cushing Academy; and Smith, Vassar, and Wellesley Colleges, and Mt. Holyoke Seminary for young women. In the majority of cases instruction, where it has been attempted, has been spasmodic, unintelligent, and half-hearted. In a few instances only, prior to 1879, when the new Hemenway Gymnasium was opened at Harvard, have fairly competent gymnasts been employed. In no case has the course adopted been so comprehensively planned or so carefully and continuously carried out as at Amherst. Ill-advised expenditures upon buildings, vague aims, and inadequate organization, have characterized the management of most of the attempts to institute departments of physical training in our superior schools and colleges.

At the request of the Vice-Minister of Education in Japan, Mr. Tanaka-Fujimaro, who visited Amherst in 1876, Dr. G. A. Leland, Captain of the Class of 1874, was designated by President Seelye to introduce the Amherst system of gymnastics into the Government schools of Japan. For three years Dr. Leland was engaged in that work to the "high satisfaction of the Government," as was officially communicated to President Seelye.

Of the three college gymnasia built in 1860, viz., those at Amherst, Harvard, and Yale, the last-named was the best arranged and most completely furnished. The gymnasium built by Princeton College in 1869 was until 1879—the date of the finest of college gymnasia as yet erected, the Hemenway Gymnasium at Harvard University—by far the best of its kind. Toward the total cost of its site and erection, $38,000, Messrs. R. Bonner and H. G. Marquand, of New York City, each contributed the sum of $10,000. The Bissell Gymnasium at Dartmouth College should be mentioned in this connection. It was built through the munificence of a Dartmouth alumnus, Mr. G. H. Bissell, of New York City, at a cost of $24,000, in 1866.

THE PRINCETON GYMNASIUM AND ITS ADMINISTRATION.

On account of its ancient pre-eminence, the Princeton gymnasium merits more than a passing mention. Thanks are due to Mr. George Goldie, for fifteen years its efficient superintendent, for the following description of this gymnasium and the methods of management there in vogue in 1882–'83:

The building was planned by George B. Post, of New York. It is of stone, and comprises 2 stories and a cellar. There are 3 rooms on the ground floor: the main room, 30 by 70 feet, contains 4 bowling alleys; the dressing-room, 78 by 14 feet, contains 221 lockers and 6 wash-basins; there is a room 70 by 10 feet for base-ball pitching, and there are 3 shower-baths, supplied with hot and cold water; also 1 water-closet and 1 urinal.

The gymnasium proper occupies the second floor. Its dimensions are 78 by 52 feet, height to beams 21 feet, to apex of roof 45 feet. It is lighted and ventilated by 5 dormer windows, 1 double dormer window at the east end, another at the west, and by 5 windows on the south side, coming to within 3 feet of the floor.

The apparatus consists of 20 sets of chest and other pulley weights; 60 pairs of Indian clubs, varying from 2 to 18 pounds in weight; 1,000 pounds of dumb-bells; 1 hand-lifting machine; 1 set of tug-of-war weights; 1 abdominal machine; 4 rowing-machines; 1 set of parallel bars, 20 feet long; 1 steel core, and 1 graduated horizontal bar; 2 inclined ladders, 25 feet long; 1 horizontal ladder, 30 feet long; 1 pair of flying rings; 8 traveling rings; 1 platform spring-board; 1 batule board; rack-bars; single, double, and flying trapezes; l'échelle; peg-pole; 2 sets of chest-poles; a grip-machine; climbing-ropes, and pole; 5 mattresses; jumping and measuring standards, platform-scales; and all the apparatus that can be used for the practice of athletic sports indoors.

The gymnasium is open from 7 A.M. to 8.15 A.M., 12 M. to 2 P.M., and 5 to 6.45 P.M. The characteristic features of the gymnastic drill are Indian club exercise, with free exercises for the trunk and legs. The duration of the class drill is thirty minutes, including three rests of two minutes each. Two hours per day are devoted to individual and special exercise on apparatus, under the supervision of superintendent. The class exercises are also led by him.

The aim of the class exercise is to give a reasonable amount of exercise to the whole muscular system, so as to secure a symmetrical development, a healthy body, and a graceful carriage. It has been employed since 1869 to the present time, i. e., 1884. From 1869 to 1876 exercise was required. At the latter date it was made optional, because the gymnasium was too limited in area, and the time allowed for exercise too short, to accommodate the increase in numbers.

In the autumn of 1884 the Indian club exercises and free-class gymnastics were made obligatory for students in the Freshman and Sophomore classes. The required exercises occupy thirty minutes each, four times weekly, from the first of November till the first of April. Mr. Goldie, after a continuous and successful service of fifteen years at Princeton, during which his pupils gained the reputation of being the most expert college acrobats in the country, has very recently assumed the charge of the gymnasium of the New York Athletic Club, whose magnificent new building, on the south-west corner of Sixth avenue and Fifty-fifth street, New York City, is by far the most complete of its kind in America.

STIMULATING INFLUENCE OF THE WAR ON PHYSICAL TRAINING.

The worth of a good physique and the educational value of physical training were most clearly demonstrated and sharply emphasized by the lessons of the late war. The unexampled interest and activity in athletic sports developed since the close of the War, have contributed most materially toward the promotion of physical training. The youth of the country have been led to engage more actively and intelligently in athletic sports than ever before. Collegiate and intercollegiate contests in great variety have attained to great prominence and favor in the estimation of the general public, as well as of the college world. The discussion of the question of athleticism in colleges will engage our attention in its proper place, but meanwhile the fact should be emphasized that the best that has been done during the last fifteen years toward the erection of gymnasia, the purchase and laying out of playing fields, and the organization of college departments of physical training, has resulted from the demands and endeavors and benefactions of the younger generation of college men, who have themselves experienced or witnessed the beneficial effects of gymnastic exercises and athletic games.

DEPARTMENT OF PHYSICAL TRAINING AT HARVARD UNIVERSITY.

Next to the athletic revival, the cause of physical education in America has received its greatest impetus, in recent years at least, from the organization by Harvard University in 1879 of a new department of physical training, in connection with the Hemenway Gymnasium, for whose erection and equipment Mr. Augustus Hemenway of Boston, a graduate of Harvard in 1876, gave the sum of $110,000. President Eliot, who had again and again pointed out the insufficiency of the old gymnasium, was a boating man in his day, and is still a bold rider and an enthusiastic yachtsman.

THE HEMENWAY GYMNASIUM.

The Hemenway Gymnasium was built according to the plans of Messrs. Peabody and Stearns, the well-known architects of Boston. Mr. Peabody was renowned as a successful athlete when a student at Harvard. Dr. D. A. Sargent, a graduate of Bowdoin College in 1875, and of the Yale Medical School in 1878, was appointed to take charge of the new department, with the title of Assistant Professor of Physical Training and Director of the Hemenway Gymnasium. The gymnasium was furnished with a full set of Dr. Sargent's developing appliances, and has ever since it was opened been managed in accordance with the system of training known as the Sargent system—a system, be it said, more comprehensive, practical, and scientific, than any hitherto attempted or adopted in any college.

Dr. Sargent's reputation and success are due to his practical knowledge of athletics (he was a stroke oar and the most accomplished athlete of his day at Bowdoin); to his experience as a teacher of gymnastics at Bowdoin and at Yale and in New York City, before he went to Cambridge; and to his inventive genius, which enabled him to embody the results of his experience and his studies in the varied series of gymnastic machines which bear his name.

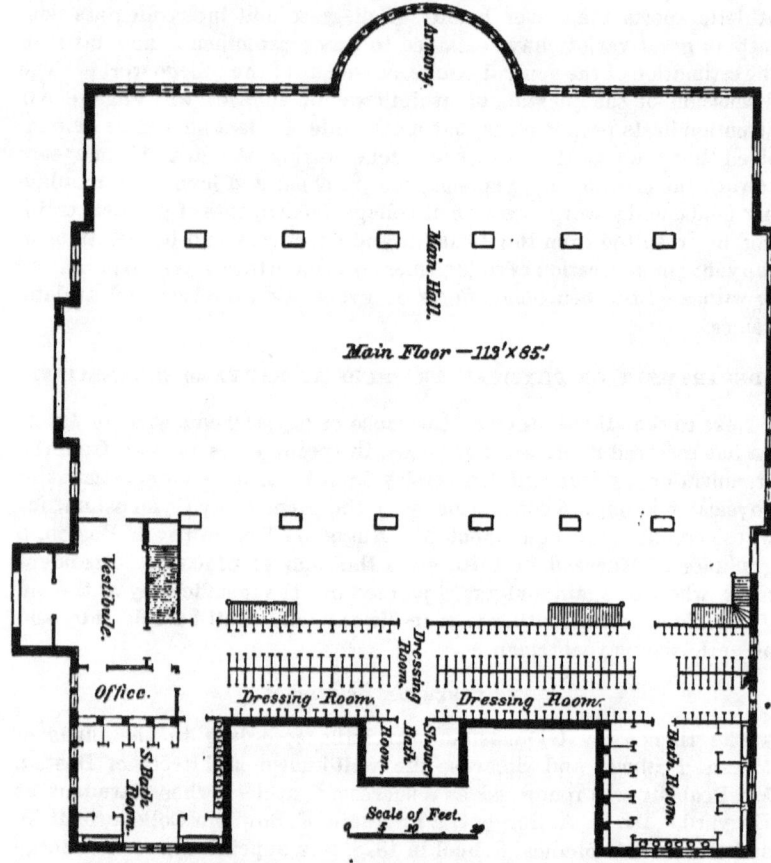

Ground plan of the Hemenway Gymnasium, Harvard University, Cambridge, Mass.

Description of the Building.

The following description, compiled from authentic sources, may serve to explain the views and ground plan of the Hemenway Gymnasium, as printed in this Report. The building, which is on the "Holmes Field," faces on Kirkland street, and is built of brick, with sandstone trim-

THE HEMENWAY GYMNASIUM.

mings, in the colonial style of architecture. The roof is covered with red slate, and is surmounted by a cupola, the top of which is 98 feet from the ground. The building is 125 feet long by 113 feet wide. Over the main window, fronting on Kirkland street, the coat-of-arms of the college is carved in freestone. The main entrance is by way of an elaborate porch. There is an outer and an inner vestibule. From the latter is a flight of stairs, made of North river bluestone, with iron balusters. On the right is an office, 12 feet by 15, finished with enameled bricks. Opening from this is the dressing-room, 103 feet by 15, containing several hundred lockers, through which steam-pipes pass for drying the clothing. On the same, or east side of the building, there are 2 bath and toilet rooms, 25 by 30 feet each, and between them is a room, 10 feet by 12, arranged for vapor and needle baths, with appliances for giving a lateral, vertical, and descending shower. Three doors open from the west side of the dressing-room into the main hall, over which extends an iron framework, arranged with sliding eye-bolts and beams, so that the swinging apparatus can be suspended from any point. On the left-hand side of the hall is an apartment for developing apparatus and a semi-circular room intended for an armory. The main hall is very elegant, the walls being of red and yellow bricks, and the wood-work of hard pine. It is 113 by 85 feet, with an open roof, having hard pine, open-timbered trusses resting on large brackets.

On the second floor there is a room, 25 by 30 feet, for the exhibition of trophies and for committee meetings; and a rowing-room, 70 by 20 feet, shut in from the rest of the building by a high wooden screen, and containing 16 rowing-machines. At the level of the second floor a gallery, 5 feet wide, that runs around the main hall, is used as a running-track. On this floor, above the north bath-room, are the director's office, 25 by 30 feet, and two examining-rooms, each 10 by 15 feet. In the basement at the north end is a room, 90 feet by 30, reserved for base-ball, lacrosse, and tennis practice, and inclosed by a heavy wire netting. In the basement are also the fencing-room, 25 feet by 30; the sparring-room, 25 feet by 30; the store-room, 25 feet by 25; the boiler-room, 15 feet by 20; the room, 15 feet by 25, containing the water-closets; some hundreds of lockers; and 8 bowling-alleys, 72 feet by 5. The whole building is heated by steam, and is ventilated by means of fly windows and a cupola.

Fittings of the Hemenway Gymnasium.

The cost of furnishing the Hemenway Gymnasium amounted to nearly $4,000. The fitting was done in accordance with Dr. Sargent's directions, very many of the appliances having been devised by him. Subjoined is a list of the apparatus of the Hemenway Gymnasium:

(1) *Heavy apparatus.*—Twelve mats; 2 vaulting bars; 3 horizontal bars, suspended; 3 pairs parallel bars, different sizes; 1 pair fixed flying rings; 2 pairs adjustable flying rings; 16 traveling rings; 2 double trapezes; 2 single trapezes; 3 flying trapezes; 1 bal-

aucing trapeze; 1 triple-barred échelle; 2 pairs hanging ropes; 2 knotted hanging ropes; 1 slack rope; 3 suspended poles; 1 spring board; 1 leaping board; 1 rope ladder; 2 peak ladders; 2 slanting ladders; 1 vertical ladder; 3 horizontal ladders; 2 plain vaulting stands; 2 adjustable vaulting stands; 1 jumping platform; 1 pole vaulting platform; 1 running platform.

The swinging apparatus is suspended from an iron framework, in which the crossties are adjustable and the eye bolts are made to move in grooves.

All the apparatus is so arranged that it can be pulled out of the way in a few moments, by a system of ropes and pulleys, thereby leaving the floor clear for class exercises.

(2) *Dr. Sargent's developing appliances.*—One foot machine; 1 ankle machine; 2 wrist machines; 1 foot rotating machine; 1 pronator machine; 1 supinator machine; 1 back and loins machine; 1 leg machine (chair form); 2 finger machines; 1 lifting machine; 2 extensor leg machines; 2 flexor leg machines; 1 abdominal machine; 1 head-balancing machine; 1 rowing machine (weight attachment); 18 rowing machines (hydraulic); 1 paddling machine; 2 sets inclined parallels; 2 sets vertical parallels; 2 sets traveling parallels; 1 pair balancing parallels; 1 adjustable ladder; 1 folding table; 1 peg pole; 4 chest expanders; 2 chest developers; 30 pairs chest weights (plain); 10 pairs chest weights (swivel pulley); 6 pairs back and side pulleys; 5 pairs high pulleys; 2 single, one-arm pulleys; 2 quarter circles; 2 traveling horizontal bars; 1 pair rack bars; 1 long inclined plane for chest and arms; 2 short inclined planes for lower extremities; 2 pairs treadles (weight attachment); 2 pairs stirrups (weight attachment); 2 bridles (weight attachment); 40 pairs Indian clubs (2¼ to 8 pounds); 40 pairs wooden dumb-bells; 36 pairs iron dumb-bells (5 to 125 pounds); 40 wands.

(3) *Dressing and bathing facilities.*—Eight hundred and forty lockers; 5 tub-bath rooms; 9 sponge-bath rooms; 1 shower-bath room (needle, vertical, and lateral shower and douche); 12 wash-bowls; private bath-room (2 tubs and 2 bowls).

Bathing and dressing accommodations are inadequate, and a swimming-bath is contemplated.

(4) *Measuring apparatus, etc., in examining room.*—One pair of scales; dynamometers, for testing strength of back, legs, arms, and chest; spirometer, for testing strength of lungs; spirometer, for testing capacity of lungs; bars and rings, for testing strength of various parts; measuring rods and tape.

The annual cost of carrying on the gymnasium is about $6,000, including the salary of the Director.

CONCERNING DR. SARGENT'S DEVELOPING APPLIANCES.

Dr. Sargent's remarks concerning the nature and purpose of the apparatus, together with his exposition of his method of physical training, are in point here:

The gymnasium, as a whole, is large enough, and has sufficient apparatus, to accommodate two hundred and fifty men at one time and allow each one all the room necessary; but if a run should be made on one kind of apparatus, although there are many duplicates, it would of course be impossible to meet it. A dressing-room, with lockers and bathing facilities enough to accommodate the whole university at one time, and give each man ample room, would require a building about twice the size of the present gymnasium, while the number of bowling-alleys demanded between three and five o'clock would more than cover the entire floor-surface of the building. Everything has been planned and arranged to meet the probable wants of the average student, and to satisfy the claims of the greatest number. Those who do nothing but bowl ought not to regard the rest of the apparatus as useless; nor does it become

INTERIOR VIEW OF THE HEMENWAY GYMNASIUM.

those who aspire to athletic fame, to undervalue the importance of light gymnastics. Every one has a right to enjoy his favorite exercise; but before carrying it too far, it behooves him to consider whether he is not riding a hobby. What is the best exercise for one man may be the worst for another; and an attempt to pursue an inappropriate course, without regard to constitutional or organic differences, has often led to physical bankruptcy and ruin.

The old-fashioned gymnasia are filled with crude appliances that have been handed down in stereotyped forms for several centuries [sic]. To use this apparatus with benefit, it is necessary for one to have more strength at the outset than the average man possesses. A man must make use of that apparatus which his physical condition permits. If he has strength enough to lift with ease his own weight, well and good; then work on the heavy apparatus will prove beneficial to him; if he has not, the liability to strains and injuries, and the enormous expenditure of nerve-power necessary to keep his muscles up to their highest tension, more than counterbalance the good effect of the exercise. When it is considered that only one man in five can raise his own weight with ease, the need of introductory apparatus to prepare one for the beneficial use of the heavy appliances becomes quite apparent. It was the realization of this need that led to the invention of the numerous contrivances that have been introduced into the Hemenway Gymnasium; the desire to strengthen certain muscles, in order to accomplish particular feats on the higher apparatus, was the original motive of their invention. The results which followed were so satisfactory that the same appliances were afterward used as a means of attaining a harmonious development.

For this last-named purpose each machine has its own use. Each is designed to bring into action one or more sets of muscles, and all can be adjusted to the capacity of a child or of an athlete. There are in all fifty-six of these numbered appliances, twenty of which are duplicated. In order to make the gymnasium complete, all the old-style apparatus has been added, with improvements in form, structure, and arrangement. The pulley weights run on steel rods in wooden boxes. In many cases the radii of the rings, bars, etc., can be readily lengthened or shortened. The side rings are made stirrup-shaped, and are covered with rubber. The hand-ropes are made of cotton, and these, together with the hanging poles and flying rings, are all capable of adjustment. In order to protect the hands the ladder rungs are polished, and the horizontal section is divided into one, two, and four feet distances. The horizontal bars are centered with steel rods and hung from the iron framework by shipper wire. The vaulting bar is also centered with a steel rod, capped with brass, and pivoted two inches below the middle line. Considering the accidents that have occurred on this apparatus from "slatting," the above-mentioned improvement will be appreciated. The parallel bars have been shaped to the form of the hand, and one pair is adjustable. The spring boards, which in most gymnasia are so difficult to manage, have been placed on iron pedestals in gliding and pivoting sockets. This improvement facilitates the action of the boards and lessens their wear and tear.

Concerning the apparatus as a whole, it may be said that everything is arranged in a progressive series. It is possible for a person to pass from the simplest movement in calisthenics up to the most difficult gymnastic feat, without experiencing lameness for a day. Easy adaptation to the capacity of the individual and facility of application for remedying local defects and weaknesses are the distinguishing characteristics of the apparatus in the new Hemenway Gymnasium.

DR. SARGENT'S VIEWS ON EXERCISE.

The object of physical training with us is not to make men active and strong, as much as it is to make them healthy and enduring. Perfect health implies a condition in which all parts of the body are properly nourished and harmoniously developed— in which the vital organs are sound, well balanced, and capable of performing their functions to the fullest extent. The researches of the physiologists have shown that whenever a certain organ or class of organs becomes relatively too small or large, causing a want of balance or harmony in their action, there is in every case far greater liability to disease. It is in imperfect, ill-balanced organizations that we find the greatest amount of sickness, and the greatest number of incurable disorders. It is the weak spot, caused by inheritance, acquired by exposure, close confinement, overwork, etc., that invites disease and death, even though the rest of the system may be in perfect condition. To attain a perfect structure, harmony in development, and a well-balanced organism, is our principal aim.

In order to go about our work intelligently, we first take a number of body measurements, which are compared with a standard for the given age. We then test the strength of various parts, examine the heart, lungs, etc., and solicit as much of the student's history as will throw light on his inherited tendencies. From the data thus obtained a course of exercise is prescribed which is in every way designed to meet the demands of his particular case. Let us take a few illustrations:

No. 1 has a flat chest and is predisposed to consumption. If he is admitted to a gymnasium and left to his own discretion, the chances are that he will exhaust his vital energy in going from one thing to another before he has given his lungs and chest the special attention which they need. His wants are best subserved by specifying the work most suitable for him, and by adopting the apparatus best adapted to his peculiar condition.

No. 2 has a weak, irregular heart and poorly-developed back and legs. Systematic rowing and running at a slow pace are admirably adapted for toning up the heart and strengthening the muscles of the back and legs, and are prescribed as special exercises with limitations.

No. 3 is nervous and excitable, inclined to do everything at a breakneck speed, thereby drawing upon the very power which it is for his interest to conserve. In this case a list of exercises is prescribed which are calculated to deaden nervous sensibility by increasing muscular strength.

No. 4 is bilious or lymphatic, and is given the opposite course from that prescribed for No. 3; and so on.

Where the muscular system only needs development, the pupil is directed at first to those appliances which are designed to strengthen his weak parts. After he has become more symmetrical his exercises are made more general. For the benefit of those who simply need exercise without special training, a number of appliances have been introduced, which are so constructed that they can be readily adjusted to the "strength of the strong and the weakness of the weak." No long instruction is needed to make this apparatus available. It is only necessary to explain the desired movements once, and the results which follow will tell how well they have been carried out. Besides the developing appliances we have a great variety of swings, bars, ladders, etc.; but before the student is allowed to use them he must give evidence of a certain amount of preparatory training.

This, in short, is the system pursued at Harvard, where there is no systematic instruction, and where, after an order of exercises has been once prescribed, everything is left to the option of the student. How well the system works may be learned from an inspection of the gymnasium records, which are always open to the public. The second examinations show results which are very suggestive, if not a little startling. They have led me to conclude that half the young men who come to college are physically in arrears, *i. e.*, their brains have been developed at the expense of their physique. The rapid gain in health, strength, and size of students and professors (though more advanced in years) during the first three or four months of their gymnastic training can only be accounted for on this ground. Our best scholars fail for want of body, not for want of brain.

. 574

The chief characteristics, then, of the Sargent system of training, as originally introduced for educational purposes at Harvard, are—

(1) It is based on a careful physical diagnosis.

(2) Exercise, diet, etc., are prescribed in each individual case in the light of such diagnosis.

(3) Besides the ordinary light and heavy gymnastic appliances, machines designed to produce definite localized effects in development can be employed to insure symmetry, and to remedy specific defects or departures from the normal standard of strength or development.

NATURE OF PHYSICAL EXAMINATION.

With the exception of some slight modifications of detail, made to suit the convenience or peculiar notions of certain examiners, the following course of procedure is followed in examining individuals, male or female, under the system:

(a) The person to be examined fills out the following "history blank" in his own handwriting:

Name,
Class and department, or occupation,
Age,   . Birthplace,
Nationality of—
  Father,
  Mother,
  Paternal grandfather,
     "   grandmother,
  Maternal grandfather,
     "   grandmother,
Occupation of father,
If parents are dead, of what did they die?
Which of your parents do you most resemble?
Is there any hereditary disease in your family?
Is your general health good?
Have you always had good health?
Have you ever had any of the following diseases:

Asthma,	Bronchitis,	Chronic diarrhea,
Dizziness,	Dyspepsia,	Dysentery,
Gout,	Rheumatism,	Neuralgia,
Pleurisy,	Shortness of breath,	Jaundice,
Palpitation of the heart,	Headaches,	Piles,
Pneumonia,	Varicose veins,	Liver complaint,
Habitual constipation,	Spitting of blood,	Paralysis?

Have you ever had any injury or undergone any surgical operation?

(b) The examiner makes a series of measurements and tests in accordance with the following form, to determine the physical peculiarities as regards weight, height, development, strength, and condition of the person under examination. The results of this examination, which is made upon the naked man, are carefully recorded, according to the *metric system*, the strength being determined by dynamometers graduated to show kilograms of force:

ITEMS NOTED AND RECORDED.

Number,	Girth of left knee,	Right shoulder elbow,
Date,	right calf,	Left shoulder elbow,
Age,	left calf,	Right elbow tip,
Weight,	right instep,	Left elbow tip,
Height,	left instep,	Length, right foot,
of knee,	upper right arm,	left foot,
sitting,	upper left arm,	Stretch of arms,
pubes,	right elbow,	Capacity of lungs,
navel,	left elbow,	Strength of lungs,
sternum,	right fore-arm,	back,
Girth of head,	left fore-arm,	legs,
neck,	right wrist,	upper arm,
chest, full,	left wrist,	fore-arm,
chest, repose,	Breadth of head,	Total strength,
belly,	neck,	Development,
hips,	shoulders,	Pilosity,
right thigh,	waist,	Color, hair,
left thigh,	hips,	eyes.
right knee,	nipples,	

(c) After comparing the results obtained by the above-mentioned tests and measurements with the standards for average healthy persons of the age given, and taking into consideration any functional or structural peculiarities which his observations or questions may have brought to light, the examiner makes his prescription regarding exercise, diet, sleep, air, bathing, clothing, &c. For the sake of convenience this prescription is frequently given in the shape of a small handbook or card, so marked by the examiner that the person receiving it is plainly directed as to the regimen he had best follow. Re-examinations are made and prescriptions are repeated or modified from time to time, according to the nature of the case.

The system of measurements above described has superseded at Amherst College that originally introduced there by Dr. Hitchcock. Dr. Sargent and his followers, including several women trained under his direction, have accumulated a great and growing mass of anthropometrical data, which cannot fail to be of value in determining the physical constants of growing males and females, especially of the student class. It is to be hoped that these data may soon be available for publication and discussion.

The subjoined tables, already published, No. 8 by Dr. Sargent, and Nos. 7, 9, and 10 by Dr. Hitchcock, are of interest in this connection.

TABLE NO. 7.—*Measures of the weight, height, chest girth, arm girth, lung capacity, and pull up, of 7,988 students of Amherst College, gathered between the academic years of 1861-'62 and 1884-'85, inclusive, noted in the English and in the metric system, and arranged and averaged by age.*

	Age of the students.									
	16.	17.	18.	19.	20.	21.	22.	23.	24.	25.
Number of students measured at each year	20	390	1,822	1,452	1,478	1,251	967	589	382	237
Weight in pounds and decimals	123.42	128.73	131.09	133.13	134.99	136.37	137.61	138.95	140.33	142.34
Weight in kilos and tenths	56.1	58.5	59.8	60.5	61.3	61.9	62.5	63.1	63.8	64.7
Height in inches and hundredths	66.70	66.77	66.95	67.12	67.47	67.50	67.58	67.70	67.77	67.90
Height in meters and millimeters	1.695	1.697	1.700	1.709	1.714	1.716	1.720	1.721	1.722	1.726
Chest girth in inches and hundredths	34.20	34.23	35.42	35.43	35.63	35.92	36.29	36.75	37.30	37.40
Chest girth in millimeters	868	870	895	890	905	918	920	934	940	947
Arm girth in inches and hundredths	10.60	11.06	11.23	11.40	11.58	11.65	11.74	11.94	11.96	11.98
Arm girth in millimeters	268	280	285	290	293	298	300	303	304	305
Lung capacity in cubic inches	225	229.9	239.3	244.1	250.4	254	256.9	260.5	263	265
Lung capacity in liters	3.68	3.80	3.97	4.02	4.11	4.18	4.20	4.26	4.30	4.30
Pull up, number of times	8.58	9.42	10.06	10.18	10.17	10.26	10.26	10.26	10.26	10.27

TABLE NO. 8.—*Strength and development of the First Ten, according to the tests made at the*

NOTE.—The items marked with an asterisk (*) are the girths whose sum is taken as total development, the average girth of the right and left fore-arms is employed in computing total development. When "total strength" is less than the "total development," it is marked minus. L. S. stands for law age is not printed, the previous record has been accepted as entitling the person to a position among

	Name and class.	Age.	Weight.	Height.	Head.*	Natural chest.*	Inflated chest.*	Waist.*	Right thigh.*	Left thigh.*
	1880.									
1	F. D. Jordan, 1880	23	73	175.7	57	95	105	78	54	54
2	Walter Trimble, L. S.	23	70	176.4	56	89	100	76	54	54
3	Richard Trimble, 1880	21	74.6	182.3	57.3	92	99	78	56	55.5
4	N. J. Stephens, 1881	22	72	177.2	53.5	93	101	76	54	53
5	R. W. G. Welling, 1881	21	80.2	188.1	57	92	99	73	56	56
6	C. H. W. Foster, 1881	20	60.9	175.9	55	91	98	70	55	54
7	James Otis, 1881	21	84	182.3	58	100	108	85	60	60
8	F. B. Keene, 1880	24	66.7	172.4	57	90	100	74	51	5L.5
9	S. W. Skinner, 1880	22	72	169.5	56.5	90	100	78	59	59
10	G. B. Morison, 1883	19	68.3	179.4	54.5	90	95	70	52	51
	Average	21.6	72.2	177.9	56.2	92.2	100.5	75.8	55.1	54.8
	1881.									
1	C. H. W. Foster, 1881	21	68.2	176.5	55.5	98	105	72	56	55
2	R. S. Codman, 1883	19	72.2	174.2	57.8	97	103	76	57.5	55.5
3	E. D. Brandegee, 1881	23	77.5	176.5	58.4	98	106.5	83	57	56.5
4	C. P. Curtis, 1883	20	68.5	178	58	90	94	75	53	53
5	N. J. Stephens, 1881		72	177.2	53.5	93	101	76	54	53
6	R. W. G. Welling, L. S.		80.2	188.1	57	92	99	73	56	56
7	G. B. Morison, 1883	20	71	179.4	55.7	89	96	73	55	54
8	James Otis, 1881		84	182.3	58	100	108	85	60	60
9	J. A. W. Goodspeed, 1884	21	64.5	165	54.5	85	96	73	50	50
10	O. J. Pfeiffer, M. S.	23	8L.2	182	58.5	95	104	84	57	56.5
	Average	2L.1	73.9	177.9	56.6	93.7	101.2	77	55.5	54.9
	1882.									
1	C. P. Curtis, 1883	21	69.5	178	57.8	94	98	73	52.5	52.3
2	James Otis, L. S	23	85.5	183	58	105	113	86	59	59.5
3	H. L. Smyth, 1883	20	73	178.6	58	96	102	78	54.5	54
4	W. S. Bryant, 1884	21	65.5	180	55.5	92	97	71	52	52
5	A. R. Crane, 1885	21	64.8	169.3	56.5	92	97	76	53.5	53.5
6	W. H. Page, 1883	21	69.5	169.5	56.5	90.5	94.5	77	56	55.5
7	L. A. Biddle, 1885	19	66.6	172	58.5	95	99.5	74	54	53.5
8	G. B. Morison, 1883	21	71.5	179.5	55.7	93	96.5	73	55	55
9	R. M. Bradley, 1882	21	66.2	177	59	88	93	75	51	51
10	John Russell, 1882	21	62.1	172.4	57.7	86.5	97	72	51	52
	Average	20.9	69.4	175.9	57.3	93.2	96.7	75.5	53.8	53.8

PHYSICAL TRAINING IN AMERICAN COLLEGES.

Hemenway Gymnasium, Harvard University, during the years 1880, 1881, 1882, 1883, *and* 1884.

ment. As the average strength of the right and left hands is used in computing the total strength, so the "total strength" exceeds the "total development," the "condition" is marked plus. When the school; M. S. for medical school. The measurements are according to the metric system. Where the the First Ten.

Right arm.	Left arm.	*Average of— Right forearm.	*Average of— Left forearm.	Development.	Lungs.	Back.	Legs.	Strength. Arms and chest.	Fore-arm.	Total strength.	Condition.	
30.5	30	27.5	27	531	40	145	230	175.2 (12/12)	85	675.2	144.2	1
35	35	27.5	27	526.5	25	155	200	224 (17/15)	70	674	147.5	2
33	32.5	27.8	27	531.1	20	159	185.5	223.8 (19/11)	75	663.3	132.2	3
34	32	29	28	525.5	22	170	190	194.4 (15/12)	86	662.4	136.9	4
32	33	28	29	526	25	175	220	160.4 (10/10)	80	660.4	134.4	5
31.5	31	28	27	513.5	22	162	197	182.7 (17/13)	90	653.7	140.2	6
36	36.5	30.8	30.8	574.3	30	170	178	210 (15/10)	59	647	72.7	7
33	31.5	28	27.5	516	25	131	186	233.4 (20/15)	68	643.4	127.4	8
35	35	28.5	27	541	23	160	167	223.2 (18/13)	67	640.2	99.2	9
32	31	27	26	502.5	20	160	165	232.2 (20/14)	55	632.2	129.7	10
33.2	32.7	28.2	27.6	528.7	25.2	158.7	191.8	205.9 (16.3/12.5)	73.5	655.2	126.4	
32	31	27.5	26.5	532	37	168	230	286.4 (25/17)	80.5	801.9	269.9	1
34.5	33.5	28.3	28	542.6	29	165	175	267.1 (25/12)	61	697.1	154.5	2
36	36	29.8	28.5	561.2	25	180	215	193.7 (12/13)	80	693.7	132.5	3
31.5	30	28.5	28	513	30	150	175	274 (25/15)	61	690	177	4
34	32	29	28	525.5	22	170	190	194.4 (15/12)	86	662.4	136.9	5
32	33	28	29	526	25	175	220	160.4 (10/10)	80	660.4	134.4	6
33.5	33	28.5	28	517.7	20	150	180	255.0 (22/14)	54	659.0	141.9	7
36	36.5	30.8	30.8	574.3	30	170	178	210 (15/10)	59	647	72.7	8
30.5	30	20	25.5	495	26	154	195	193.5 (15/15)	63	631.5	136.5	9
32.5	32.5	30	29.8	550	25	160	175	194.9 (12/12)	71	625.9	75.9	10
33.2	32.7	28.6	28.2	533.7	26.9	164	193.3	223 (17.6/13)	69.5	676.9	143.2	
32.5	32	29	28.5	521.1	16	250	425	326.6 (30/17)	66	1085.6	564.5	1
38.5	39.5	32	31.8	590.5	27.5	230	375	222.3 (16/10)	65	919.8	329.3	2
34.5	35.5	29	28	541.5	20.5	240	275	270.1 (23/14)	65.5	871.1	329.6	3
31.5	32	28.5	28	511.5	18	200	325	229.2 (22/13)	60	832.2	320.7	4
35.5	33.5	27	26.5	524.5	20	210	300	220.8 (20/15)	67.5	824.3	209.8	5
34	34	28.5	28.5	526.5	12	175	290	278 (26/24)	60	810	289.5	6
31	30	27	27	522.5	20	225	300	199.8 (15/15)	58	802.8	280.3	7
33	32.5	28.5	28	522.2	21	210	270	243.1 (21/13)	56	800.1	277.9	8
31	30.5	26.5	26	505	22	200	260	258.2 (25/14)	59	799.2	294.2	9
31	30.5	26.5	26	504.2	21	220	370	124.2 (10/10)	62	797.2	293	10
33.2	33	28.2	27.8	526.9	20.1	216	319	237.8 (20.8/14.5)	61.9	854.8	327.9	

TABLE NO. 8.—*Strength and development of the First Ten, according to the tests*

	Name and class.	Age.	Weight.	Height.	Head.*	Natural chest.*	Inflated chest.*	Waist.*	Right thigh.*	Left thigh.*
	1883.									
1	C. P. Curtis, 1883		69.5	178	57.8	94	98	73	52.5	52.3
2	A. R. Crane, 1885	22	64.5	169.3	57	95.5	101	76	52	53
3	G. B. Morison, 1883	22	71	179.8	56.5	94	100	72	53.5	53.5
4	H. L. Smyth, 1883		73	178.6	58	96	102	78	54.5	54
5	E. A. S. Clarke, 1884	21	87.6	181	57	102	106	87	62	62
6	F. A. P. Fiske, L. S	24	56.6	167.8	56.5	89	93	71	48	47.5
7	C. J. Hubbard, 1883	26	79.1	184.5	58	93	102	82	56	56
8	W. H. Page, 1883	22	66.2	169.5	56.5	90.5	96	73	56	55
9	W. S. Bryant, 1884		65.5	180	55.5	92	97	71	52	52
10	A. L. McRae, special	22	85.5	186	61	98	108	82	58	58
	Average	22.1	71.8	177.4	57.4	94.4	100.3	76.5	54.4	54.3
	1884.									
1	S. L. Foster, 1885	21	71.8	168.5	58	95	104	77	56	56.5
2	R. W. Boyden, 1885	21	73.2	172	57	97	104	77	56	56
3	R. S. Gorham, 1885	21	67.6	172.3	56.5	94	103	75	54	53
4	C. P. Curtis, L. S		69.5	178	57.8	94	98	73	52.5	52.3
5	Arthur Keith, 1885	19	76.5	176	57	98	103	81	57	57.5
6	T. C. Bachelder, L. S	23	69.2	171	58.5	102	107	80	57	55.5
7	A. R. Crane, 1884		64.5	169.3	57	95.5	101	76	52	53
8	W. J. Bowen, 1887	23	71.7	172	56	95	100	76	57	57
9	E. A. S. Clarke, 1884		87.6	181	57	102	106	87	62	62
10	F. A. P. Fiske, L. S		56.6	167.8	56.5	89	93	71	48	47.5
	Average	21.6	70.8	172.8	57.1	96.1	101.9	77.3	55.1	55

PHYSICAL TRAINING IN AMERICAN COLLEGES.

made at the Heménway Gymnasium, Harvard University, &c.—Continued.

Right arm.	Left arm.	*Average of—		Development.	Strength.					Total strength.	Condition.	
		Right forearm.	Left forearm.		Lungs.	Back.	Legs.	Arms and chest.	Fore-arm.			
32.5	32	29	28.5	521.1	18	250	425	326.6 $\binom{30}{17}$	66	1085.6	564.5	1
36.5	35.5	28	27.5	534.5	25	250	325	290.2 $\binom{26}{19}$	73.5	963.7	429.2	2
33	32	29	28	523.5	25	200	350	291.1 $\binom{25}{16}$	69	935.1	411.6	3
34.5	33.5	29	28	541.5	20.5	240	275	270.1 $\binom{23}{14}$	65.5	871.1	329.6	4
37	36.5	30.8	31	580.3	31.5	205	345	184 $\binom{10}{11}$	98	863.5	283.2	5
29.5	29	27	26.8	490.5	19	255	330	175.5 $\binom{15}{16}$	78.5	858	367.5	6
33.8	33.2	28	28	542	28.5	225	300	213.6 $\binom{16}{11}$	89	856.1	314.1	7
33.5	33.6	28.8	28.7	522.9	19.5	200	275	291.3 $\binom{25}{19}$	67	852.8	329.9	8
31.5	32	28.5	28	511.5	18	200	325	229.2 $\binom{22}{13}$	60	832.2	320.7	9
35	35	29.5	29	564.5	24	230	350	145.2 $\binom{9}{8}$	67	816.2	251.7	10
33.7	33.4	28.8	28.3	533.2	22.9	225.5	330	241.7 $\binom{20.1}{14.4}$	73.3	893.4	360.2	
38	37	29.8	29.5	551.3	20.5	270	375	531.3 $\binom{58}{16}$	76	1272.8	721.5	1
36	35	31.3	30.8	549.3	19	290	330	409.9 $\binom{40}{16}$	93	1141.9	592.6	2
36	34	31.5	29.5	537	15	240	400	371.8 $\binom{35}{20}$	72	1098.8	561.8	3
32.5	32	29	28.5	521.1	18	250	425	326.6 $\binom{30}{17}$	66	1085.0	564.5	4
34	33.5	29.5	28.8	550.5	32	300	360	252.4 $\binom{20}{13}$	84	1028.4	477.9	5
36.5	36	31	30	563.5	28	245	300	332.2 $\binom{30}{18}$	89	994.2	430.7	6
36.5	35.5	28	27.5	534.5	25	250	325	290.2 $\binom{26}{19}$	73.5	963.7	429.2	7
33.5	33	29	29	536.5	25.5	190	340	243.8 $\binom{17}{17}$	73.5	872.8	336.3	8
37	36.5	30.8	31	580.3	31.5	205	345	184 $\binom{10}{11}$	98	863.5	283.2	9
29.5	29	27	26.8	490.5	19	255	330	175.5 $\binom{15}{16}$	78.5	858	367.5	10
34.9	34.1	29.7	29.1	541.4	23.3	249.5	353	311.8 $\binom{28.1}{16.3}$	80.3	1018	476.5	

581

TABLE No. 9.—*Bodily measurements of the students of Amherst College for the years* 1881–'82 *to* 1883–'84, *inclusive, averaged by years of age.*

[This table gives the average results of the study of 461 students during the past three years in the more than fifty measures and tests that are applied. They are grouped under the different years from 17 to 25, inclusive, and the results are given in kilograms, meters, and millimeters, except the "capacity of lungs," which is in liters, and the "chest strength," the unit of which is the bodily weight as raised in a "dip" and a "pull up."]

	Years of age.								
	17.	18.	19.	20.	21.	22.	23.	24.	25.
Weight	59.8	59.7	61.1	61.3	63.2	62.7	63.1	64.7	62.2
Height	1.71	1.70	1.71	1.71	1.72	1.71	1.72	1.72	1.72
Knee	472	466	469	464	477	474	480	467	473
Sitting	897	889	900	891	904	902	902	916	915
Pubes	869	857	858	844	863	860	863	847	857
Navel	1.02	1.00	1.02	1.01	1.02	1.02	1.02	1.01	1.02
Sternum	1.40	1.38	1.39	1.39	1.40	1.39	1.41	1.4	1.40
Girth:									
Head	568	568	568	569	575	572	575	572	573
Neck	337	341	348	350	354	351	358	356	357
Chest, full	887	903	923	922	935	933	934	942	925
Chest, repose	853	865	877	883	896	895	899	908	880
Belly	703	717	714	723	736	735	747	753	741
Hips	872	875	893	897	903	896	901	911	900
Thighs	501	501	512	513	523	513	525	527	509
Knees	356	354	355	356	357	355	358	358	357
Calves	337	340	344	346	351	346	345	360	345
Insteps	236	237	238	240	243	241	242	247	238
Right upper arm contracted	275	279	291	284	296	294	301	297	277
Upper arms	242	247	252	253	257	254	261	258	250
Elbows	244	243	246	248	251	248	253	254	247
Fore-arms	251	253	257	261	265	261	266	264	260
Wrists	163	162	162	163	166	166	167	167	164
Breadth:									
Head	152	152	153	153	155	154	156	155	155
Neck	106	106	107	108	109	107	109	108	110
Shoulders	414	428	425	428	435	441	437	438	423
Waist	247	247	258	258	256	259	259	266	260
Hips	319	321	325	324	329	323	330	332	326
Nipples	188	192	195	197	202	202	201	201	190
Shoulder elbows	372	367	367	369	375	371	376	378	370
Elbow tips	465	460	460	456	461	462	466	461	454
Length of feet	260	257	258	257	262	261	262	261	258
Stretch of arms	1.77	1.77	1.77	1.77	1.80	1.79	1.80	1.78	1.77
Horizontal length	1.73	1.72	1.72	1.72	1.73	1.73	1.73	1.73	1.71
Strength of lungs	10.0	13.0	13.5	13.0	12.0	12.0	12.6	12.0	10.7
of back	132	132	139	146	153	151	159	154	138
chest, dip	3.6	5.2	5.8	6.2	7.0	7.0	8.2	7.3	5.6
pull up	7.6	7.9	8.8	8.9	9.0	9.1	8.8	8.8	9.4
of legs	166	161	172	180	193	198	197	183	164
of fore-arm	33.9	34.8	36.1	38.4	40.0	39.9	40.9	40.7	37.1
Capacity of lungs	3.86	3.91	4.03	4.01	4.10	4.40	4.29	4.14	4.00
Pilosity	2.1	2.2	2.2	2.3	2.4	2.6	2.7	2.3	2.7
Number measured	47	100	90	97	50	30	26	11	10
Total					461				

TABLE No. 10.—*Statistics of bodily growth and development secured from the class of 1884, in Amherst College, during junior and senior years.*

	Averages taken in 1882.	Averages taken in 1884.	Difference.	Largest individual measure.	Smallest individual measure.	Largest individual increase in two years.
Weight	60.5	62.4	4¼ lbs.	82.5	50.5	15 lbs.
Height	1.71	1.72	½ in.	1.86	1.53	1¼ in.
Sitting	918	921	⅛ "	1.00	820	1 "
Sternum	1.39	1.40	½ "	1.54	1.24	1 "
Girth:						
Head	568	578	⅜ "	615	541	1 "
Neck	347	356	⅓ "	400	320	1½ "
Chest, full	924	932	⅓ "	1.01	840	2⅛ "
Chest, repose	877	879	⅛ "	1.02	795	2⅛ "
Belly	710	739	¼ "	865	670	3 "
Hips	891	907	¾ "	1.04	816	4 "
Thighs	508	526	¾ "	650	475	3½ "
Knees	353	363	⅓ "	415	322	1¾ "
Calves	342	351	⅓ "	406	312	1½ "
Insteps	240	239	1/25 "	270	212	¾ "
Contracted arm	290	296	¼ "	370	257	1¾ "
Arm at rest	253	256	⅛ "	346	220	1 "
Elbows	246	259	½ "	292	223	1¼ "
Fore-arms	258	266	¼ "	305	235	1 "
Wrists	161	165	⅛ "	185	152	½ "
Breadth:						
Head	154	154	0 "	170	143	½ "
Neck	102	109	¼ "	122	98	½ "
Shoulders	420	437	½ "	488	411	3 "
Waist	252	257	⅛ "	298	280	¾ "
Hips	321	327	⅛ "	379	294	1 "
Shoulder elbows	367	375	¼ "	419	337	1 "
Elbow tips	456	459	⅛ "	521	410	1½ "
Length of feet	256	260	⅛ "	289	236	¼ "
Stretch of arms	1.77	1.79	¾ "	1.99	1.59	2¼ "
Horizontal length	1.72	1.74	¾ "	1.87	1.56	1½ "
Strength	474	501	27	860	316	176

This is not presented as showing remarkably large results. These figures are not compared with the picked men, such as soldiers, sailors, sporting men, or the volunteer or paid gymnasts who are paraded to announce a system, a method, or a theoretical basis, but are the exact measurements of a whole class in Amherst College, taken with an interval of two years, with the sole object to show the growth and development in an "average lot" of young men between twenty years and six months and two years older, engaged in college study, discipline, and training.

In this table the first column of figures indicates the average measures of the class as taken in February, 1882, and the second column the same in February, 1884, both from 79 men. The data are all expressed in millimeters, except "weight," which is in kilograms, and "strength," which is an arbitrary datum constructed by multiplying the weight of the body into the indications of strength known as "chest tests," and added to the tests of the "back, legs, fore-arms, and lungs."

The third column gives the difference or increase between the two series, expressed in fractions of an inch.

The fourth column gives the largest individual measurements found in February 1884, and the fifth column the smallest of the same date.

The sixth column gives the largest individual increase gained in the two years.

The item of "height" is of interest, in that we see a slow and apparently small growth in two years. We, however, can very easily compare the results of the college students with those obtained by Dr. J. H. Baxter, Medical Purveyor, U. S. A., during the late civil war. His measurements were from 190,621 drafted and enlisted men, and those at Amherst from 1,806 students at college between 1861 and 1878.

	Years of age.								
	17.	18.	19.	20.	21.	22.	23.	24.	25.
	Inches.	Inches.	Inches.	Inches.	Inches.	Inches.	Inches.	Inches.	Inches.
Dr. Baxter	65.65	66.39	67.07	67.51	67.58	67.92	68.01	68.02	68.05
Amherst College	66.71	67.38	67.72	67.88	67.86	68.11	68.17	68.35	68.34

In both these tables we see a rapid increase from 17 to 20, and a slower and more uniform rate afterward.

The chest measure is large for the Senior age, it being 36.75 inches for the class of 1884, while the Senior average for 20 years has been but 35.97 inches.

The abdominal girth expresses a healthy growth either in the fat or well developed nutritive organs.

The increase of joints and muscles in both extremities is significant and symmetrical, and while the average arm girth increase (biceps) is .25 inch, and the largest individual increase is 1.75 inches, the development is shown in the test of strength, which has increased from 474 to 501, showing the greater hardening and compactness of the muscular fiber, a much more valuable acquisition than the greater girth.

Probably the brain acquires its full size early in life. This is corroborated by these results. The increase of head girth is three-eighths of an inch, and that of the breadth nothing.

These results go to show that the "stretch of arms" is more than the "perpendicular height," as is latterly admitted to be the true proportion of the body. The difference is more than two inches. That the finger-reach has increased three-quarters of an inch and the height one-half an inch, may show that the one maximum is gained before the other.

This study of these seventy-nine men is one of their unconscious additions to anthropology, and is their contribution to a knowledge of what constitutes the most complete manhood.

INSTITUTIONS THAT HAVE ADOPTED MORE OR LESS COMPLETELY THE SARGENT SYSTEM.

The gymnasia at the following named institutions have been wholly or partially furnished with Dr. Sargent's apparatus since 1879. Those in which his system of measurements and directions are employed are indicated by an asterisk (*).

[M. against the name of an institution indicates that it is for males; F., for females; M. and F., for males and females. A † indicates that the gymnasium is in charge of a regularly educated physician.]

1. *†Amherst College, Amherst, Mass. M.
2. *Boston University, Boston, Mass. M. and F.
3. *†Cornell University, Ithaca, N. Y. M. and F.
4. *†Harvard University, Cambridge, Mass. M.
5. *†Haverford College, Haverford, Pa. M.

PHYSICAL TRAINING IN AMERICAN COLLEGES. 57

6. *†Johns Hopkins University, Baltimore, Md. M.
7. *Lehigh University, South Bethlehem, Pa. M.
8. Massachusetts Institute of Technology, Boston, Mass. M.
9. *Nashville University, State Normal College, Nashville, Tenn. M. and F.
10. *National Deaf-Mute College, Washington, D. C. M.
11. *Smith College, Northampton, Mass. F.
12. *†Swarthmore College, Swarthmore, Pa. M. and F.
13. Tufts College, College Hill, Mass. M.
14. Wellesley College, Wellesley, Mass. F.
15. English High and Public Latin School, Boston, Mass. M.
16. Marlboro Street School, Boston, Mass. F.
17. Mount Vernon Street School, Boston, Mass. F.
18. Berkeley School, New York City.
19. Fifth Avenue School, New York City.
20. Dr. Brearley's School, New York City. F.
21. *†William Penn Charter School, Philadelphia. M.
22. Gunnery School, Washington, Conn. M.
23. St. Mark's School, Southborough, Mass. M.
24. High School, Providence, R. I. M. and F.
25. Siglar's Preparatory School, Newburg, N. Y. M.
26. Cook Academy, Havana, N. Y. M.
27. Willard's Academy, Saxton's River, Vt.
28. McLean Insane Asylum, Somerville, Mass. M. and F.
29. Cadets' Armory, Boston, Mass. M.
30. *†Hartford Theological Seminary, Hartford, Conn. M.
31. Theological Seminary, Princeton, N. J. M.
32. Newton Theological Institution, Newton, Mass. M.
33. *†Young Men's Christian Union, Boston, Mass. M.
34. Young Men's Christian Association, Baltimore, Md. M.
35. Young Men's Christian Association, Providence, R. I. M.
36. Young Men's Christian Association, Chicago, Ill. M.
37. Young Men's Christian Association, Washington, D. C. M.
38. Young Men's Christian Association, Lawrence, Mass. M.
39. Young Men's Christian Association, Bangor, Me. M.
40. *†Sanatory Gymnasium, Philadelphia, Pa. M. and F.
41. Sanatory Gymnasium, Providence, R. I.
42. *†Sanatory Gymnasium, Cambridge, Mass. F.
43. New York Athletic Club, New York City. M.
44. Olympic Athletic Club, San Francisco, Cal. M.
45. Montreal Athletic Club, Montreal, Canada. M.
46. Saint Louis Athletic Club, Saint Louis, Mo. M.
47. Rochester Athletic Club, Rochester, N. Y. M.
48. Norfolk Athletic Club, Norfolk, Va. M.

It is proposed to introduce the Sargent system of directed exercise into Vassar College, for women, at Poughkeepsie, N. Y., and the University of Vermont at Burlington, Vt. It has just been adopted for the new gymnasium of Lafayette College at Easton, Pa. The largest and best of the gymnasia belonging to a woman's college is that at Bryn Mawr College, Bryn Mawr, Pa. It will be opened probably in September, 1885, under the charge of a directress trained for the position by Dr. Sargent.

CONCERNING TEACHERS OF THE SARGENT SYSTEM.

So great is the demand for competent teachers of physical training that Dr. Sargent opened a school for teachers in the autumn of 1884, with an attendance of sixteen pupils.

The following circular sets forth the nature, aims, and methods of the Physical Training School for Teachers, corner of Church and Palmer streets, Cambridge, Mass.:

Within the past few years the demand for competent teachers in physical training has been so great that salaries ranging from one to three thousand dollars a year have been offered to those that are capable of filling the desired positions.

Most of the applicants for these places have been poorly qualified, both mentally and physically, for the work that was expected of them, and they have failed to meet the requirements of the position for want of a proper preparatory training.

The numerous requests that I have received for teachers trained in accordance with the Harvard system have induced me to open a school for this purpose.

The object of this school will be to drill pupils in the theory and practice of physical training, and to prepare them to teach in this much neglected branch of education.

Course.— The course will extend over two years. Medical graduates and those that are prepared to pass a satisfactory examination in the preliminary work will be required to attend only one year.

Applicants.— All applicants must have good health, a sound physique, and have had the advantages of at least a common school education.

Course for first year.— Believing that all teaching should be preceded by inquiries into the "nature, capabilities, and requirements of the being to be taught," the fundamental principles of anatomy and physiology will form the basis of the first year's work.

The studies in these branches will be supplemented by such studies in biology, zoölogy, chemistry, and physics, as are necessary to understand the laws of health, growth, and development.

Practice for the first year.— The practice for the first year will consist of special exercises for the development of the teacher:—Massage, free movements, calisthenics, light gymnastics—the last including wooden and iron dumb-bells, wands, and Indian clubs; chest weights, class exercises, voice training, and introductory exercises on the heavy apparatus; practical carpentry, the art of splicing, serving, and knotting ropes, and the mechanical working of the gymnasium; what to do in case of emergencies.

Course for second year.— The studies for the second year will consist of inquiries into the relation of body and mind:—The conservation of energy, animal mechanics, mental hygiene from the physical basis, anthropometry and the laws of form and proportion, vital statistics, semeiology, physical diagnosis; the hygiene of occupations and of schools; natural heritage; variations in exercise, food, sleep, bathing, clothing, and climate, considered as to their mental and physical effects upon different constitutions; the analysis of sports, games, and educational exercises; the relation of the organism to the structure, the structure to the individual, and the individual to the public; the science and art of teaching.

Practice for second year.— The practice for the second year will consist of class exercises with bar bells, chest weights, and Indian clubs, marches, the organization of classes and the division into squads, school work, athletic sports, heavy gymnastics, practice with the dynamometers; the application of developing appliances for the relief of natural weaknesses; the adaptation of exercise and training to individual needs; practice in teaching.

Reading course.— Special arrangements will be made with those who desire to take the reading course at home, though attendance at the gymnasium is advised.

Summer course.— For the benefit of all that are engaged in teaching throughout the year, a course of reading and practice will be prescribed, and a summer course of lectures, examinations, and exercises will be given.

Equivalents.— A good physique, fine muscular development, proficiency in physical exercises, and experience in teaching, will be accepted as equivalents for a certain amount of time.

Certificates.— In every case the applicant must pass a satisfactory examination in all of the work prescribed, and have taken a medical degree from a medical school in good standing, in order to receive a full certificate.

In other cases certificates will be given indicating the time spent at the school, the work done, and the nature of the service that each teacher is capable of performing.

Sessions.— The course will be open to men and women, but the physical exercises will be conducted in different gymnasia. The gymnasium for women will be in Cambridge, the gymnasium for men in Boston.

The winter session will begin November 1, and continue until June 1. The summer session will begin the first Monday after July 4, and continue five weeks.

Terms.— For season ending June 1, 1885: One-half course in theory and practice, $100; one-half course in reading, prescribed, $50; one-half course in summer practice, ending second week in August, $50.

In no case will a summer course be given unless preceded by a reading course extending over six months. All payments made in advance. For further particulars address—

D. A. SARGENT, M.D.,
Cambridge, Mass.

THE NUMBER AND COST OF COLLEGE GYMNASIUM BUILDINGS IN THE UNITED STATES.

In passing to consider the number and cost of the college gymnasia erected and fitted since those of Amherst, Harvard, and Yale were built in 1860, we may note that to Princeton College, probably, belongs the honor of having the first college building devoted exclusively to gymnastic purposes. This embryo structure, if we may be allowed the term, as befits an embryo, was a very small affair, and owed its existence to the zealous endeavors of a few students of the college in 1856. It was a small "single-boarded structure of wood," and was painted red, "that," as its historian tells us, "it might resist the storms of heaven as its founders had resisted the objections of an unpropitious Faculty." It remained "a stoveless shanty" till 1860, when a stove and a new set of apparatus were put into it. In 1865, during the summer vacation, the people of the town reduced it to ashes, on account of a report that a tramp sick with yellow fever had slept in it over night.

The era of gymnasium building which opened in 1860 may be conveniently divided into three periods, viz.: first period, 1859–'60 to 1870, inclusive; second period, 1871 to 1880, inclusive; third period, 1881 to the present writing, February, 1885.

FIRST PERIOD.

Institution with which gymnasium is connected.	When built.	Cost.	
(a) Institutions for superior instruction.			
Amherst College, Massachusetts	1859–'60	$15,000	
Dartmouth College, New Hampshire	1866	24,000	
Harvard University, Massachusetts	1860	10,000	
College of New Jersey (Princeton College), N. J.	1869	38,000	
Washington University, Missouri	?	7,000	
Wesleyan University, Connecticut	1863	5,000	
University of Wisconsin, Wisconsin	1868	5,000	
Yale College, Connecticut	1860	13,000	
Pennsylvania College, Pennsylvania	1870	3,000	120,000
(b) Institutions for secondary instruction.			
Claverack College and Hudson River Institute, New York	1861	6,000	
West Newton English and Classical School, Massachusetts	1860	500	
Williston Seminary, Massachusetts	?	¹20,000	26,500
Total for the first period			146,500

Williams College, Massachusetts, and Bowdoin College, Maine, for young men, and Vassar College, for women, in New York, each fitted up a gymnasium during this period, in a building since devoted to other purposes.

SECOND PERIOD.

Institution with which gymnasium is connected.	When built.	Cost.
Institutions for superior instruction.		
Beloit College, Wisconsin	1874	$5,000
University of California, California	1878	12,000
Harvard University, Massachusetts	1879	110,000
Smith College, Massachusetts	1880	4,000
Vanderbilt University, Tennessee	1879	22,000
Newton Theological Institution, Massachusetts	1876	4,000
Hartford Theological Seminary, Connecticut	?	¹8,000
Total for the second period		165,000

¹ Estimated.

PHYSICAL TRAINING IN AMERICAN COLLEGES. 61

THIRD PERIOD.

Institutions with which gymnasium is connected.	When built.	Cost.
(a) *Institutions for superior instruction.*		
Amherst College, Massachusetts	1883–'84	$65,000
Bryn Mawr College, Pennsylvania	1884	18,000
Cornell University, New York	1882–'83	40,000
Dickinson College, Pennsylvania	1884	8,000
Johns Hopkins University, Maryland	1883	10,000
Lafayette College, Pennsylvania	1884	15,000
Lehigh University, Pennsylvania	1882	40,000
Massachusetts Agricultural College, Massachusetts[1]	1883	6,000
University of Minnesota, Minnesota[1]	1884	34,000
Nashville University, State Normal College, Tennessee.	1884	5,500
National Deaf-Mute College, District of Columbia[2]	1881	14,600
Tufts College, Massachusetts	1882–'83	10,000
University of Wooster, Ohio	1882–'83	4,200
(b) *Institutions for secondary instruction.*		
Shattuck School, Minnesota	1880	20,000
Total for third period		290,300
Total for second period		165,000
Total for first period		146,500
Grand total		601,800

CONCERNING SCHOOL AND COLLEGE GYMNASIA NOT OCCUPYING AN ENTIRE BUILDING.

It is impossible, owing to meager returns to our inquiries, to state accurately the amount of money expended for buildings and apparatus by institutions not noted in the above lists; but we may safely "guess" that $150,000 have been expended since 1860 on the class of gymnasia under consideration, in addition to the $600,000 accounted for above.

Funds are either in hand or are being raised for gymnasia at Phillips Exeter Academy, New Hampshire; University of Michigan, Michigan; University of Pennsylvania, Pennsylvania; and Williams College, Massachusetts. New gymnasia are projected at the United States Military and Naval Academies.

[1] Used at present for military drill.
[2] This is unique among our college gymnasia, as it contains, on the ground floor, a swimming pool, which is 40 by 26 feet, 6 feet deep at one end, sloping upward to a depth of 3 feet at the other.

TABLE No. 11, PART I.—*Statistics of the principal college and school gymnasia of the United States.*

NOTE.—Vital statistics are kept at the institutions marked *. L. G. indicates light gymnastics; H. G., heavy gymnastics; S. G., Sargent's gymnastics; Mil, military drill; Cal., calisthenics; °, optional; †, required; M. F., member of the Faculty.

	Institutions having a structure devoted to the purposes of physical training and personal hygiene.	Date of the erection, or fitting up of the building.	Cost of the building and its fittings.	Main material of the building.	Number of stories in the building.	Number of rooms in the building.	Dimensions of the main hall, in feet.	Kind of drill adopted.	Date of adoption of drill.	Number of hours' drill per week for individuals.
1	University of California, Cal	1878	$12,000	Wood			Octa'l, 80	L. G.°; Mil.°	1880	2
2	Wesleyan University, Conn	1863–'64	5,000	do	1	1	70 by 40	L. G.°		
3	Yale College, Conn	1859–'60	13,000	Brick	2 & cellar	4	110 by 60	L. G.°; H. G.°		
4	Northwestern University, Ill			do	2	6				
5	Johns Hopkins University, Md.*	1883	10,000	do	1 & annex 2½		90 by 40	S. G.°	1883	2
6	Amherst College, Mass.*	1863–'64	65,000	do	2 & basement	18	80 by 64	L. G.; S. G.	1860	
7	Harvard College, Mass.*	1870	110,000	do	2 & basement	16	113 by 90†	S. G.°	1879	2
8	Massachusetts Agricultural College, Mass.*	1883	6,000	Wood		4	120 by 60	Mil.°	1867	3
9	Smith College, Mass	1880	4,000	do	2			L. G.°; S. G.°		2
10	Tufts College, Mass	1862–'63	10,000	Brick	1 & basement	4	90 by 45	S. G.		
11	Carleton College, Minn.*	1863–'64				4	40 by 40			
12	University of Minnesota, Minn	1884	34,000	Wood	3	9	120 by 140	Mil.°	1869(1)	2
13	Shattuck School, Minn	1880	20,000	Stone	2 & cellar	9	34 by 60	Mil.°; L. G.°	1862	2
14	Washington University, Mo		7,000	do	1 & cellar	4	70 by 50	L. G.°	1870	2
15	Dartmouth College, N. H	1866	24,000	Brick	2 & cellar	5	75 by 45	L. G.°	1867	2 fr.; 1 soph.
16	College of New Jersey, N. J.*	1869	38,000	Stone	2 & cellar	4	78 by 52	L. G.°; H. G.°	1869	
17	Cornell University, N. Y.*	1882–'83	40,000	Brick	1 & annex 2	4	150 by 60	S. G.; Mil.°	S. G., 1864	3(†)
18	University of Wooster, O	1882–'83	4,200	do	1	1	48 by 96	L. G.°		1†
19	Lafayette College, Penn.*	1883–'84	15,000	do	1 & basement	8	76 by 41	L. G.°; S. G.	1884	2
20	Lehigh University, Penn.*	1882	40,000	Stone	2 & cellar	8	75 by 45	S. G.°; L. G.°	1883	
21	Pennsylvania College, Penn	1870	3,000	Wood		1	50 by 90	L. G.°		
22	Univ. of Nashville State Nor. Coll., Tenn	1884	5,500	Brick	1	3	80 by 30	S. G.	1884	
23	Vanderbilt University, Tenn	1879	22,000	do	1 & cellar	5	90 by 60	L. G.°		open 6 hr's.

TABLE No. 11, PART II.—*Statistics of the principal college and school gymnasia of the United States.*

NOTE.—Vital statistics are kept at the institutions marked *. L. G. indicates light gymnastics; H. G., heavy gymnastics; S. G., Sargent's gymnastics; Mil., military drill: Cal., calisthenics; °, optional; †, required; M. F., member of the Faculty.

	Institutions having a structure devoted to the purposes of physical training and personal hygiene.	Students of whom drill is required.	Drill is in charge of—	Number of lockers in dressing-room.	Bathing facilities. a Bath-tubs. b Bowls. c Shower-baths.	Number of— a Water-closets. b Urinals.	Items regarding play-grounds.	Remarks concerning the character and amount of the instruction given in anatomy, physiology, and hygiene.	Number of students in 1882-'83. (M., males; F., females.)
1	University of California, Cal.	All able-bodied males.	U. S. officer	60	c 2	a 1			143 M.; 72, F.
2	Wesleyan University, Conn.		No instruction						176 M.; 15 F.
3	Yale College, Conn	1st year men, 2d term.	Special teacher	70	a 7, b 4, c 1	a 1, b 2	Ball grounds	Lectures and recitations req'd.	1,080 M.
4	Northwestern University, Ill.								294.
5	Johns Hopkins University, Md.*	Candidates for B. A.	Director, M. F.	228	a 2, b 6, c 2	a 2, b 2	Clifton, 4 A.	Lectures and text-book req'd.	352 M.
6	Amherst College, Mass.*	All able-bodied	Director, M. F.	270	a 12, c 6	a 2, b 3	2 to 3 A. (1881)	Req'd inst. given 1st and 2d yrs.	1,428. (?)
7	Harvard College, Mass.*	...do...	Director, Mil., M. F. (!)890				10 A		112 M.
8	Mass. Agric. College, Mass		U. S. officer				Ball grounds		284. F.
9	Smith College, Mass		Instructress				Tennis courts.		160 M.
10	Tufts College, Mass.						Ball grounds		175 M.; 155 F.
11	Carleton College, Minn.*								146 M.; 77 F.
12	University of Minnesota, Minn		U. S. officer						
13	Shattuck School, Minn.*	All boys	U. S. officer and special teacher.		8 baths	a 16, b 10	Ample playgrounds.	Anatomy, physiology, and hygiene are required studies.[1]	
14	Washington University, Mo	1st and 2d year males.	Special teacher	60	Small	a 3, b 5	Yard 100 x 100 ft	Lectures required	880 M.; 490 F.
15	Dartmouth College, N. H	...do...	Tutor in math			b 1	Village Green.	Lectures, optional and req'd.	339 M.
16	College of New Jersey, N. J.*	...do...	Director, Sept.	221	b 6, c 3	a 1, b 1	Ath. grounds	Lectures required	500 M.
17	Cornell University, N. Y.*		Director, M. F.; U. S. officer.	285	a 6	a 2, b 1	Ample grounds		407.
18	University of Wooster, O.		Class leaders						
19	Lafayette College, Penn.*	All classes	Medical director				Ample grounds	Lectures required	395 M.; 161 F.
20	Lehigh University, Penn.*								249 M.
21	Pennsylvania College, Penn	All students	Director, M. F.	246	a 10, b 2, c 17	a 3, b 6		Lectures required	150 M.

PHYSICAL TRAINING IN AMERICAN COLLEGES. 65

22	Univ. of Nashville State Nor. Col., Tenn.		Special teachers	Some		Some		Entrance examination includes anat., phys., and hygiene.	70 M.; 92 F.
23	Vanderbilt University, Tenn		A student		a 5	b 6	Ample grounds	Lectures elective	480 M.; 7 F.
24	Beloit College, Wis	All students	U. class leaders						222 M.
25	University of Wisconsin, Wis		Class leaders				Ample grounds	Lectures elective	314.
26	Nat. Deaf-Mute Col., D. C.*	All male students	Director, M. F. (1)	Swim'g b'th			Ball grounds		51 M.

[1] In 1882–'83 all candidates for admission were required to undergo a physical examination by a physician.

TABLE No. 12, PART I.—*Statistics of institutions having gymnasium or drill halls.*

NOTE.—Vital statistics are kept at the institutions marked *. L. G. indicates light gymnastics; H. G., heavy gymnastics; S. G., Sargent's gymnastics; Mil., military drill; Cal, calisthenics; °, optional; ʳ, required; M. F., member of the Faculty.

	Institutions having gymnasium or drill halls, but in structures used also for other purposes.	Date of building or fitting up.	Cost of fittings, etc.	Material.	Number of rooms.	Dimensions of gymnasium in feet.	Character of Attings, M. Machines.	Kind of drill adopted.	Date of adoption of drill.	Number of hours drill per week for individuals.
1	Augustana College, Ill	1883	Unfitted	Wood	1	88 by 96		Mil		
2	De Pauw University, Ind			Brick	1	100 by 50		L. G		
3	Iowa College, Ia		Unfitted		1	42 by 70		Mil.ʳ		
4	Kansas State Agricultural College, Kan		Unfitted		2	35 by 35		L. G		
5	Central University, Ky									
6	Boston University, Mass	1882–'83	$900	Brick	2	35 by 20	Sargent M.	S. G.°; H. G.°; Cal.°	S. G., 1883	2
7	Wellesley College, Mass.*	1882	$1,200 to $1,500	do	2		do	L. G.ʳ; S. G.°	1882	1½
8	Vassar College, N. Y.*							L. G.ʳ; S. G.		
9	Haverford College, Penn.*		1,000	Brick	2	82 by 25	Sargent M.	S. G.°	1850	
10	Connecticut Literary Institution, Conn.	New.			1			Mil.ʳ		
11	Morgan Park Military Academy, Ill	1870	1,500	Wood.	3	40 by 60		Mil.ʳ		4
12	West Newton English and Classical School, Mass.	1860	500	do	1	40 by 30	Old style.	L. G.ʳ		
13	Phillips Academy, Mass	1818						L. G.°		
14	Public Latin School, Boston, Mass	1881	1,500	Brick	1	40 by 80	Sargent M.	Mil.ʳ; L. G.°; S. G.	1860	
15	Williston Seminary, Mass	1860–'65?	20,000	do	2	130 by 60		L. G.ʳ	Mil. 1865	
16	Concordia Seminary, Mo	New.			1	Spacious		L. G.°		
17	Claverack College, N. Y	1861	6,000	Wood.	1	50 by 80		Mil. for males; Cal. for fem.		
18	William Penn Charter School, Penn	1884	1,200	Brick	2	56 by 28	Sargent M.	S. G.ʳ	1885	2
19	Eng. and Classical School, Providence, R. I.	1875		do	1	90 by 40		L. G.ʳ; Mil.	1886	2
20	Belleview High School, Va	Recently								

TABLE No. 12, PART II.—*Statistics of institutions having gymnasium or drill halls.*

	Institutions having gymnasium or drill halls, but in structures used also for other purposes.	Students of whom drill is required.	Drill is in charge of—	Number of lockers in dressing-room.	Bathing facilities. a Bath-tubs b Bowls. c Shower baths.	Number of— a Water-closets. b Urinals.	Items regarding play-grounds.	Remarks concerning the character and amount of the instruction given in anatomy, physiology, and hygiene.	Number of students in 1882–'83. (M, males; F, females.)
1	Augustana College, Ill.							Instruction given	72 M.
2	De Pauw University, Ind		U. S. officer					Instruction given	503—400 M.; 103 F.
3	Iowa College, Ia							Instruction given	304—154 M.; 150 F.
4	Kansas State Agric'l College		U. S. officer					Required instruction given	347—233 M.; 114 F.
5	Central University, Ky								
6	Boston University, Mass		Two sp'l teachers	24	Some		None	Instruction given	601—469 M.; 132 F.
7	*Wellesley College, Mass		Director, special teacher, M. D.		Good	Good	Ample gr'nds; also a lake.	Required instruction given	485 F.
8	*Vassar College, N. Y		Special teacher					Required instruction given	318 F.
9	*Haverford College, Penn		Medical director					Optional; instruction given	140—65 M.; 75 F.
10	Conn. Literary Institution, Conn							Instruction given	
11	Morgan Park Milit'y Acad., Ill.						Ball grounds	Instruction given	111—75 M.; 30 F.
12	W. Newton Eng. and Class. Sch							Some instruction given	267 M.
13	Phillips Academy, Mass		Special mil. inst.						381 M.
14	Public Latin School, Boston		Special instructor					Some instruction given	
15	Williston Seminary, Mass								
16	Concordia Seminary, Mo								
17	Claverack College, N. Y							Instruction given	248—138 M.; 110 F.
18	William Penn Charter School, Penn.	All boys	Medical director				Yard	Excellent day school	
19	English and Classical School, Providence, R. I.	All boys	Special teachers					Physiology taught	
20	Bellevue High School, Va.						Ball grounds		50. (†)

DESCRIPTIONS OF THE PRINCIPAL GYMNASIA.

THE PRATT GYMNASIUM AT AMHERST COLLEGE.

The new gymnasium at Amherst College, which was completed during the summer of 1884, is styled the Pratt Gymnasium, in honor of C. M. Pratt, of Brooklyn, N. Y., a graduate of the college in 1879, who contributed nearly $40,000 for its erection. The building, which faces westerly, is situated within the college precincts, on, or rather in, a sidehill sloping toward the south. The structure, which is 120 feet by 80 in the clear, is of brick, has a slated roof, and comprises two stories and a basement. E. L. Roberts, 46 Broadway, New York City, was its architect. Through the kindness of Dr. E. Hitchcock, its director, we are

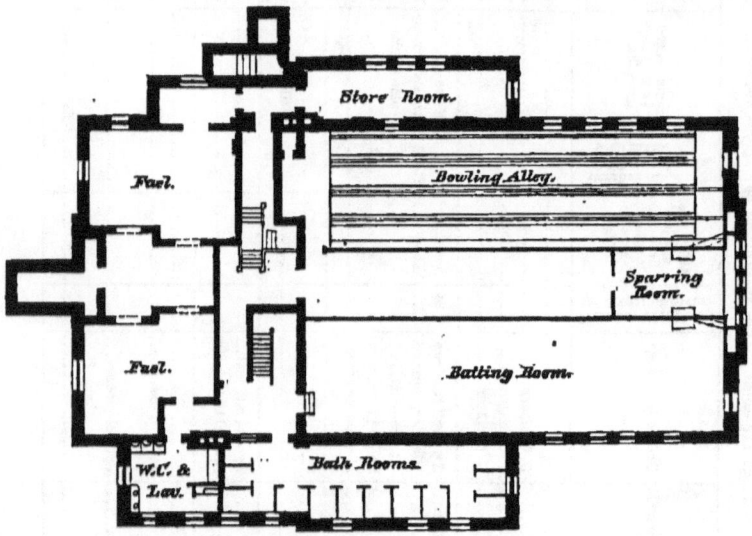

Pratt Gymnasium—Basement Plan.

enabled to give the floor plans of the Pratt Gymnasium and a view of the building, and to furnish an itemized statement of its cost. The rooms on the first floor, besides the front and side entrance halls, are 6 in number: main hall and annex, 80 feet by 64; dressing room, 38 feet by 40, with 270 heated and ventilated lockers; a tepidarium, or dry-rub room, 15 feet by 12; a shower room, 14 feet by 12, opening from the tepidarium, and containing 6 shower baths; the professor's room, 20 feet by 18, fitted as a study and office; and a statistics room, 18 feet by 12, for the physical examination of students.

On the second floor are: the billiard room, 48 feet by 24, containing 3 billiard tables; a small professor's room, 14 feet by 9; the resort, or club-room, 25 feet by 14, for the headquarters of the *Student* (the col-

THE PRATT GYMNASIUM.

lege journal) and reading room; 2 rooms, respectively 16 feet by 10, and 32 feet by 16, for the custodians of the building to live in; a furniture room, 20 feet by 10; a spacious visitors' gallery; and a running

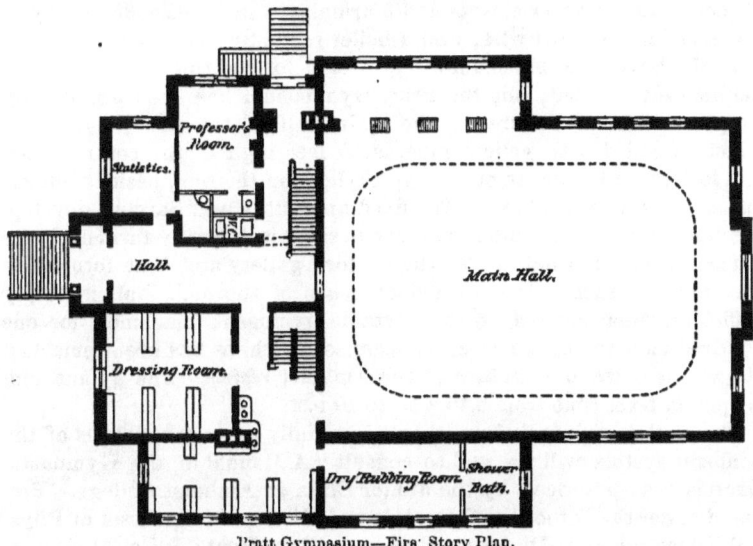

Pratt Gymnasium—First Story Plan.

track, 207 feet long, extending around the main hall at an elevation of 11 feet from its floor.

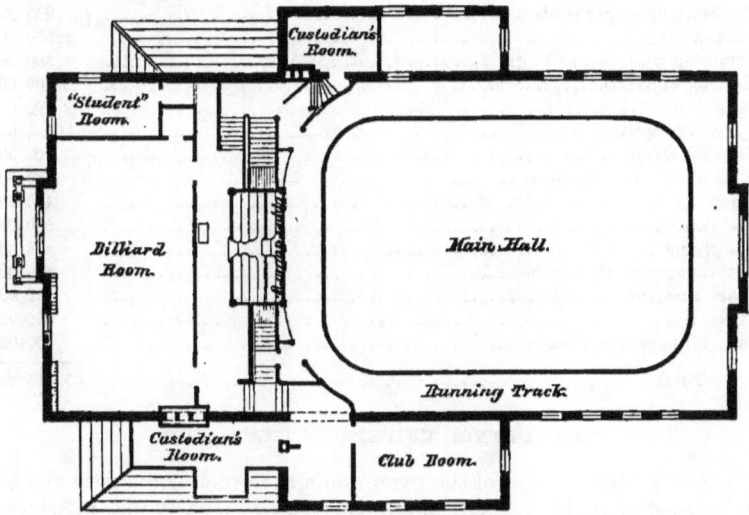

Pratt Gymnasium—Second Story Plan.

In the basement, which is high-studded and lighted by windows on all sides, there are 7 rooms, viz.: the bowling room, 76 feet by 21, with

3 alleys 70 feet in length; a sparring room, 23 feet by 13; a "cage," or room for base-ball and tennis practice, 76 feet by 21; a bath-room, 58 feet by 12, containing 6 tub and 6 sponge baths; a room, 16 feet by 13, containing 2 water-closets and 3 urinals; a store-room, 38 feet by 9; a fuel cellar, 28 feet by 24; and a boiler room, 24 feet by 24.

In the Barrett Gymnasium all provision for lighting after dark was deliberately omitted; but the Pratt Gymnasium has been abundantly supplied with gas fixtures. The main hall of the new gymnasium, which is ceiled with yellow pine, is 40 feet high in the central part, and is lighted by means of a large skylight in the roof, besides numerous side and end windows. The fixed apparatus and Sargent developing appliances, with which this gymnasium is liberally furnished, are placed in the main hall under the visitors' gallery and that formed by the running track. The open floor space of the main hall is amply sufficient, when cleared of the portable gymnastic machines, for one hundred men to engage in class exercise, which, as has been remarked already, is a peculiar feature of the Amherst *régime*. The gymnasium is open in term time from 8.15 A.M. to 10 P.M.

Those who wish to inform themselves fully as to the details of the Amherst system will do well to consult "A Manual of the Gymnastic Exercises as practiced by the Junior Class in Amherst College. Prepared under the Direction of Dr. Edward Hitchcock, Professor of Physical Education and Hygiene. Boston: Ginn, Heath & Co. 1884."

The following itemized statement concerning the cost of building and furnishing the Pratt Gymnasium is of interest:

The building as per contract	$49,825 00
Excavation	1,500 00
Retaining wall, and railings	1,300 00
Heating apparatus	3,700 00
Plumbing	2,790 00
Gymnastic apparatus	1,824 61
Bowling alleys	1,200 00
Billiard tables and fixtures	630 00
Piano	460 00
Gas fixtures	560 68
Gas piping	424 00
Anthropometric apparatus	100 00
Other furniture	149 00
Tiling	850 00
Safe, for papers and books	100 00
Total	65,413 29

THE CORNELL UNIVERSITY GYMNASIUM.

The following account of the gymnasium at Cornell University and of its method of working, was kindly furnished by Lieut. Walter S. Schuyler, U. S. A., Professor of Military Science and Tactics at the university, in the absence of the professor of physical culture.

Buildings.—The main building, completed in 1882–'83, is of brick, with heavily buttressed walls, the self-supporting roof tiled without and ceiled within. To this structure was annexed the frame building formerly used as a gymnasium, refitted and practically rebuilt. In this addition are 6 shower baths, a toilet room, closets, an office for the director, a withdrawing room for use in physical examinations, a small store room, and, on the second floor, a set of 250 lockers for use of students. The whole was designed to serve the double purpose of gymnasium and armory.

The main building comprises the armory and gymnasium hall, with the floor, 60 by 150 feet, laid solidly in cement; an office for the military professor; a military store room; and over these rooms and the lobby, a gallery for spectators. On occasion, the gallery accommodates an orchestra, and the office is arranged for use as a ladies' dressing room.

As the main hall must be used alternately as a gymnasium and a drill room, nearly all of the apparatus is made detachable and portable, and on drill days is, so far as necessary, removed into the annex, or hauled up to the iron suspension frame by the janitor. The removal occupies but a few minutes, and after drill the muskets are locked in arm racks and the apparatus replaced in short order, so that class work with dumb-bells and clubs, as well as general exercise, begins in half an hour after the recall from drill.

The present locker and bath accommodations having been found inadequate for the rapidly increasing student body, an additional building has been planned to supply this deficiency, and also to give room for special exercises. This annex will be of two stories with a basement. The latter will contain four bowling alleys. On the ground floor will be six bath rooms of various kinds, a rubbing room, and a dressing room; also a hall, 30 by 52 feet, for an upper classmen's general exercising room, fitted with about 100 lockers, and a small store room. The attic floor will comprise a base-ball cage, 19 by 75 feet, in which certain rowing machines will be placed, and small store closets between the several windows protecting the same.

Equipment.—The gymnasium is equipped with apparatus of the most approved make and adjustment. The heavier pieces are mainly from the Boston establishment; some have been manufactured in the university shops, and there are a few "Gifford" and other patent appliances. The machines are arranged about the room with a view to orderly and systematic work, and on each is posted a card of direction as to its use.

System.—The affairs of the associated departments of military science and physical culture are regulated by a council composed of the president of the university, one other member of the board of trustees, the professor of physiology, etc., the professor of military science, and the professor of physical culture.

The system now in vogue was adopted last year on trial, and thus far has been found to work well. As soon as possible after the opening of the fall term, all members of the new class are subjected to a systematic examination by the professor of physical culture, the measurements and other statistics being recorded in a book prepared for the purpose. Military drill is required of all members of the Freshman

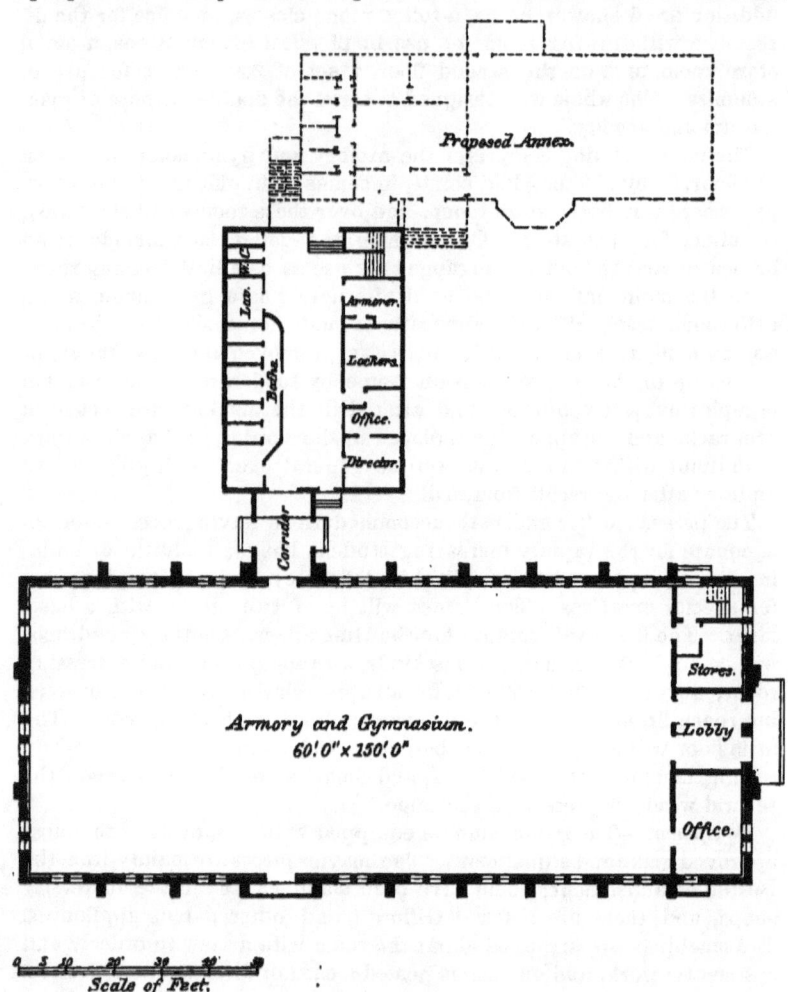

Plan of Cornell University Gymnasium.

and Sophomore classes; but such students as are found, upon the examination referred to, to imperatively need special gymnastic training, are at once transferred from the military to the gymnastic department, and are required to pursue a course of training laid down for them by the examiner, this course comprising five exercises per week, on the apparatus specially adapted to their individual needs.

For all other students work in the gymnasium is optional, and under the advice and direction of the professor and his assistant. Many of the men whose development is not sufficiently defective to warrant their transfer from the military department, are advised by the examiner as to their deficiencies. To each is given a card showing a comparison between his own statistics and the average to be expected in a subject of corresponding stature and weight.

The professor of physical culture is also the medical examiner for all those wishing to get excused from military exercises on the ground of physical disability. The applicants for such exemptions for limited periods are not more numerous than is to be expected in a battalion aggregating two hundred men.

Students absenting themselves from their assigned gymnastic or military exercises for any cause other than illness, must conform to the regulations governing absence from other university duties.

This system, outlined above, will probably be, in time, so modified as to require work in the gymnasium during the winter term of the entire Freshman class. During that term there is no drill.

The professor of physical culture is aided by a skilled assistant who conducts the class exercises and supervises all practice with the apparatus. He also gives instruction in boxing and acts as coach for the outdoor athletics.

The exercises of the women students are conducted in the gymnasium of Sage College, by the professor in person, with the assistance of the matron.

During the past year there were about twenty students transferred from the military department for compulsory exercise, and the result of their practice, as shown by comparison of the measurements made at the beginning and end of the year, is most gratifying, the total increase of the class (thirteen measured) in the one item of "lung capacity" being over forty cubic inches.

In addition to this class upon which the exercise was compulsory, the students to a large number have availed themselves of the privileges of the gymnasium with greater or less regularity, and in every case to good effect. Perhaps the best evidence of this is to be found in the records of Cornell in the State intercollegiate contests during the spring of 1885.

It is found by examination of the statistics that the topography of the country supplies, in a sense, the place of a gymnasium for the students at large, the average increase of leg and lung dimensions during their first year being unprecedented in college statistics.

The military drill gives a special training in discipline and personal carriage which proves beneficial, and the effect of which is observed by all who visit our campus.

Plan of the gymnasium.—It may be readily seen that we have a main gymnasium hall equal in space and equipment to any in the country, except, perhaps, that of Harvard; and after the completion of the additional buildings as planned, our facilities will be second to none.

It appears from the printed forms accompanying Lieutenant Schuyler's account, that the system of measurements and of obtaining the "history" of an individual is the same as that used at Harvard and at Amherst, and that cards are furnished each student exercising in the gymnasium, containing specific printed directions in regard to the apparatus he must use and the time he must use it.

THE LEHIGH UNIVERSITY GYMNASIUM.

The Lehigh University Gymnasium, at South Bethlehem, Pa., is situated on the university campus and faces west. The building was planned by Addison Hutton, architect, 400 Chestnut street, Philadelphia. Dr. Sargent of Cambridge rendered valuable service in perfecting the plans, which embody features suggested by his experience as director of the Hemenway Gymnasium. The building, of Potsdam

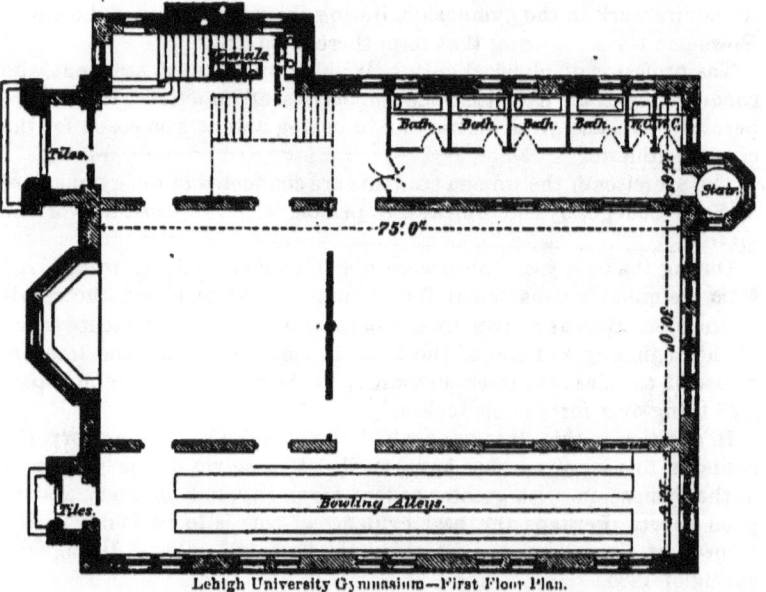

Lehigh University Gymnasium—First Floor Plan.

sandstone, is an elegantly finished structure, and occupies a commanding site, being on the highest part of the university grounds. It was erected in 1882 out of the university funds, at a total cost, including fittings and furniture, of $40,000, and comprises two stories of stone and a third of wood. The basement contains the engine, gauged to a pressure of 30 pounds, with a boiler having a capacity of 100 gallons. The average pressure required is 8 pounds, and on the coldest days not over 15 pounds. Thus, with the numerous radiators throughout the building, it is possible to maintain easily a comfortable temperature in the

LEHIGH UNIVERSITY GYMNASIUM, (INTERIOR VIEW.)

coldest weather. As represented in the front view of the exterior, there are two entrances on the ground floor, viz., the main entrance, on the left, and the entrance to the bowling alleys, on the right. The two bowling alleys are contained in a room 74 feet by 13½. Besides the bowling alleys and the vestibule, which is 30 feet by 20, there are on the first floor a billiard room, 30 feet by 30, containing a pool table and a billiard table; an assembly room, 44 feet by 30, for students' meetings, which, although furnished with settees, can also be used for fencing and sparring; and a bathing and dressing room, 38 feet by 13½, containing 4 long tubs, 2 water closets, and 126 ventilated closets, or lockers, for clothing. A small side room, containing 2 wash bowls and 3 urinals, opens from the vestibule on the left.

On the second floor, which is reached by a broad main stairway in front and a retired stairway in the tower at the rear, there are four rooms, viz.: the director's office, 16 feet by 7, fitted with electric bells, and so arranged with glazed casements as to command a view of the whole floor as well as the stairway from the vestibule; the examining

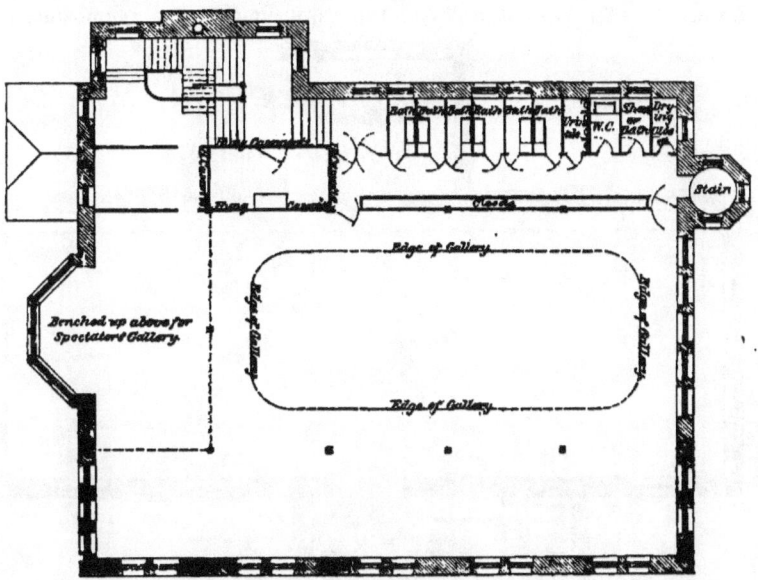

Lehigh University Gymnasium—Second Floor Plan.

room, 10 feet by 7, fitted with scales, measuring rods, dynamometers, and the appliances for making the various strength tests and recording the results of the examinations; a bath room, 44 feet by 13½, containing 6 soapstone sponge-bath tubs, 3 urinals, a water closet, shower room with communicating drying closet, and 120 lockers; and the main hall, or exercise room, 75 feet by 45. The main hall is 40 feet high in the center, and is lighted by a bay-window containing 12 large panes, 36 large windows, 52 smaller windows, besides 8 large skylights of ground glass in the roof, each containing 4 panes, 2 feet by 7.

The visitors' gallery, having benches for spectators, and the running track of 38 laps to the mile, take the place of a third story.

The main hall is fitted with 23 pairs of chest weights, 22 pieces of Dr. Sargent's apparatus for individual development, and the usual gymnastic apparatus, such as parallel and horizontal bars, flying and traveling rings, trapezes, ladders, spring-board, Indian clubs, dumb-bells, etc.

The ceiling of the main hall and of the dressing room is of oiled yellow pine.

Thanks are due to President T. H. Lamberton and Director W. H. Herrick for the pains taken to provide the views, plans, and description herein given of the Lehigh Gymnasium. This gymnasium is, taken all in all, a model structure, on account of its elegance, convenience, and commodiousness.

GYMNASIUM OF BRYN MAWR COLLEGE.

The architectural design, both as to the exterior and interior, is the outgrowth of a careful study of the requirements of a gymnasium for

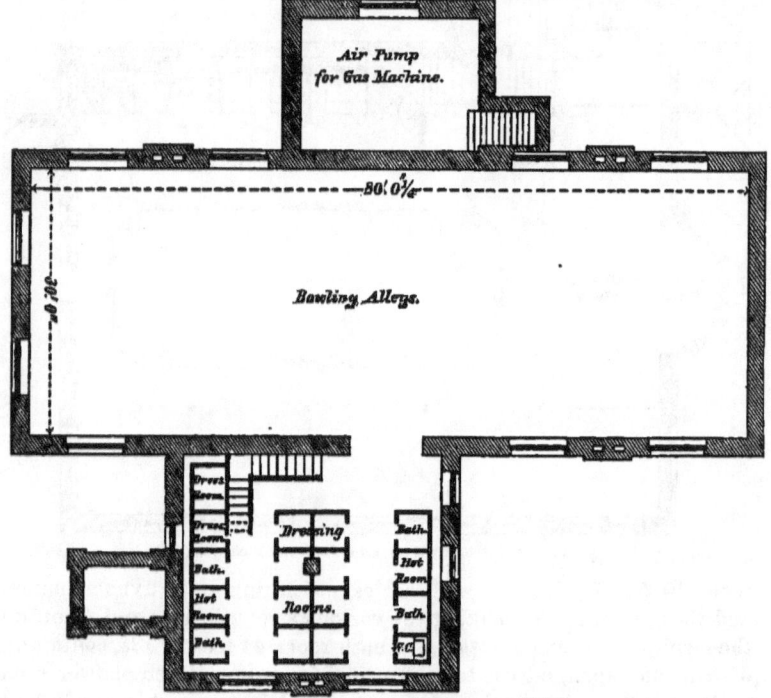

Bryn Mawr College Gymnasium—Basement Plan.

girls, limited in its execution by due regard to economy. The walls of the basement extend 5 feet above the ground line, and are built of dark-

BRYN MAWR COLLEGE GYMNASIUM.

BRYN MAWR COLLEGE GYMNASIUM—INTERIOR VIEW.

gray granite. Above the basement the walls are made of red bricks laid in red mortar, and no plaster appears on their inner surfaces.

The main floor of the building contains the principal hall, 80 feet long by 30 feet wide, 22 feet high to the collar beams, and open to the roof above, the timbers of which are exposed and finished to show the natural grain and color of the wood. Around this hall, at a height of 10 feet from the floor, is placed a gallery, 4 feet wide and supported upon iron cantalevers inserted into the walls, to be used as a track for walk-

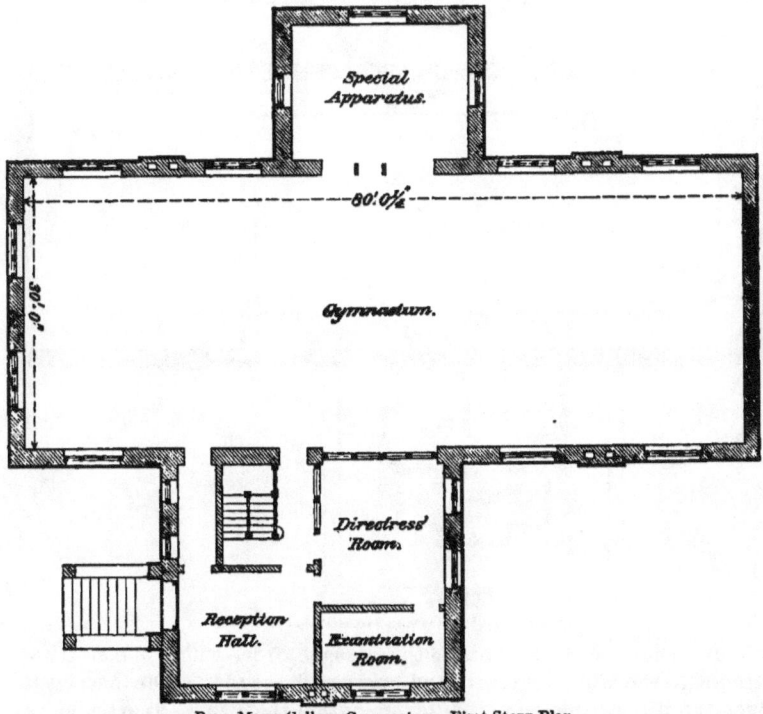

Bryn Mawr College Gymnasium—First Story Plan.

ing or running. The floor of this gallery is of narrow pine boards, and along its front is an iron balustrade of a pleasing design, surmounted by a wooden hand-rail. Upon the north side of the main hall and separated from it by curtains, is a small room, 14 by 20 feet in size, intended for special apparatus.

Upon the south side of the main hall, where are the rooms of administration, there is a reception room, 12 feet 6 inches wide by 15 feet long, entered by the front door. Beyond this room visitors cannot pass without the express permission of the directress. Opening from this is the directress's room, 16 feet long by 14 feet wide, which is separated by glass partitions from the main hall and from the passage leading to it and to the stairways. Adjoining this is the examination room, designed for the examination and record of the physical development of each student using the gymnasium. From the reception room extends a passage way, which is usually closed, and through which alone visitors may be admitted to the main hall. Another doorway from the re-

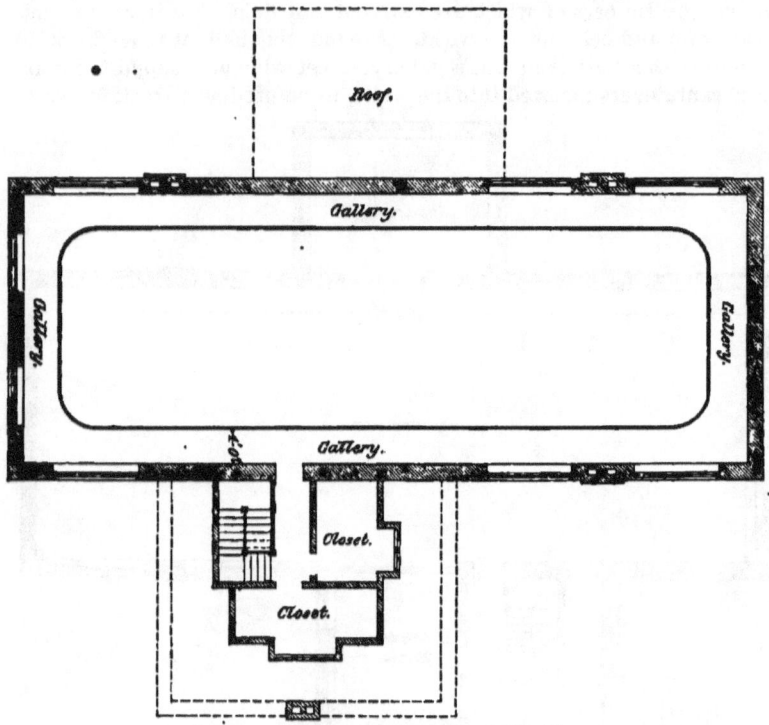

Bryn Mawr College Gymnasium—Second Story Plan.

ception room admits students to the passage, from which one stairway ascends to the walking track, and another descends to the basement. Over the directress's room and examination room is an apartment reserved for the use of the directress.

The basement contains an apartment which is of the same dimensions as the main hall above. It is 9 feet high, well supplied with windows, which are colored and arranged to open inward, so as to secure abundant light and air, with complete privacy. It is further ventilated by 8 large flues, in which a current is kept up at all times by steam-heated coils of pipe. One half of this apartment is reserved for a bowling alley, the other for dressing rooms. Adjoining this apartment and beneath the administration room, is a space allotted to bath rooms and dressing rooms. The bath rooms are 4 feet square; they are lined with lead on the bottom, and on the sides to the height of 5 feet. They are supplied with hot and cold water, with a sprinkler, and are designed for sponge baths only. They are entered from a hot room, into which the bather steps after the bath. The floor of the entire basement is laid with hollow tiles and covered with asphaltum, so as to make a thoroughly dry surface.

In the arrangement of the whole building great attention has been given to the admission of an abundance of light and to thorough ventilation. The entrance is so arranged as to secure the greatest privacy possible, in order that the students may take exercise without the slightest fear of intrusion.

THE LAFAYETTE COLLEGE GYMNASIUM, EASTON, PA.

The gymnasium has one story and a basement, is built of brick, with a slate roof, and a tower at each corner.

The basement contains the dressing room, provided with lockers,

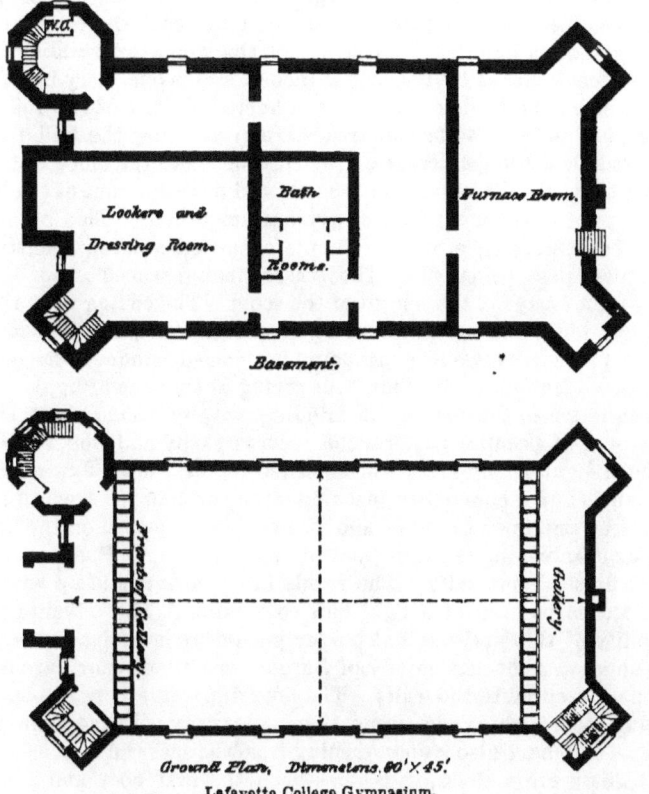

Lafayette College Gymnasium.

and bath rooms provided with bowls and sponge, shower, individual, and needle baths. The main floor has a gallery across each end, one used by visitors, the other by the medical director. It is lighted by four large windows on either side, and above by four dormer windows on each side in the roof; a rose window over the main entrance; and two dormer windows on the north end. There are also windows in the towers; these open into the main tower and increase the light.

The ventilation is carried on by means of three flue shafts, with openings at the floor. The heating is by steam, direct radiation. The ceiling shows the roof timbers and is ceiled with wood above.

THE JOHNS HOPKINS UNIVERSITY GYMNASIUM.

This gymnasium is conveniently situated near to the university buildings, in Baltimore. The main building is a parallelogram in plan, running north and south. An L wing, containing dressing rooms, baths, director's office, and examination room, extends easterly from the south end of the main building. Exclusive of the wing, the building covers a lot 40 feet 2 inches by 103 feet 2 inches, and is one story high. The wing, which is a remodeled structure of ancient date, is of two and a half stories, and is 18 by 45 feet in area. Upon entering the hall through the vestibule a wide staircase on the right leads to the office and examining room of the director. On the left, and near the front of the hall, is the entrance to the main hall, or gymnasium proper. This room is 38 by 89 feet, and is covered by a simple open-timbered roof, constructed with queen-post principals. The trusses, being spaced about $13\frac{1}{2}$ feet apart, form 7 bays in the length of the room. The ceiling in the center is 45 feet high, and at the sides 24 feet high "to plate." Each side wall is pierced by 7 large semicircular-headed windows, the sills of which are 6 feet above the floor, thus giving abundance of light. There is a ventilator in the roof at its middle point, by which, together with four stoves of peculiar pattern, the room is easily and well ventilated. Artificial light is supplied, when needed, by bracketed fixtures on the wall panels and a chandelier just under the ventilator. The rafters are all dressed and open to view, and the ceiling is formed on the back of them by narrow tongued-and-grooved cypress lining. Rafters and ceiling are finished naturally. The inside brick-work is laid up with flush joints and is painted of a light-buff color in oil. The advantage and durability of this style of finish over plastering is indisputable. The fixed apparatus consists chiefly of Sargent machines, which are for the most part secured to the walls. The floor apparatus is portable. The dressing rooms, which communicate by a doorway with the main hall at its south end, have also a door opening from the east end of the entrance hall. There are 4 dressing rooms—2 on the first floor and 2 on the third—containing in all 226 lockers. On the first floor are 6 set bowls, with hot and cold water, 2 baths, and 2 water-closets, all of approved pattern.

We have here produced the plans and descriptions of the Johns Hopkins University and the Dickinson College gymnasia for the purpose of showing that commodious and well-fitted gymnasia can be had at a comparatively slight cost. If an institution can afford to decorate its campus with an elegant building, architecturally considered, well and good. But it should not be supposed that it is necessary to expend thirty or forty thousand dollars in order to provide gymnastic and bathing facilities for 250 or 300 students. In our opinion, the Lehigh and Amherst gymnasia cost more than was necessary, needless expense

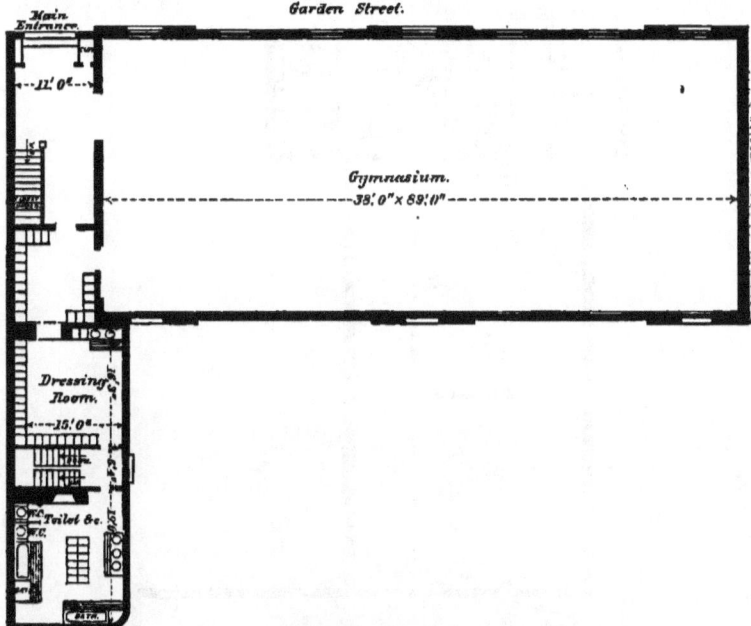

Plan of Johns Hopkins University Gymnasium.

having been incurred in finishing the walls with costly linings of wood. The total cost of the Johns Hopkins Gymnasium, with all its accessories and fittings, including apparatus, was not far from $10,000.

THE DICKINSON COLLEGE GYMNASIUM.

The Dickinson College Gymnasium, at Carlisle, Pa., was completed in 1884. The building has a frontage of 120 feet on a village street, and is conveniently accessible from all the college buildings. In plan it is a parallelogram, with a wing at each end. The main hall is 40 by 75 feet on the floor, and is accessible from the campus by means of a spacious entrance hall through the east wing, which is 23 by 62 feet, two stories high, and contains the dressing rooms, baths, offices, examining room, etc. The opposite, or west wing, is 23 by 87 by 20 feet, one story high, and contains the bowling alleys, three in number. This wing is entered from the main hall. The building is constructed of brick, with stone sills, and is covered by a simple open-timbered roof, the trusses being placed about 15 feet apart and forming bays, each of which is pierced by a large window, admitting ample light and serving for a good natural ventilation. The walls are finished with flush joints for painting, and the woodwork throughout is finished "naturally" in oil, and is of the best material. To complete the building, including bowling

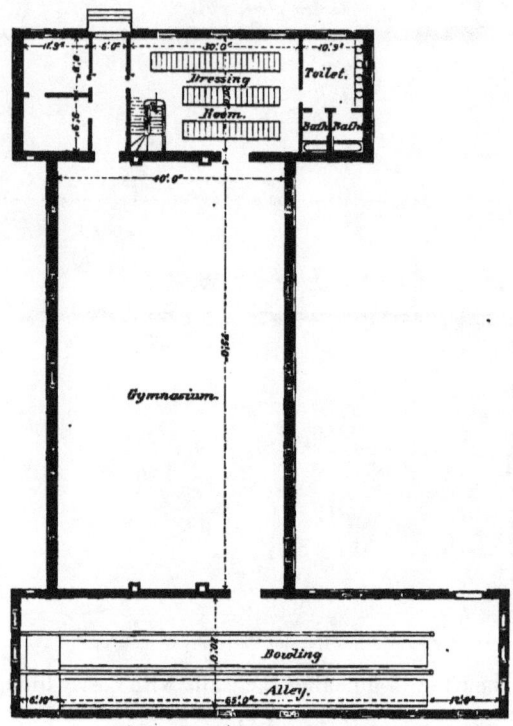

Plan of Dickinson College Gymnasium.

alleys, but exclusive of plumbing and the fittings of the dressing room and main hall, cost $7,300.

THE BUILDING OF THE NEW YORK ATHLETIC CLUB.

The building of the New York Athletic Club is not a gymnasium only; it is a fully equipped club house. Situated on the south-west corner of Sixth avenue and Fifty-fifth street, it extends 75 feet on the avenue and 95 on Fifty-fifth street, and is four stories high.

The basement contains six bowling alleys and a rifle range. In the first story there are facilities for Turkish and Russian bathing, and a swimming bath 66 feet long by 20 wide. The second story contains a reception hall, parlor, reading room, billiard rooms, and a restaurant.

BUILDING FOR THE NEW YORK ATHLETIC CLUB.

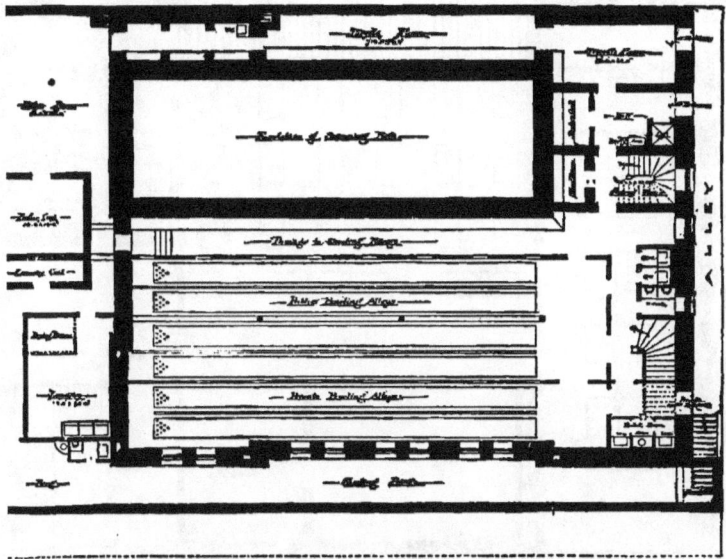

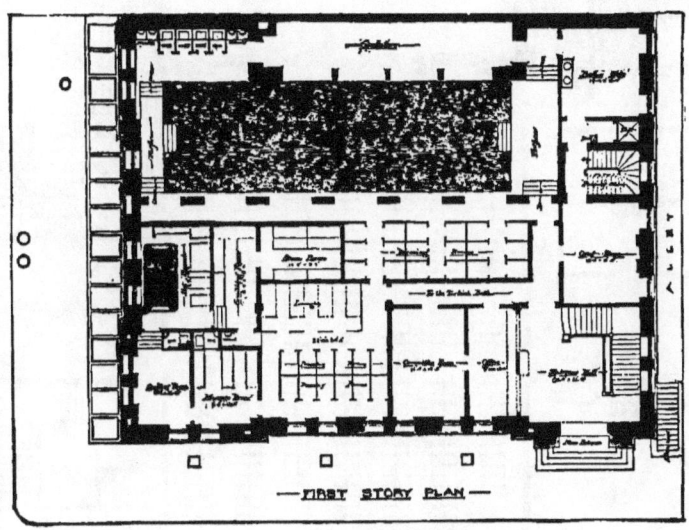

Building of New York Athletic Club.

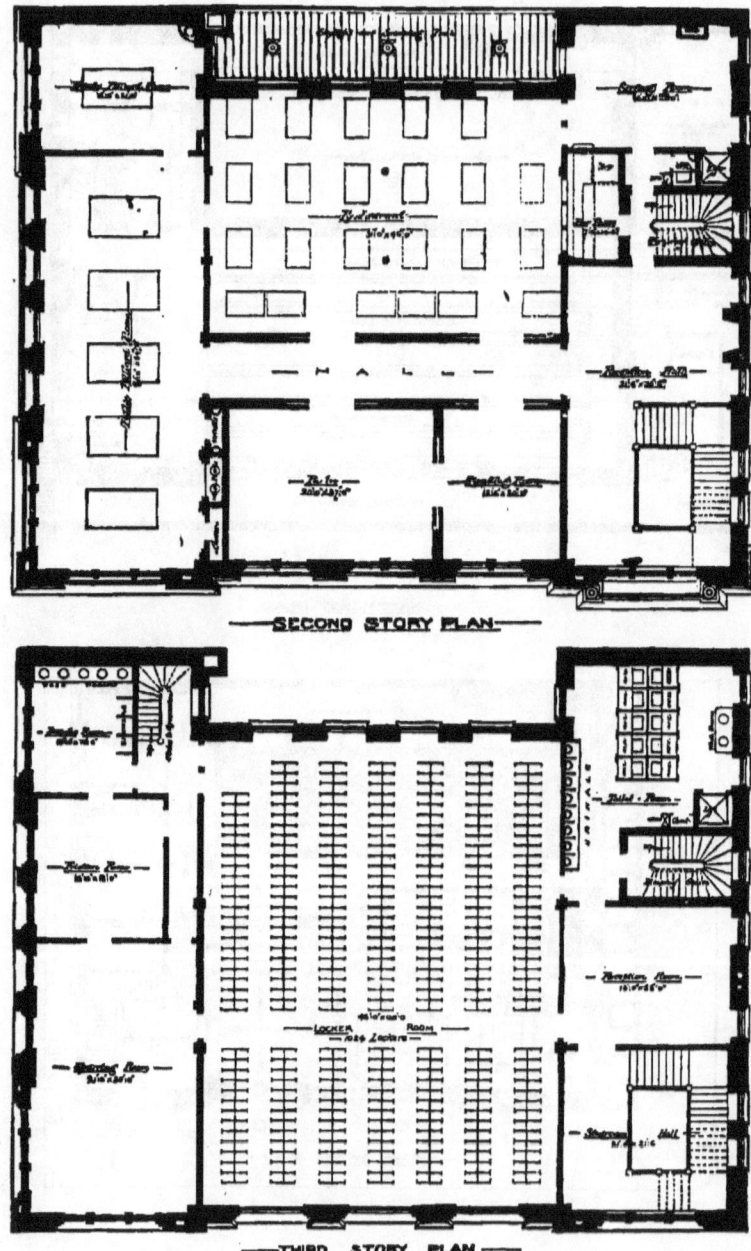

Building of New York Athletic Club.

On the third floor are a thousand lockers, a lavatory, *douche* room, reception room, and sparring room. The entire area of the fourth floor is occupied by the gymnasium; it is 22 feet from floor to ceiling, light and airy. Around this hall, 12 feet from the floor, extends a track for the use of runners; twenty-two laps of it make a mile.

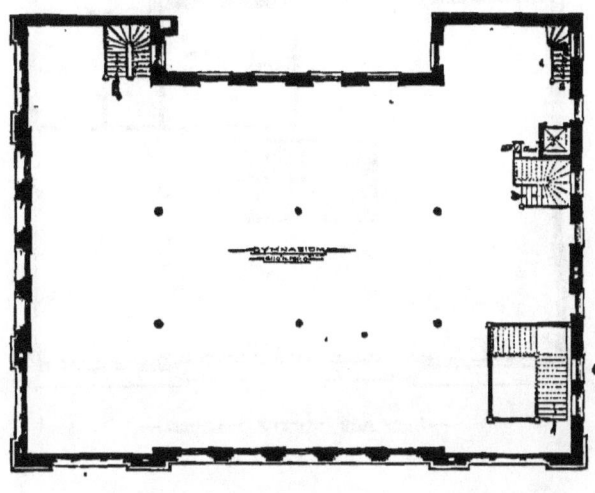

FOURTH STORY PLAN

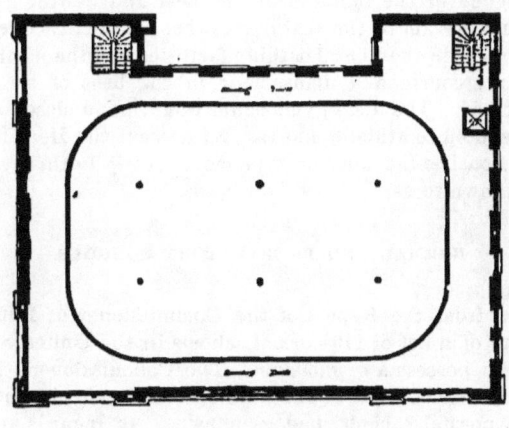

GALLERY PLAN

Building of New York Athletic Club.

The cost of the building was $250,000. The club is in a flourishing condition, with fifteen hundred members and three hundred more wait-

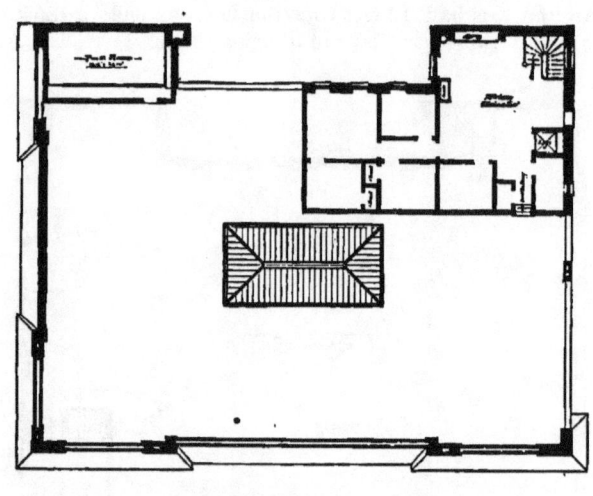

Building of New York Athletic Club.

ing anxiously to get in. The initiation fee is $50, and the annual dues $30. Mr. William R. Travers is the president.

The tendency of the builders of our best and newest gymnasia is to incorporate certain of the features of those of ancient Greece. This is most manifest in the liberal bathing facilities and the means afforded for social intercourse and amusement in the best of the gymnasia above described. The ideal gymnasium would be in close proximity to the fields devoted to athletic sports. At present the Hemenway Gymnasium approaches the ancient type more nearly in this respect than any other known to us.

NORMAL AND PREPARATORY SCHOOLS.

It appears from the Report of the Commissioner of Education for 1873 that out of a list of 119 normal schools in the United States only 17 claimed to possess a gymnasium. The Commissioner's Report for 1882–'83 shows that 19 out of 119 public normal schools, and 16 out of 114 private normal schools, had gymnasia. As regards preparatory schools, the same Report notices the fact that 56 out of 157 of them had gymnasia.

YOUNG MEN'S CHRISTIAN ASSOCIATION GYMNASIA.

GENERAL CHARACTER.

As a class, the gymnasia belonging to the Young Men's Christian Associations are better furnished and officered than those belonging to the two classes of schools above mentioned. Since 1869, when the New York Young Men's Christian Association opened a gymnasium in its new building, "physical culture" has been a prominent feature in Association work. The Young Men's Christian Association Year Book for 1884, p. 141, states that "83 associations report attention to physical culture; 68 of these through gymnasia and 23 through other means, including base ball, rambling, rowing, and swimming clubs, bowling alleys, health lifts, and classes in calisthenics." Since this statement applies to the United States and Canada, and only two of the Canadian associations report gymnasia, 66 appears to be the correct number for the United States, or rather 67, since the Boston Young Men's Christian Union Gymnasium properly belongs in this category, even though its managers and patrons represent a different type of theology from that of the affiliated associations.

In the days of primitive Christianity "gymnastical sports and exercises" were classed with the "madness of the theater, huntings, and horse-racings," and those addicted to them were required "either to leave them off or be rejected from baptism." Superintendents of gymnasia probably correspond as closely as any class of modern men to the ancient "curators of the common games and practicers in the Olympic games," who, with "charioteers, gladiators, minstrels, harpers, dancers, and vintners," were commanded by the apostolic constitutions either to quit such callings or be rejected from baptism.

The gymnasia of the Young Men's Christian Associations in the following named cities have their own salaried superintendents, as is shown by the published lists of officers: Baltimore, Md.; Boston, Mass.; Brooklyn, N. Y.; Buffalo, N. Y.; Chicago, Ill.; Cleveland, Ohio; Indianapolis, Ind.; Newark, N. J.; Newburyport, Mass.; New York, N. Y.; Philadelphia, Pa.; Pittsburg, Pa.; Providence, R. I.; San Francisco, Cal., and Washington, D. C.

The Young Men's Christian Association gymnasia, as a class, do not compare favorably with college gymnasia, and chiefly so because they are placed in an out-of-the-way corner of the building, and are ill ventilated and poorly lighted. This criticism does not apply to all of them; but in too many cases the gymnasium, even in imposing and commodious Young Men's Christian Association buildings, is placed at or below the level of the ground. The Brooklyn association is to be commended for its plan of erecting a gymnasium annex, which is now building at an estimated cost of between $90,000 and $100,000. It is the intention of the projectors of this Brooklyn gymnasium to make it the best of its class.

BOSTON YOUNG MEN'S CHRISTIAN UNION GYMNASIUM.

At present the best specimens of the type are those of the Boston Young Men's Christian Association and the Boston Young Men's Christian Union. The Union gymnasium is on the whole the more worthy of the two of imitation, since it contains a large number of the Sargent developing appliances, and is under the medical direction of Dr. Sargent himself.

The following extracts from a recent circular indicate what are the distinctive features of this gymnasium:

The Union gymnasium is 136 feet long, 22 feet high, and has a floor space of 6,200 square feet, exclusive of dressing and bath rooms.

The room is well lighted on every side, thoroughly ventilated, has indirect steam heat, and the exercising floor is above the street level.

The dressing rooms are large and spacious, and contain over 900 lockers.

The bathing facilities are ample, there being 13 sponge-bath rooms, 8 bowls, 3 tubs, and 1 shower room.

A running track has been arranged on the main floor with a course of 26 laps to a mile, unobstructed by apparatus, and open to runners at all times during gymnasium hours.

The management aim to make the gymnasium beneficial to all ages and to all conditions.

By the use of the adjustable weights and appliances, the exercises can be adapted to the "strength of the strong and the weakness of the weak."

Dr. Sargent will examine those who desire it, and make out a book with specific directions for exercise, diet, sleep, bathing, etc., based upon the data ascertained from the examination. Each book is furnished with a blank form; and those who wish may have their measurements entered, and their condition compared with the average man of the same age, weight, etc.

Terms, including the Union membership (one dollar), and entitling to all its privileges:

For one year, entitling to use of gymnasium, after 7 P.M., and on holidays for such time as it may be open $5 00
For one year, entitling to use of gymnasium at all times when open 8 00
Keys, to be refunded on return of same 50

There is no extra charge for consultation with, and examination by, Dr. Sargent, instruction, use of baths and dressing closets in the large dressing rooms.

Dr. Sargent will give during the fall and winter season a course of practical talks on "the theories and principles of physical training."

The gymnasium is open from 8 A.M. to 9.45 P.M.

THE BROOKLYN YOUNG MEN'S CHRISTIAN ASSOCIATION GYMNASIUM.

This gymnasium, the best of its class, is now (1885) in course of construction. It constitutes a separate building in the nature of an annex to the Young Men's Christian Association building, whose entrance is on Bond street. The gymnasium building, which is 100 feet deep, has a frontage on Hanover place of 60 feet. The structure, which was

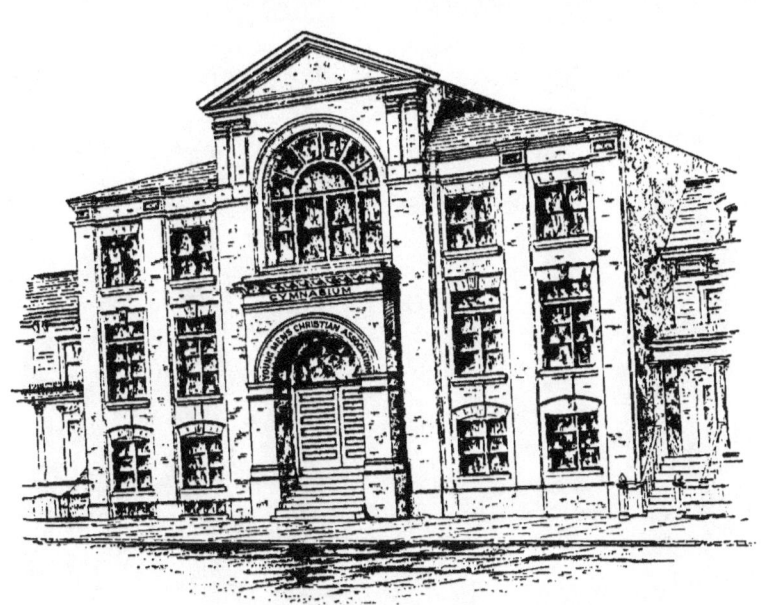

Hanover Place Front.

BROOKLYN Y. M. C. A. GYMNASIUM.

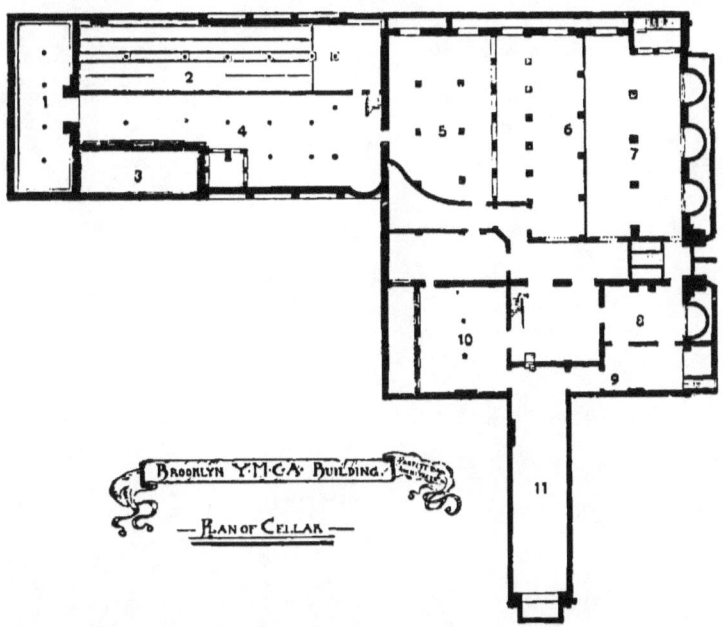

1. Boiler room, engine room, workshop, and well.
2. Four 80-feet bowling alleys.
3. Bottom part of swimming tank.
4. Coal cellar—to hold 300 tons.
5. Extra locker space.
6. Cellar.
7. Mechanical class room.
8. Room to stall bicycles.
9. Passage-way to boys' quarters—separate entrance, direct from the street.
10. Boys' meeting room.
11. Boys' gymnasium and play room.

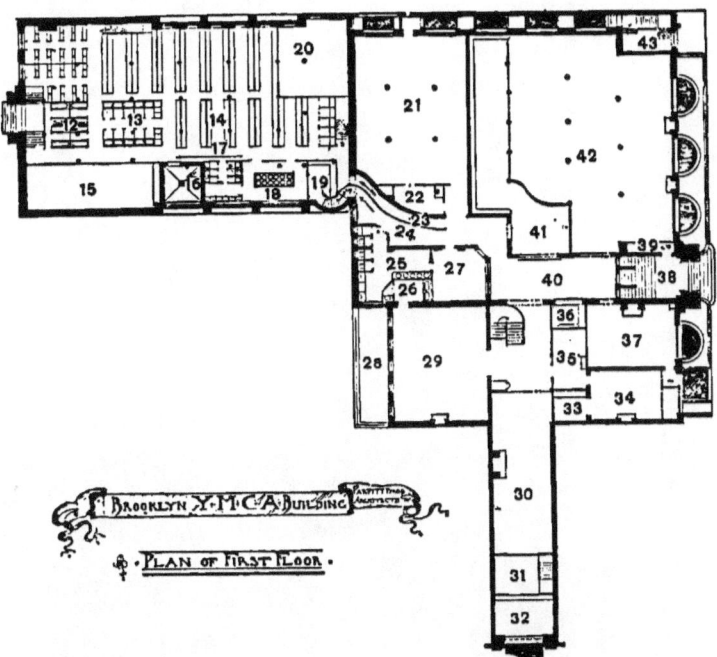

12. Six hot and cold bath tubs.
13. Ten sponge baths.
14. Eight hundred locker space.
15. Swimming bath, 14×45.
16. Russian, shower, needle, and douche bath room.
17. Lavatory.
18. Washbowls.
19. Gymnasium instructor's office.
20. Bowling alley room.
21. Small lecture hall—for prayer meetings, Bible classes, &c.
22. Inquirers' room.
23. Private passage to gymnasium.
24. Passage to lavatories.
25. Lavatories.
26. Ladies' lavatory.
27. Cloak room; also for keeping of valuables of gymnasium members.
28. Area reserved for light and conservatory.
29. Members' parlor.
30. Reception and amusement room.
31. Inner vestibule.
32. Outer vestibule and main entrance to the building.
33. Office for committees.
34. General Secretary's private office.
35. Assistant Secretary's office.
36. Treasurer's office.
37. Board room.
38. Grand stairway to the main auditorium, with two fire-proof vaults beneath.
39. Ticket office.
40. Hallway.
41. Librarian's office and library.
42. Reading room.
43. Side entrance to janitor's rooms and exit from main hall.

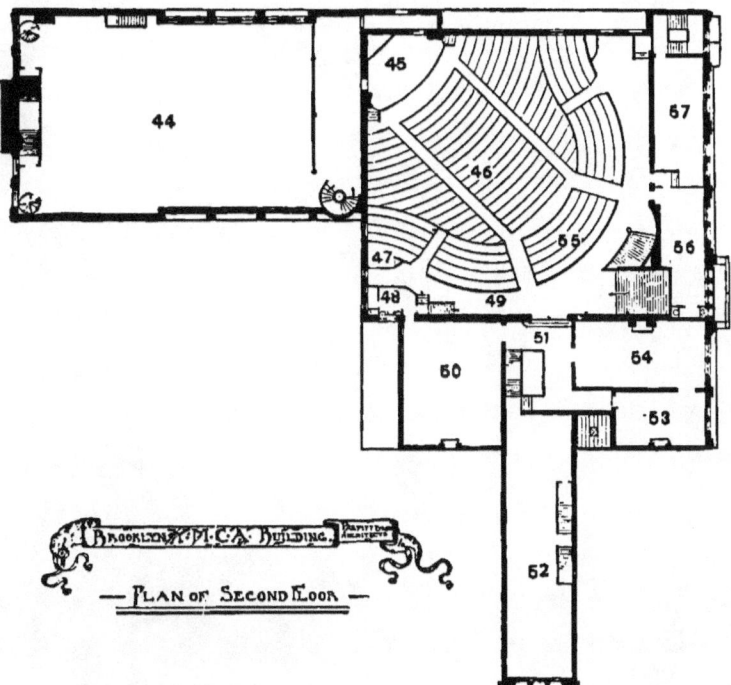

44. Floor of gymnasium—all clear space.
45. Platform or stage.
46. Parquette.
47. Air vent.
48. Lavatories.
49. Lower foyer.
50. Class room.
51. Landing and passage.
52. Class room, or office for rent.
53. Class room.
54. Class room.
55. Balcony.
56. Ladies' retiring or cloak room.
57. Gentlemen's retiring or coat room.

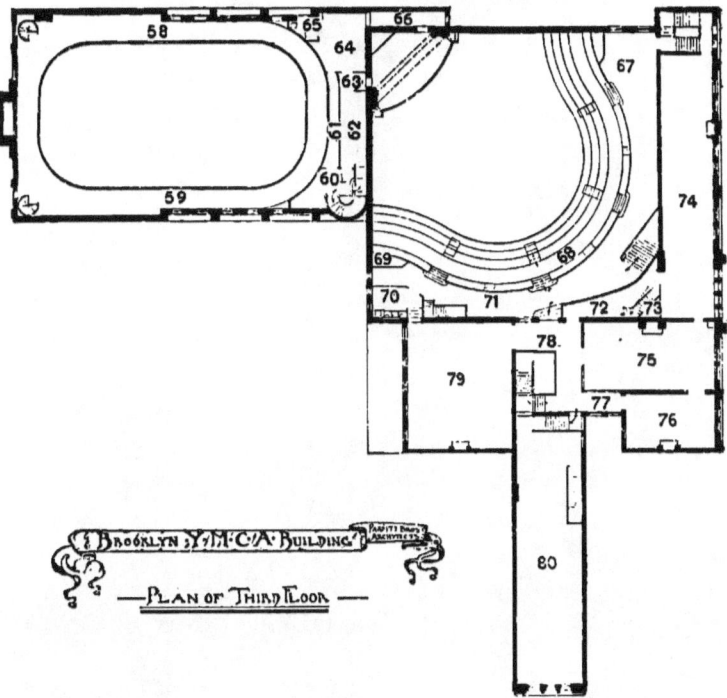

58. }
59. } Elevated running track in gymnasium.
60. Spectators' gallery.
61. Passage-way to retiring rooms of music hall.
62. Gentlemen's retiring room.
65. Lavatory.
66. Ladies' private entrance to the stage.
67. Side exit from hall.
68. Dress circle.
69. Air vent.
70. Lavatory.
71. Upper foyer.
72. Passage to janitor's room.
73. China closet.
74. Dining hall.
75. Class room.
76. Class room.
77. Passage.
78. Passage.
79. Class room.
80. Class room.

planned by Parfitt Brothers, architects, Brooklyn, is built of brick and terra cotta and Long Meadow red sandstone.

The first floor contains a locker room with about 200 public and 100 private lockers; also hot-water baths, sponge baths, large shower baths, and a swimming bath 45 feet by 14, besides lavatories and an instructor's office. In the basement are 4 bowling-alleys 80 feet long, 2 60-horse-power boilers, and a coal cellar of 300-tons capacity. A well 50 feet deep and 5 feet in diameter, calculated to yield 100 gallons of water per minute, has here been dug for the use of the baths, bowls, and closets.

The gymnasium is in the second story. It is 24 feet high, 54 feet wide, and 98 feet deep. The running track, which is suspended from the roof, is 5 feet wide and has 22 laps to the mile. Its floor is 8 feet above that of the gymnasium. The ceiling, which is of the open-roof description, is supported on 6 elliptical arches of wood, each built of 12 sections of 1 by 6 inch pieces of wood laid one over the other, bent and bolted into the shape desired.

It is worth noting that in the Bond street building the Brooklyn Young Men's Christian Association will provide a gymnasium and playroom especially suited for boys.

Future builders of gymnasia will do well to study the means employed in this gymnasium and in the Cornell University Gymnasium for supporting the roof by arches instead of by pillars, as much valuable floor-space has been sacrificed in the Hemenway, Pratt, and Lehigh gymnasia through the use of pillars and posts. Suspended running-tracks are to be preferred when they are practicable.

Following is as complete a statement as we are able to make of the facts regarding gymnasia belonging to the theological schools of America. The gymnasium belonging to the Hartford Seminary is the best of its class.

TABLE No. 13.—*Gymnasia in theological schools in the United States, 1882–'83.*

Institution and number of students in 1882–'83.	Location.	Gymnasium in—		Gymnasium.	Room.	Material.	Style of drill.	Instruction.
		Separate structure.	Room.					
Andover Theological Seminary (41).	Andover, Mass.	Yes; shared with Philipe Academy.		Date of erection, 1816; cost of structure, $13,500; originally built for other purposes.	Has bowling-alleys.	Brick.	Light gymnastic; optional.	
Auburn Theological Seminary (47).	Auburn, N. Y.		2 rooms, 30' by 15'; fitted; simple apparatus.				Optional	None given.
Christian Biblical Institute (23).	Stanfordville, N. Y.		Students have "rude extemporized apparatus" in a single room.				do	Instruction given by lectures on hygiene. Steele's "Fourteen Weeks in Human Physiology."
Franciscan College (a few ecclesiastical students).	Santa Barbara, Cal.						Students "find plenty of recreation in walking, working in flower gardens, or riding."	
Hartford Theological Seminary.	Hartford, Conn.	Yes; main hall 40' by 28½'.	There are 4 rooms: main hall; dressing room; bath room, bowls and shower bath; retiring room, water closet and urinal.	Date of erection, 1880; cost of structure, $8,000 (estimated); originally built for gymnasium.		Brick.	"Sargent;" required, 30 to 60 minutes daily.	Dr. Sargent measures and prescribes. A special teacher instructs.
Lane Theological Seminary.	Walnut Hills, Cincinnati, Ohio.		Has a room scantily furnished				Optional	Incidental lectures.

618

Meadville Theological School.	Meadville, Pa.		Has a "health lift," use of which is discouraged.			No special instruction.
Newton Theological Institution (62).	Newton, Mass.	Yes; of 1 story, with ordinary gymnastic fittings.		Date of erection, 1876; cost of structure, $4,000; originally built for gymnasium.	Has 2 bowling-alleys; dimensions, 30' by 50'.	Wood. Optional	No special instruction.
Theological Seminary of the Reformed Church in America.	New Brunswick, N. J.		Room on ground floor, 80' by 50'; good supply of ordinary appliances.	Date of erection, Jas. Suydam Hall built 1874; cost of structure, $80,000; originally built for chapel and dormitory.		Brick. ...do	No instruction.

* Calisthenics favored. Beneficiaries required to pass a physical examination and be sound bodily.

NOTE.—The Western Theological Seminary of the Presbyterian Church, at Allegheny, Pa., has a gymnasium in a basement room. This is used by students at their option.

ARCHITECTS AND FURNISHERS OF GYMNASIA.

The following list of architects who have planned gymnasia is given for the convenience of those who may have occasion hereafter to build or remodel gymnasia:

Peabody & Stearns, of Boston, Mass., planned the Hemenway Gymnasium.

E. L. Roberts, 46 Broadway, New York City, planned the Pratt Gymnasium.

Addison Hutton, 400 Chestnut street, Philadelphia, planned the Lehigh University Gymnasium and the Bryn Mawr Gymnasium.

F. C. Withers, New York City, planned the National Deaf-Mute College Gymnasium.

G. B. Post, New York City, planned the Princeton College Gymnasium.

J. R. Richard, ———, planned the Dartmouth College Gymnasium.

Charles Babcock, Professor of Architecture, Cornell University, planned the Cornell Armory and Gymnasium.

C. W. Clinton, New York City, planned the New York Athletic Club Building.

Parfitt Brothers, Brooklyn, N. Y., planned the Brooklyn Young Men's Christian Association Gymnasium.

Charles L. Carson, corner Charles and Lexington streets, Baltimore, planned the Johns Hopkins University Gymnasium and the Dickinson College Gymnasium.

The names of the most reliable manufacturers of gymnastic apparatus are:

American—

Dr. D. A. Sargent, Cambridge, Mass.

Boston Gymnasium Construction and Supply Company, A. H. Howard, Secretary, 9 Ashburton place, Boston, Mass.

Fred. Medart, 1206 North Main street, St. Louis, Mo.

John Gloy, 27 Johnson street, Chicago, Ill.

Foreign—

Julius Dietrich & Hannak, Chemnitz, Saxony.

A. Buczilowsky, 17 Köthen street, Berlin, Prussia.

A. A. Stempel, 75 Albany street, Regent's park, London, N. W., England.

Oscar Knofe, 26 Pancras road, King's cross, London, W. C., England.

MILITARY DRILL AND DISCIPLINE A PHYSICAL TRAINING.

"Solitary men dreaming in their corners," as well as the most severely practical men of affairs, when proposing schemes for the betterment of the "discipline of the common weal" through educational reforms, have frequently, perhaps usually, urged the value of military drill and discipline as a means of training young men.

VIEWS OF LUTHER AND POLE.

Martin Luther, while praising bodily exercises as a means to health and as a safeguard against "the temptations of the fiend," does not fail to commend them as needful for rendering "us Germans fit and always prepared for joining the army and for battle. For verily our boys will have to defend land and people and to be warriors."

Reginald Pole, when outlining to Master Lupset his idea of the "most noble institute that ever was devised in any common weal," declares that the nobility should "be constrained, by lawful punishment, to exercise themselves in all such things and feats of arms as shall be for the defense of our realm necessary; the which they should do with the same diligence that the plowmen labor and till the ground, for the common food."

VIEWS OF MILTON.

John Milton, in his tractate on education, imagines an "institution of breeding, which should be equally good both for peace and war." "The exercise which I first commend," he says, "is the exact use of their weapon, to guard and to strike safely with edge or point. This will keep them healthy, nimble, strong, and well in breath; is also the likeliest means to make them grow large and tall, and to inspire them with a gallant and fearless courage, which being tempered with seasonable lectures and precepts to make them of true fortitude and patience, will turn into a native and heroic valor, and make them hate the cowardice of doing wrong. They must be also practiced in all the locks and gripes of wrestling, wherein Englishmen are wont to excel, as need may often be in fight to tug, to grapple, and to close. And this perhaps will be enough wherein to prove and heat their single strength." He further recommends that all the youth, while engaged in study "under vigilant eyes," should "about two hours before supper, by a sudden alarm or watchword, be called out to their military motions, under sky or covert according to the season, as was the Roman wont; first on foot, then, as their age permits, on horseback to all the art of cavalry; that having in sport, but with much exactness and daily muster, served out the rudiments of their soldiership in all the skill of embattling, marching, encamping, fortifying, besieging, and battering with all the helps of ancient and modern stratagems, tactics, and warlike maxims, they may, as it were out of a long war, come forth renowned and perfect commanders in the service of their country." The effect of classical studies and the lessons derived from the experiences of civil war are strangely mingled in this tractate.

MILITARY GYMNASTICS IN ENGLAND.

Gymnastics, in the Greek or German sense, have never been popular in the public schools of England, or with the devotees of manly sports outside of them; but volunteer military companies have sprung up at the schools and universities in recent years. In 1822, Captain Clias, who had been instrumental in introducing gymnastic training for recruits into the Swiss and French armies, introduced gymnastics into the British army and navy. For the period of two years and a half he was Professor of Gymnastics in the Royal Military Academy, at Woolwich. He occupied this post until September, 1825, when instruction in gymnastics was intrusted to non-commissioned officers. After a long period of disuse military gymnastics were revived in England—after the Crimean war. In 1861 a central school of gymnastics was established at Aldershot for the purpose of supplying instructors to the army. This action was taken in accordance with the recommendations of the report of a commission appointed in 1859 to examine into the systems of military gymnastics then in vogue on the Continent. Later, by order of Lord de Grey, gymnasia were built at all barracks.

MACLAREN'S SYSTEM OF GYMNASTICS.

The late Archibald Maclaren drew up the code of instruction which was adopted by the authorities. Mr. Maclaren's writings and teachings on physical education are the best that England has yet produced. The principles of physical training, as expounded by Mr. Maclaren, are essentially the same as those which lie at the basis of the Sargent system. The followers of each labor for the same ends, though by methods not always identical. A series of physical measurements, periodically made and carefully registered, was employed by Mr. Maclaren from the first. Similar measurements, it will be remembered, were instituted by Dr. Hitchcock, at Amherst, in 1861, the same year that Mr. Maclaren began his work in the British army. The Amherst measurements were, indeed, intended to determine the rate of growth and development; but they served for statistical rather than diagnostic purposes. Mr. Maclaren used the data obtained by his examinations in determining the kind and amount of exercise to be required of his pupils.

PUBLICATIONS BY MR. MACLAREN.

Besides his "Military System of Gymnastic Exercises for the Use of Instructors", originally published in 1862, two other works by Mr. Maclaren, viz., "Training in Theory and Practice", and "Physical Education", have been published respectively by Macmillan & Co. and the Clarendon Press. The latter work well deserves the unstinted praise bestowed upon it by that high authority on hygiene, Dr. E. A. Parkes, who says of it that it "should be in the hands of every one." Its Part I, comprising 101 pages taken up with an essay upon "Growth and Development," is a lucid and admirable exposition of the modern views of physical training, and contains apt characterizations of the German and French systems of military gymnastics, which were adopted respectively in the years 1845 and 1847. Dr. Ball, in Buck's *Hygiene and Public Health*, New York, 1879, declares that Mr. Maclaren's code

PHYSICAL TRAINING IN AMERICAN COLLEGES. 95

of instruction is much less elaborate than the French system, while it is more thorough and practical than the German, and is based upon the sound principle that the first requisite is to develop physical power by a simple and *gradually progressive* course of exercises, after which the practical application of this acquired power to the special duties of the soldier becomes a comparatively easy task.

DR. PARKES ON MACLAREN'S CODE.

As yet no such comprehensive system as that contained in the Maclaren code has been adopted for the United States Army. The best summary account of this code that has come under our notice is the following, contained in the sixth edition of Parkes's "Practical Hygiene", pp. 584–585:

The instructions have two great objects: (1) To assist the physical development of the recruit; (2) to strengthen and render supple the frame of the trained soldier. Every recruit is now ordered to have three months' gymnastic training during (or, if judged expedient by a medical officer, in lieu of part of) his ordinary drill. Two months are given before he commences rifle practice, and one month afterward. This training is superintended by a medical officer, who will be responsible that it is done properly, and who will have the power to continue the exercises beyond the prescribed time, if he deems it necessary. The exercise for the recruit is to last only one hour a day, and in addition he will have from two to three hours of ordinary drill.

The trained infantry soldier is ordered to go through a gymnastic course of three months' duration every year, one hour being given every other day. The cavalry soldier is to be taught fencing and sword exercise in lieu of gymnastics.

The exercises have been arranged with great care, and present a progressive course of the most useful kind. The early exercise commences with walking and running; leaping, with and without the pole, follows; and then the exercises with apparatus commence, the order being the horizontal beam, the vaulting bar, and the vaulting horse. All these are called exercises of progression. The elementary exercises follow, viz., with the parallel bars, the pair of rings, the row of rings, the elastic ladder, the horizontal bar, the bridge ladder, and the ladder plank. Then follow the advanced exercises of climbing on the slanting and vertical pole, the slanting and vertical rope, and the knotted rope.

Finally, the most advanced exercises consist of escalading, first against a wall, and then against a prepared building.

It might be thought that so complete and methodical a system as that of Mr. Maclaren, its good results being well known, would have commended itself to the teachers of boys. But so late as 1869, Mr. Maclaren calls attention to the fact that, excepting the two military colleges of Woolwich and Sandhurst, and Radley College, not one of the large educational establishments in England was provided with a regularly organized gymnasium with properly qualified teachers. The case stands only slightly better now.

EARLY SCHEMES FOR MILITARY TRAINING IN THE UNITED STATES.

On January 21, 1790, President Washington transmitted to the first Senate of the United States a comprehensive report from General H.

Knox, the Secretary of War, on a plan for "a national system of defense adequate to the probable exigencies of the United States, whether arising from internal or external causes." In passing we may remark that this was seven months prior to the penning of Dr. Rush's eulogy of agricultural and mechanical labor as an amusement. Among the principles on which Secretary Knox based his plan are the following:

That every man of the proper age and ability of body is firmly bound, by the social compact, to perform personally his proportion of military duty for the defense of the state.

That all men of the legal military age should be armed, enrolled, and held responsible for different degrees of military service.

PLAN OF SECRETARY KNOX, 1790.

The plan called for the enrollment of those liable to bear arms into three classes, described as follows:

The first class shall comprehend the youth of eighteen, nineteen, and twenty years of age, to be denominated the advanced corps. The second class shall include the men from twenty-one to forty-five years of age, to be denominated the main corps.

The third class shall comprehend, inclusively, the men from forty-six to sixty years of age, to be denominated the reserved corps.

Of the advanced corps.

The advanced corps are designed not only as a school in which the youth of the United States are to be instructed in the art of war, but they are, in all cases of exigence, to serve as an actual defense to the community.

The whole of the armed corps shall be clothed, armed, and subsisted at the expense of the United States; and all the youth of the said corps in each State shall be encamped together, if practicable, or by legions, which encampments shall be denominated the *annual camps of discipline*. The youth of *eighteen* and *nineteen* years shall be disciplined for *thirty* days successively in each year; and those of twenty years shall be disciplined only for ten days in each year.

At the age of twenty-one years, every individual having served in the manner and for the time prescribed, shall receive an honorary certificate thereof, on parchment, and signed by the legionary general and inspector. And the said certificate, or an attested copy of the register aforesaid, shall be required as an indispensable qualification for exercising any of the rights of a free citizen, until after the age of ―― years. No amusements should be admitted in camp but those which correspond with war: the swimming of men and horses, running, wrestling, and such other exercises as should render the body flexible and vigorous.

This plan failed of adoption, although the need of a well-trained militia had been sharply and abundantly emphasized by the events of the revolutionary war. The failure of this plan was attributed to the great expense and the administrative difficulties which it was believed it would entail.

MR. HARRISON'S PLAN, 1817 AND 1819.

In 1817, in a report on the reorganization of the militia, made to the House of Representatives by Mr. Harrison, it was recommended that "military instruction should not be given in distant schools, but that it should form a branch of education in every school within the United

States; that a corps of military instructors should be formed to attend to the gymnastic and elementary part of education in every school in the United States, whilst the more scientific part of the art of war should be communicated by professors of tactics, to be established in all the higher seminaries."

It does not appear that this scheme, or anything like it, ever received the sanction of law, although it was again brought forward for adoption in 1819.

UNITED STATES MILITARY ACADEMY.

Meanwhile the United States Military Academy at West Point, in New York, had been instituted for the professional training of army officers. Yet the bitter lessons of the war of the Revolution had to be enforced by those of the war of 1812 before Congress could be induced to make anything like adequate provision for such training.

WASHINGTON'S VIEWS.

His experiences as commander-in-chief in the war of the Revolution caused Washington when President to suggest to Congress in 1793, and again in 1796, the establishment of an academy for "the study of those branches of the military art which can scarcely ever be obtained by practice alone." Washington's suggestions bore no immediate fruit, but his views on this subject were adopted by his successor.

REPORT OF SECRETARY JAMES MCHENRY, 1800.

Mr. McHenry, of Maryland, Secretary of War under President John Adams, made an elaborate report in 1800, recommending the establishment of a military academy, to consist of the fundamental school, the school of engineers and artillerists, the school of cavalry and infantry, and the school of the navy. Mr. McHenry's ideas were far in advance of his time, and were little regarded until after the war of 1812. In 1802 the United States Military Academy was established by law, but in name only, for, prior to 1817, there was but little system or regularity observed in the instruction given. Cadets were admitted without examination, and without the least regard to their age or qualifications. Sylvanus Thayer, who became superintendent in 1817, in the course of the five years following established in all its essential features the course of instruction which has become identified with the name of West Point.

PHYSICAL TRAINING AT WEST POINT AND ANNAPOLIS.

Bodily training, under the heads of military instruction and sword exercise, has received marked attention from the first. Dancing is now regularly taught, and gymnastics and swimming have at times been regular branches of instruction. The United States Naval Academy dates from the year 1845. Both at West Point and at Annapolis the course of study is characterized by an extended, varied, and exacting system of bodily exercise, as embraced in the various drills and branches of practical instruction. Weaklings in body are prevented from entering either academy by the requirement, which has been in force for many years, that all applicants failing to pass a satisfactory physical examination at the hands of a medical board shall be rejected. Idlers and dolts lose their commissions. The absolute control and constant supervision and inspection to which all cadets are subjected, as regards deportment, dress, studies, exercise, recreation, diet, and rest, are productive of a vigorous manliness which is much less uniformly found in the graduates of other institutions. In all other professional schools and in the majority of our colleges the training is less steadily and successfully directed toward securing mental power, moral strength, and bodily ability.

The writer is strongly convinced that the best that has yet been accomplished in the United States, in the province of physical training, has been accomplished at West Point and at Annapolis; and, while recognizing fully that the systems there in operation could not be imposed, without undergoing many modifications, upon any considerable portion of the collegiate youth of the country, he cannot forbear recommending a careful study of those systems to all who are responsible for the training of boys between the ages of twelve and twenty.

It is eminently to be desired that the data on record in the War and Navy Departments touching the physical condition, academic standing, and professional success and career of all cadets, from the time of their admission to the academy till the termination of their service by discharge, resignation, or death, should be statistically digested and discussed. The publication of these records could not fail to be helpful to those engaged in the study of the natural history of the student class: it would be of very great pedagogical value.

The published reports of Medical Director A. L. Gihon, U. S. N., upon the hygiene of the Naval Academy and on the rates of growth of cadets before and after entering the academy, serve admirably to indicate what might be done in this direction. A satisfactory comparison of the results thus far obtained under the Amherst, Sargent, Maclaren, West Point, and Annapolis systems of physical training is as yet hardly feasible.

CAPTAIN PARTRIDGE'S MILITARY SCHOOLS, 1820–'53.

Alden Partridge, captain of engineers in the United States Army, who was the immediate predecessor of General Sylvanus Thayer as Superintendent of the Military Academy, seems to have been the first person to found an institution modeled after that at West Point. Captain Partridge left the Military Academy in 1817, and in 1818 resigned from the military service of the Government. In a lecture delivered by him in 1820 on what he conceived to be the deficiencies of superior education as then conducted, Captain Partridge spoke as follows:

Another defect in the present system is the entire neglect, in all our principal seminaries, of physical education. The great importance and even absolute necessity of a regular and systematic course of exercise for the preservation of health, and confirming and rendering vigorous the constitution, must be evident to the most superficial observer. It is for want of this that so many of our most promising youths lose their health by the time they are prepared to enter on the grand theater of active and useful life. That the health of the closest applicant may be preserved, when he is subjected to a regular and systematic course of exercises, I know from practical experience; and I have no hesitation in asserting that in nine cases out of ten it is just as easy for a youth, however hard he may study, to attain the age of manhood with a firm and vigorous constitution, as it is to grow up puny and debilitated, incapable of either bodily or mental exertion.

PHYSICAL TRAINING UNDER CAPTAIN PARTRIDGE.

Captain Partridge opened his American Literary Scientific Academy at Norwich, Vt., his native town, September 4, 1820. In a card published in April, 1825, on the eve of his departure for Middletown, Conn., for the purpose of reopening his seminary in that place, Captain Partridge set forth the results of his labors at Norwich. He claimed that his plan of "connecting mental improvement with a regular course of bodily exercises and the full development of the physical powers, the whole conducted under a military system of discipline," had succeeded beyond his most sanguine expectations. Out of 480 pupils who had entered the seminary from 21 States, only one had died there. "Many of my pupils, and those the closest applicants to study," he says, "walk with facility forty miles per day. On a recent excursion to the summit of the most elevated of the White Mountains, with a party of 50 of my pupils, a large portion of them walked, on the last day, 42 miles. Belonging to this party was a youth of but twelve years of age, who walked the whole distance, 160 miles, carrying his knapsack, and returned in good health." It would be interesting to know the ultimate stature of this youth.

Captain Partridge remained only three years at Middletown. He was doubtless impelled to abandon his seminary there from the refusal of the legislature of Connecticut to charter the institution as a college. He was instrumental, in 1834, in rehabilitating the institution at Norwich, which became known as "Norwich University", and in establishing military schools at Portsmouth, Va., in 1839, at Brandywine Springs, Del., 1853, and at Bristol, Pa., in 1853, the year of his death.

MILITARY SCHOOLS BEFORE 1861.

A considerable number of military schools and colleges, additional to those above mentioned, were organized before the War of the Rebellion. The more important of them were established in the Southern States, and were in several cases subsidized by the State. This was notably the case in Virginia, South Carolina, Louisiana, Kentucky, and Alabama. The Virginia Military Institute, at Lexington, Va., the Military Institute at Frankfort, Ky., and the Louisiana State Institute, at Alexandria, La., should be mentioned in this connection. It has been estimated that "one-tenth of the Confederate armies was commanded by the *élèves* of the Virginia Military Institute, at Lexington, embracing 3 major-generals, 30 brigadier-generals, 60 colonels, 50 lieutenant-colonels, 30 majors, 125 captains, 200 to 300 lieutenants". General "Stonewall" Jackson was long a professor in the Virginia Military Institute. General W. T. Sherman, of the United States Army, was in 1861 the head of the Louisiana State University, which had been organized on a military basis in the previous year. At the North the military plan of education was chiefly adopted by the proprietors of private schools for boys. Among the principal schools of this description established prior to 1861 we may mention, Russell's Collegiate and Commercial Institute, at New Haven, Conn.; the Highland Military Academy, Worcester, Mass.; Claverack College, Claverack, N. Y.

EFFECT OF THE WAR IN STIMULATING MILITARY DRILL.

Once the war opened, military drill assumed a new and unprecedented interest in the eyes of school authorities. The educational literature of that period teems with schemes for the introduction of gymnastics and military drill into public school courses. As early as 1861 military drill was introduced into a portion of the public schools in the city of Bangor, Me.; and the State of New Jersey, about the same time, made an appropriation of money for military instruction in her normal school.

MILITARY DRILL IN BOSTON SCHOOLS.

Elementary military drill was experimentally introduced into the Public Latin, English High, Eliot, and Dwight Schools for boys in Boston in 1863. It has since been eliminated from the grammar schools, to which class the Eliot and the Dwight belong, but has been introduced into all the high schools of the city for males. Two drills a week, of an hour each, are required of all boys able to carry a musket.

The new Public Latin and English High School house in Boston, which was opened in February, 1881, is provided with a large and elegant drill hall, and a commodious and well-furnished modern gymnasium. The gymnasium remains practically worthless, through the inability or unwillingness of the school authorities to grapple with the problem of securing proper instructors. The publications of the Boston school committee contain several elaborate reports, filled with commendable expressions of sentiment on the subject of physical education; also a few notes and regulations regarding gymnastic and calisthenic exercises; but their actual working programme embraces almost nothing worthy of imitation as regards genuine development and training of the bodily powers. Military drill has also been introduced, to a limited extent, into the public schools of other American cities; notably in those of Baltimore, Md., and Washington, D. C.

MILITARY TRAINING ORDAINED BY THE MORRILL ACT, 1862.

Congress, under the stress of war, passed, in July, 1862, the so-called Morrill Act, granting thirty thousand acres of the public lands for each of its Senators and Representatives to every State which should "provide at least one college where the leading object shall be, without excluding other scientific and classical studies, and including military tactics, to teach such branches of learning as are related to agriculture and the mechanic arts." Under the provisions of this act, as originally passed and since amended, there have been detailed, as we are informed by the Adjutant-General of the army, one hundred and forty-two different officers of the army for the purpose of teaching military tactics and science. The following extracts and tables are taken from the Report of the Adjutant-General, published October 30, 1883:

ARMY OFFICERS AS MILITARY INSTRUCTORS AT COLLEGES.

The tables subjoined exhibit the apportionment of details, corrected to October 1, 1883, and the data contained in the reports of the several officers performing the duties of professors of tactics and military science.

The law authorizing the detail of officers of the army at a limited number of colleges and universities evidently contemplated that the services of the military professors would be the means of securing a number of youths well instructed in military knowledge, who when occasion required could efficiently exercise command in the militia of their respective States. A better plan could scarcely have been devised, and, carried out faithfully, will prove a powerful factor in insuring the thorough efficiency of that branch of the military service.

Section 1225 of the Revised Statutes empowers the President, upon the application of a college or university having capacity to educate at the same time not less than 150 male students, to detail an officer of the army to act as president, superintendent, or professor thereof. In establishing the minimum number of students that could be educated at a college or university, the law no doubt contemplated that not only such institutions should have capacity for educating a certain number of youths, but that at least the minimum number prescribed be actually under instruction. This point the War Department has no means of verifying except from the reports required of the military professor; and a glance at the second table submitted shows that a minority of the colleges or universities named therein actually educate 150 students. It is earnestly recommended that, if necessary to prevent cavil, the law be amended so as to require applications for the detail of a military professor to be accompanied by satisfactory proof that at least 150 male pupils above the age of fifteen are actually present at the institution.

The colleges and universities at which officers of the army may be detailed should be designated by the governor of the State in which located, as being most interested in the progress of the State and its institutions, and possessing greater means of information necessary to wisely determine the question of selection.

The section of the Statutes above referred to prescribes that the officer detailed shall act as "president, superintendent, or professor." He should, therefore, be a recognized member of the Faculty, with equal vote, and not simply a prefect of discipline. This is of the utmost importance to secure the best results, as well as to preserve the dignity of the position of the professor of tactics and military science.

Drills should not be held outside of regular hours, but considered as part of the curriculum of instruction.

Finally, I am of opinion that officers should be forbidden to instruct in any other branch of education, except in so far as the instruction has direct reference to military knowledge.

TABLE No. 14.—*Apportionment of details at colleges, universities, etc., under section 1225, Revised Statutes.*

States, by groups.	Aggregate population of States and groups.	No. of officers to which entitled.	No. on duty in State or group.	Officers detailed.	Colleges, &c., at which detailed.	Expiration of detail.
Maine	648,945			Second Lieut. Edgar W. Howe, Seventeenth Infantry	Maine State College, Orono	July 1, 1885.
New Hampshire	346,984					
Vermont	332,286			First Lieut. H. E. Tuiberly, First Cavalry	University of Vermont, Burlington	July 1, 1884.
Massachusetts	1,783,012			Second Lieut. V. H. Bridgman, Second Artillery	Massachusetts Agricultural College, Amherst	July 1, 1884.
Connecticut	622,683					
Rhode Island	270,528					
	4,010,438	3	3			
New York	5,083,810	3	3	First Lieut. H. W. Hubbell, jr., First Artillery	Union College, Schenectady, N. Y	July 1, 1886.
				First Lieut. W. S. Schuyler, Fifth Cavalry	Cornell University, Ithaca, N. Y	July 1, 1886.
				First Lieut. C. A. L. Totten, Fourth Artillery	Cathedral School of St. Paul, Garden City, L. I.	July 1, 1886.
Pennsylvania	4,282,786			First Lieut. W. P. Duvall, Fifth Artillery	Pennsylvania Military Academy, Chester	July 1, 1884.
				First Lieut. J. W. Pullman, Eighth Cavalry	Allegheny College, Meadville, Pa	July 1, 1886.
				Second Lieut. J. A. Leyden, Fourth Infantry	Pennsylvania State College, Center County	July 1, 1886.
New Jersey	1,130,983			Second Lieut. F. L. Dodds, Ninth Infantry	Rutgers College, New Brunswick, N. J	July 1, 1885.
Delaware	146,654					
Maryland	934,632					
	6,495,055	4	4			
West Virginia	618,443					
Virginia	1,512,806			Second Lieut. Geo. Le R. Brown, Eleventh Infantry	Hampton Nor. and Agric. Inst., Hampton, Va.	July 1, 1884.
North Carolina	1,400,047			Second Lieut. J. Batchelder, Twenty-fourth Infantry	Bingham School, Orange County, N. C	July 1, 1886.
	3,531,296	2	2			
South Carolina	995,622			Second Lieut. E. M. Weaver, jr., Second Artillery	South Carolina Military Institute, Charleston	July 1, 1886.
Georgia	1,539,048					
	2,534,670	1	1			

PHYSICAL TRAINING IN AMERICAN COLLEGES.

State	Population	No.	Officer	Institution	Date
Florida	267,351		Second Lieut. Arthur L. Wagner, Sixth Infantry	East Florida Seminary, Gainesville, Fla.	July 1, 1885
Alabama	1,262,794				
Mississippi	1,530,145	1	Second Lieut. W. L. Buck, Thirteenth Infantry	Agricultural and Mechanical College of Mississippi, Starkville.	July 1, 1886
Louisiana	940,103				
Texas	2,071,695 1,592,574	1	First Lieut. Charles J. Crane, Twenty-fourth Infantry	Agricultural and Mechanical College of Texas, near Bryan.	July 1, 1885
Arkansas	802,564				
Tennessee	2,395,138	1	Second Lieut. R. W. Dowdy, Seventeenth Infantry	University of the South, Sewanee, Tenn.	July 1, 1886
Kentucky	1,542,463	1	First Lieut. C. R. Tyler, Sixteenth Infantry	Agric'l and Mech'l College of Ky., Lexington.	July 1, 1886
Ohio	1,648,708	1	First Lieut. George Ruhlen, Seventeenth Infantry	Ohio State University, Columbus.	July 1, 1884
Indiana	3,198,239	2	Second Lieut. J. B. Goe, Thirteenth Infantry	Indiana Asbury University, Greencastle.	July 1, 1886
Michigan	1,978,362	1	Second Lieut. H. A. Schroeder, Fourth Artillery	Michigan Military Academy, Orchard Lake.	July 1, 1886
Illinois	1,636,331 3,078,769	1 2	Second Lieut. C. G. Starr, First Infantry; Second Lieut. C. McClure, Eighteenth Infantry	S. Illinois Normal University, Carbondale; Illinois Industrial University, Champaign	July 1, 1886 July 1, 1886
Wisconsin	1,315,460	1	Second Lieut. G. N. Chase, Fourth Infantry	University of Wisconsin, Madison.	July 1, 1885
Missouri	14,366,352 2,168,804	2	Second Lieut. John J. Haden, Eighth Infantry	University of Missouri, Columbia	July 1, 1884
Kansas	995,966		First Lieut. Albert Todd, First Artillery	Kansas State Agricultural College, Manhattan.	July 1, 1884
Colorado	194,649				
Iowa	3,359,410 1,624,620	2	First Lieut. E. C. Knower, Third Artillery; First Lieut. S. R. Jones, Fourth Artillery	Iowa State University, Iowa City; Cornell College, Mount Vernon, Iowa.	July 1, 1886 July 1, 1886
Minnesota	780,806				
Nebraska	452,433				
California	2,857,859 864,686	1	Second Lieut. J. A. Hutton, Eighth Infantry	University of California, Berkeley	July 1, 1886
Oregon	174,767				
Nevada	62,265 1,101,718				

TABLE No. 15.—*Data contained in the reports of the officers detailed as military instructors at the institutions named.*

Universities and colleges.	No. of students. Over 15 years of age.	Under 15 years of age.	Total average attendance.	Average attendance. Artillery drills.	Infantry drills.	Aptitude of pupils.	Interest manifested by Faculty.
Maine State College, Orono	54		54		40	Good	Very good.
University of Vermont, Burlington.	73		73	15	64	Excellent	Excellent.
Massachusetts Agricultural College, Amherst.	65		65	28	61	Good	Marked.
Union College, Schenectady, N. Y.							
Cornell University, Ithaca, N. Y.	227		227	27	185	Good	Good.
Cathedral School of St. Paul, Garden City, Long Island, N. Y.							
Pennsylvania Military Academy, Chester.	112	19	131		131	Very good	Commendable and unremitting.
Allegheny College, Meadville, Pa.							
Pennsylvania State College, Center County.							
Rutgers College, New Brunswick, N. J.	126		126		35	Good	Good.
Hampton Normal and Agricultural Institute, Virginia.	310	33	343	42	170	Very good	Satisfactory.
Bingham School, Orange County, North Carolina.							
South Carolina Military Institute, Charleston.							
East Florida Seminary, Gainesville, Fla.	51	27	78	27	48	Good	Very great.
Agricultural and Mechanical College of Mississippi, Starkville.	185	6	191	(*)	(*)	Good	Rather negative.†
Agricultural and Mechanical College of Texas, near Bryan.	229	5	234	16		Good	Good.
University of the South, Sewanee, Tenn.	104	22	126	20	51	Fair	Satisfactory.
Agricultural and Mechanical College of Kentucky, Lexington.	143	20	163		119	Good	Good.
Ohio State University, Columbus	280	(*)	280	42	150	Fair	Very satisfactory.
Indiana Asbury University, Greencastle.	280	30	310	117	117	Good	Very good.
Michigan Military Academy, Orchard Lake.	78	16	94	45	64	Not good	Not good.
Southern Illinois Normal University, Carbondale, Ill.	64		64	17	58	Very good	Not good.
Illinois Industrial University, Champaign.	214		214	65	70	Good	Very satisfactory.
University of Wisconsin, Madison.							
University of Missouri, Columbia.	400	25	425	14	31	Good	Fair.
Kansas State Agricultural College, Manhattan.	117	2	119		20	Good	Good.
Iowa State University, Iowa City.	151		151	22	102	Average	Very indifferent.
Cornell College, Mount Vernon, Iowa.							
University of California, Berkeley.							

* Not stated.

†Great interest shown and much assistance given in military discipline; found essential to control of pupils.

PHYSICAL TRAINING IN AMERICAN COLLEGES.   105

Though the Report of the Commissioner of Education does not group military schools by themselves, an examination of his Report for 1882–'83 shows that there were at least thirty institutions, other than those mentioned in the above list, in which military drill and discipline formed an essential feature.

During the year ending July 1, 1884, there were thirty-three officers of the army on duty at colleges, universities, and schools of superior instruction for young men.

ATHLETIC SPORTS IN THE UNITED STATES.

THE PRESENT CONTRASTED WITH THE PAST.

The grim and unjoyous ideals of the generations that conquered the wilderness and laid the foundation of the Republic have ceased to actuate the mass of the community, if we may judge from the practices which now obtain all over the country with regard to recreation and amusements.

The value of play is a favored theme with writers on hygiene and education. The ardor and activity displayed by the undergraduate world in games and exercises once frowned upon by Faculties and boards of trust because of their " vain, idle, and flesh-pleasing " qualities, have become so great that it is the fashion in certain quarters to speak of many colleges as if they were schools for ball-players, oarsmen, and athletes. There would be more point to such satire if the interest in athletics, which seems to strengthen year by year, were confined to the student class, instead of pervading the community as a whole. It is too often overlooked that the growth of college athletics has been stimulated and shaped by forces whose effects are equally, if not more strongly, marked on the non-scholastic classes of our population. Exhibitions and contests of every description which would not have been licensed or tolerated, much less pecuniarily supported, thirty years ago, now yield quick and large returns in popularity and cash to their promoters. Never, before the War and the profound changes that it has wrought upon the American mind and manners, would it have been possible for a single college class, or even a single college, to have raised $5,000 in one year for the maintenance of its representative athletes. Such a draft upon the imagination, as well as upon the pockets of the college public, would inevitably have gone to protest, and for precisely the same reasons that would have entailed disfavor and bankruptcy upon almost any of the professional athletic organizations which now flourish so on every hand that simply to name and classify them would prove wearisome.

ATHLETICS STIMULATED BY THE WAR.

The disbanded armies of the Republic furnished a large contingent of students who had been subjected to strenuous physical training, to the preparatory schools and colleges during the decade succeeding the war. The influence exerted by this contingent in reviving and developing the interest in physical culture, whose beginnings in the fifties and early sixties we have already noted, has been, perhaps, even more potent in the department of athletics than in those of gymnastics and military drill. The history of athletics in America has not yet been written, and it is not our purpose to attempt it here; but it would be a grave omission in a survey of physical training in American colleges and universities not to consider the salient features and tendencies of college athletics.

COLLEGE ATHLETICS.

The growth of college athletics within very recent years has led to a very general and somewhat heated discussion regarding them. In the last year (1884), especially, the question of their regulation has become a burning one with more than one Faculty. That the question should have assumed its present proportions is due to the fact that the athletic interest has been developed and organized chiefly through the efforts of the students themselves, and in accordance with their own notions of what is fitting and desirable. The general weakening, amounting sometimes to absolute break-down, of paternal government in our colleges, serves to complicate the difficulties in those institutions where the governing boards find themselves suddenly called upon to regulate abuses whose development they have been too short-sighted to prevent.

COLLEGE ATHLETIC ORGANIZATIONS.

Athletics have been carried to a higher degree of development and specialization at Yale, Harvard, and Princeton, than at any other colleges in the country. The accompanying statement (Table No. 16) has been prepared from authoritative returns made to the compiler of this Report. It is intended to set forth the status of the athletic interest in the colleges named during the year 1882–'83. It is followed by a summary statement (Table No. 17), which indicates in a measure the number and activity of the athletic organizations maintained by the students of seven less prominent colleges. It will be noticed that these are chiefly eastern colleges. Neither the general nor college public at the South manifests much interest in athletics or gymnastics. The best gymnasium building in the South is at Vanderbilt University, Nashville, Tenn., and a languid interest in athletics, more particularly in boating, exists at the University of Virginia. Military drill is in vogue in many places in the South, but athletic *organizations* comparable with those below noted do not exist. It may be said, in general, concerning western colleges, that physical education, both on its formal or gymnastic side and on its recreative or athletic side, is still in its embryonic stage.

CIRCULARS OF INFORMATION FOR 1885.

TABLE No. 16.—*Statement concerning the athletic organi-*

Names of student organizations for athletic sports, in 1882–'83—	Year it was established.	Number of members in 1882–'83.	Nature and value of property owned.	Cost of maintenance in 1882–'83.	Amount of funds raised. [1] Earnings. [2] Subscriptions, &c.
At Yale College, New Haven, Conn., with 1,080 students.					
Base-ball club	1865	1,000		$6,863 38	[1]$5,457 15 [2]1,797 00
Boat club	1852	1,000	a $16,000 b 5,000	7,348 86	[1]1,322 11 [2]5,926 87
Foot-ball club	1872	1,000		2,689 80	[1]1,329 65 [2]382 00
Lacrosse club	1882	1,000		574 00	[1]225 05 [2]349 95
Athletic association	1876	1,000		400 00	
Tennis club	1882	1,000		25 00	
Dunham Boat Club	1879	22	b 700		
Bicycle club	1883	29			
Hare-and-hounds club	1882	56			c 1,238 25
Yacht club	1882	43			
Totals				17,901 04	18,048 03
Balance					146 99
At Harvard University, Cambridge, Mass., with 1,428 students.					
Base-ball association	1865	Whole university.	Uniforms, bats, balls.	4,500 00	[1]2,600 00 [2]1,900 00
Boat club	1866	400	d 3,500 b 4,500	5,000 00	[1]2,764 00 [2]3,342 00
Foot-ball association	1873	Whole university.		3,655 62	[1]2,050 00 [2]857 00
Lacrosse association	1878	30 players.		350 00	[1]175 00 [2]175 00
Athletic association	1874	775	322	1,653 00	[1]1,025 00 [2]2,775 00
Tennis association	1880				
Bicycle club	1879 or 1880	91		150 62	[1]150 62
Cricket club		60		233 20	[2]233 20
Polo club	1883	12			
Shooting club	1883	60			
Totals				15,542 44	18,046 82
Balance					2,504 38
At Princeton College, Princeton, N. J., with 500 students.					
Base-ball association					
Boating association		Open to all students without payment of dues.	a 3,500 b 1,500	1,200 00	[1]1,200 00
Foot-ball association				1,975 00	[1]2,045 94 [1]130 52
Lacrosse association				322 11	[2]101 00
Athletic association	1870			755 06	[1]816 32
Totals				4,252 17	4,293 78
Balance					41 61

a Boat house.   b Boats, &c.   c Balance from previous year.

zations at Yale, Harvard, and Princeton in 1882-'83.

Times represented in contests in town in 1882-'83.	Times represented in contests out of town in 1882-'83.	Number of contests won by them.	Number of contests lost by them.	Remarks.
18	14	20	12	Hamilton park, valued at $80,000, was rented for matches and practice purposes at a rental amounting to one-quarter of gross gate receipts. The Yale Field Corporation now owns twenty-nine acres of land inclosed and fitted for field and track athletics. The names of the colleges whose athletes contested with those of Yale in championship matches in 1882-'83 are Amherst, Brown, Harvard, and Princeton. (This list is incomplete.) In the six years ending 1882-'83 the Yale foot-ball team did not suffer a defeat, and the base-ball club held the college championship for five years of the six, i. e., during the entire period of its belonging to the American Base-Ball Association.
....	1	....	1	
3	3	6	....	
18	11	14	15	The colleges represented in athletic contests with Harvard in 1882-'83 were Amherst, Bowdoin, Brown, Dartmouth, Columbia, Haverford, McGill University (of Montreal), Massachusetts Institute of Technology, University of New York, Princeton, Trinity, Wesleyan University, Williams, and Yale. The boat club pays an annual rental of $800 for the boat-house, which belongs to the university.
....	3	3	....	
7	2	8	1	
2	3	3	2	
3	1	....	....	
....	4	....	3 and 1 draw	
15	7	10	9	Princeton's contestants were chiefly drawn from the following named institutions: Amherst, Brown, Columbia, Cornell, Harvard, University of New York, University of Pennsylvania, Rutgers, and Yale. The athletic association pays a nominal rent for its grounds, which include in ten acres, a foot-ball field, a base-ball field, a quarter-mile running track, five dressing rooms, and two grand stands.
....	5	2	3	
4	5	8	1	
3	4	4	3	
3	1	....	....	

d Small house at New London.   e By theatricals for the club.

TABLE No. 17.—*Summary statement concerning athletic organizations at Amherst, Bowdoin,*

List of student organizations for athletic sports, in 1881–'83—	Year it was established.	Number of members in 1882–'83.	Nature and value of property owned by them or for them.	Cost of maintenance in 1882–'83.	Funds raised among students.
At Amherst College, Mass., with 352 students.					
Base-ball club					
Foot-ball team					
Athletic association					
Bicycle club					
Tennis club					
At Bowdoin College, Brunswick, Me., with 215 students.					
Boating association	1871	73	Boat-house, $875; boats, &c., $800.	$50 00	$70 00
Base-ball association	1868	57	Uniforms, $150	430 00	211 00
Athletic association	1874	98		30 00	
Tennis association	1883	50	8 tennis courts, $175		30 00
At University of California, Berkeley, Cal., with 143 male students.					
U. C. Base-Ball Club		9			
U. C. Foot-Ball Club	1882	15			
At Columbia College, New York City, with 1,522 students.					
Boat club			Rents a $0,000 boat-house	4,500 00	
Foot-ball association					
Athletic association	1873	95		400 00	400 00
Bicycle club	1880	30			
Cricket club		33			
Tennis club	1883	20			
At Dartmouth College, Hanover, N. H., with 329 students.					
Base-ball association	1860	339	Uniforms, &c., $250	832 75	755 25
Foot-ball association	1881	339	Uniforms, &c., $150	175 50	175 50
Athletic association	1875	339			
At Rutgers College, New Brunswick, N. J., with 129 students.					
Boating association	1871	31	Boat-house, $1,500; carried away by freshet of 1882.		
Base-ball association					
Foot-ball association					
Tennis association					
At Wesleyan University, Middletown, Conn., with 176 male students.					
Foot-ball association	1881		Uniforms, &c., $130	261 30	219 50
Rowing association		60	Boats, &c., $1,000; boat-house rented for $150.	805 68	300 00

PHYSICAL TRAINING IN AMERICAN COLLEGES.

Columbia, Dartmouth, Rutgers, University of California, and Wesleyan University.

Funds raised among outsiders.	Times represented in contests, in 1882-'83, in town.	Times represented in contests, in 1882-'83, out of town.	Number of contests won by them.	Number of contests lost by them.	Remarks.
....	7	8	6	9	Athletics are encouraged. Some members of the Faculty make money contributions. Men in teams are excused from certain exercises in the gymnasium. Professional trainers are occasionally employed.
....	1	....	....	....	Bicycling and foot ball are also engaged in. Members of teams are excused from certain recitations.
$219 00	5	3	4	4	
30 00	1	....	....	....	
....	2	1	2	1	
....	....	5	4	1	Class nines cost $20 for maintenance, and class foot-ball teams, $25.
....	4	....	4	....	
....	6	6	6	6	
....	3	7	1	9	
....	20	....	5	15	
....	....	2	(a)	....	
77 50	7	5	9	3	There were also tennis, bicycle, and hare-and-hounds clubs established in 1881. The nine has leave of absence for about a week yearly.
....	1	1	1	1	
....	....	....	....	....	The authorities do not interfere with athletics, except that each man on the "'varsity nine and eleven is required to file a certificate to the effect that his parent or guardian is willing for him to play."
....	12	8	11	9	
....	7	3	6	4	
98 00	1	3	3	1	Crews and teams have been excused from college exercises, to some extent, for inter-collegiate matches. The crew has sometimes employed a professional trainer. A gymnastic exhibition has usually been given during commencement week. The authorities have not provided for any systematic instruction or drill in gymnastics or athletics.
350 00	1	1	....	1	

a Drawn games.

CONCERNING PLAY GROUNDS.

GENERAL FACILITIES.

At most country colleges ample facilities in the way of grounds are furnished for the playing of base ball, foot ball, and tennis. The playing fields are usually within the college precincts. Since track athletics, *i. e.*, walking, jumping, sprint and hurdle races, have become popular, very considerable sums have been spent on the grading and on the improvement of athletic fields, in the way of providing stands for spectators, dressing rooms for the contestants, and "cinder tracks" for pedestrian purposes. Haverford College has a fine cricket field; Lehigh University has an inclosure containing a grand stand, dressing rooms, and a quarter-mile cinder path, together with fields for ball and lawn tennis; the University of Pennsylvania, in Philadelphia, has recently furnished a well-appointed athletic field; and the Johns Hopkins University, in Baltimore, has one nearly completed.

HARVARD'S PLAYING FIELDS.

The grounds devoted to field sports at Harvard belong to the university, and are well known among collegians as Holmes Field and Jarvis Field. They are adjacent to the Hemenway Gymnasium, and together embrace not far from ten acres of level land. Holmes Field was put in order in 1883–'84 at an expense of nearly $6,000, toward which the university contributed $2,000, the remainder being raised by subscription. The following statement, printed in the Harvard *Advocate*, January 4, 1884, is given for the purpose of affording information to institutions that may hereafter find it necessary to improve their play grounds:

RECEIPTS.

From subscriptions	$3,814 00
From Harvard University	2,000 00
	5,814 00

EXPENDITURES.

For grading field, and making and furnishing material for track, etc., as specified in agreement of July, 1883	$4,541 00
For 6 M. feet kyanized spruce, at $23	138 00
For grass seed	152 50
For manure	195 00
For teaming lumber	14 00
For watering track	4 00
For spreading and spading manure	112 50
For carpentering and other work	14 00
For sawing spruce stakes	4 00
For 52 loads of coal ashes, at 10 cents	5 20
For use of horses and carts	96 50
Carried forward	5,276 70

Brought forward	$5,276	70
For services	106	75
For screening cinders, etc	100	00
For 146 loads ashes, at 15 cents	21	90
	5,505	35
Balance in bank	308	65
	5,814	00

To the balance in the bank must be added $160, which is due the athletic association from the sale of cinders and gravel, and some money from subscriptions, which has not as yet been deposited.

THE YALE ATHLETIC FIELD.

As showing what undergraduate zeal and alumni aid, when combined, can accomplish toward promoting athletic interests, the following condensed abstract of the report of the Yale Field Corporation is given:

For many years Yale men have known that their college was one of the few which made no provision whatever for the outdoor sports of its students. Though situated near the center of a rapidly growing city, it relied entirely on such arrangements as its undergraduates could make from year to year.

In the spring of 1880 a movement was started in the Junior class which led to a university meeting, at which a committee of students was appointed to find out whether a suitable field for college sports could be purchased, and, if so, whether it was probable that money could be raised to pay for it. The committee reported favorably on both points, and was authorized to take the necessary steps to secure a field. Two months later this committee associated with itself the "Advisory Committee on Athletics," then composed of four graduates. During the following year the sum of $15,000 was collected and twenty-nine acres of land were purchased.

On the 27th of May, 1882, the "Committee on Purchase of Yale Athletic Grounds" was merged in the "Yale Field Corporation," which was formed to "manage grounds to be used by persons connected, or who shall have been connected, with Yale College, for athletic games, exercises, and recreations in said college, and to take, buy, own, and hold property, real and personal, necessary or proper therefor."

The members of this corporation are all persons who prior to its incorporation had paid $5 to the treasurer of the field fund, and all students and instructors who since that time have paid a like sum to the treasurer of the corporation. The management is vested in a board of twelve directors, of whom four are undergraduate officers of college athletic associations, six are graduates, and two are instructors in the university.

On the 1st of June, 1884, the field was thrown open to the college, and during the fall it has been used for foot ball and lacrosse, and has given general satisfaction. It lies on the south side of Derby avenue, due west of the campus, and distant one and one-half miles.

Some have objected to this field on account of its distance from the college. The reason why it was selected was because there was no suitable field nearer which could be bought. Every available spot within two miles of the college was carefully examined and considered, and those who know what there was to choose from have never questioned the wisdom of the choice. In point of fact, the new field is one sixth of a mile nearer South College than the grounds heretofore used, and the directors think that the Chapel street cars will soon run to the entrance. The location adopted, moreover, is in less danger from the opening of new streets than any other site available.

The preparation of the field for use has gone forward rather slowly. The reasons are numerous. It has been hard to raise money, and the expenses have been heavy.

Many questions have arisen concerning the treatment of soil, raising of turf, building of the track, etc., about which it was extremely difficult to procure trustworthy advice, and to proceed without it was simple experiment. The *personnel* of the committee and board of directors has undergone many changes. The members were from different cities, and those who are graduates have been so closely occupied with their own affairs that the time required for this work has not been easily spared.

Soon after the land was purchased the fences, trees, and buildings were cleared away, and about fourteen acres were graded for use. The soil was then enriched by plowing in two crops of grass and the addition of large quantities of wood ashes with other fertilizers; and by seeding and sodding, a strong turf was secured over an area about equal to that of the New Haven Green. The plan for lay-out submitted by Mr. Frederick Law Olmsted was adopted, with some modifications suggested by those practically acquainted with college athletics. At the entrance a roadway 200 feet long by 30 feet wide, flanked by a stone wall, was constructed, and drives four-fifths of a mile in length have been laid out within the grounds. The running track lies at the south-east corner of the field, and was built under the superintendence of Mr. Robert Rogers. It is a quarter of a mile long, and the straight-away length of its sides is 372.5 feet, while the width is 15 feet in the narrowest and 20 feet in the widest part. No pains were spared in its construction or in procuring the right kind of cinders and other materials of which it is made. The grounds are inclosed on three sides by 2,762 feet of fence, the fourth side being bounded by the river. The water supply is furnished by a good well and by 1,580 feet of pipe, which extend through the grounds from the city main. The grand stand, situated at the north side of the field and overlooking the principal ball ground, is the gift of Mr. William H. Crocker, '82 S. It seats 850 persons, and will afford a perfect view of the intercollegiate games to be played directly in front of it. The field is now ready for base ball, foot ball, track athletics, lacrosse, and tennis, and a tract of about four acres has been set aside for cricket, though it is not yet graded. When completed it will afford room and opportunity to all students for all games which they wish to play.

The plans adopted for further improvement include the grading of the cricket field, the planting of a hedge just inside the fence, the erection of two club houses, containing baths and dressing rooms for those who take part in the games, and some minor matters which will add to the beauty and convenience of the grounds.

The field lies on the farther bank of West River, on a bluff that rises forty feet above the water and extends westward. The side and eastern edge of this bluff are covered by a growth of chestnut, oak, and hickory, and near the entrance gate are two large pines. Through the grove one sees the city, and toward the south catches glimpses of the harbor and sound. The Edgewood hills rise on the side opposite the river, and West, Pine, and East Rocks, and farther away Mount Carmel, may be seen to the northward and north-east. With these natural advantages the field can be made a pleasant place for all friends of the college to visit. * * *

The following financial statement is submitted by the treasurer:

RECEIPTS.

Subscriptions paid	$32,209 35
Amount borrowed	20,685 78
Proceeds of buildings sold, rents, etc.	289 12
	53,184 25

DISBURSEMENTS.

For land	$21,394 50
For track	3,330 02
For grand stand	6,658 67
Carried forward	31,383 19

642

Brought forward		$31,383 19
For grading and preparation of field		13,558 41
For interest and discount		1,908 62
For expense account:		
Superintendence	$1,893 62	
Collection expenses, travel, etc.	2,299 66	
Fence	907 12	
Water pipes	673 88	
Seed	559 75	
		6,334 03
		53,184 25

The above statement shows that the corporation is in debt $20,685.78. It was thought best to borrow money to prepare the field for use rather than delay the work longer. The estimated expense of grading the remainder of the ground, erecting cottages, planting a hedge, and carrying out the rest of the plan already adopted, is, in round numbers, $10,000. At least $30,000 is therefore needed at once.

It is estimated that the cost of employing a superintendent and keeping the field in order after it is finished will be fully met by the money received for admission to the games. When the students use their own field the expenses of maintaining athletics can be materially reduced.

Any persons disposed to aid the corporation in meeting its obligations and continuing the work are earnestly requested to communicate with the treasurer, Mr. Henry B. Sargent, New Haven, Conn.

By order of the board of directors.

           MASON YOUNG, *President.*
           HENRY C. WHITE, *Secretary.*

NEW HAVEN, Conn., *December* 20, 1884.

During 1883–'84, Mr. W. C. Camp, who had distinguished himself as an accomplished athlete and as a scholar during his course at Yale, was engaged by the graduate advisory committee on athletics and the athletic association of the undergraduates to supervise the field sports of Yale students, at a salary of $1,200. Mr. Camp's assiduous and intelligent coaching and training contributed much to Yale's athletic triumphs in 1883–'84, when the Yale crew, foot-ball team, and ball nine each gained the championship prizes of the year.

THE YALE SYSTEM OF ATHLETICS.

Physical training at Yale means athletics, toward the regulation of which the Faculty exercise a minimum of influence. It is rather singular that Yale, which has been so averse to anything approaching an elective system of studies, should have developed a most unrestricted elective system of athletics.

The fairest and most intelligent paper elicited by the recent discussion of athleticism which has come under our notice, is the production of an ardent friend and defender of the Yale system of athletics. In it the whole system is so well set forth, its advantages are so cogently argued, and the attacks of its critics so temperately met, that it seems best to quote copiously from it. Its exposition of the reciprocal relations of body-work and brain-work should be *grasped* by every teacher.

Those who may desire to consult the paper as originally printed will find it published, in two parts, in the *Popular Science Monthly* for February and March, 1884.[1]

I. ADVANTAGES.

* * * If we can show that college athletics supply this need [of exercise] to quite a large body of students, and supply it regularly and systematically, we may secure a patient consideration of their good effects long enough to add a discussion of their accompanying evils. In this discussion we hope to prove that the evils have been exaggerated; that they are not so great as would be the evils of a college life without a system of athletics; and, lastly, that such evils as do inhere in the present system are capable of remedy.

* * * Though we admit the truth of all the wise sayings with regard to a "sane mind in a sound body," we are yet too apt to regard the sound body as a mere accident of inheritance or environment. So we read the proposition as a hypothetical one, viz., "If the body is sound the mind will be sane." Few but physicians read it as indicating a connection between body and mind, by means of which we can make, or help to make, a good healthy brain by making a good sound body. In the fact that the brain always seems to direct the body, we are prone to forget that the body carries the brain and feeds it with its own life. If the body has good blood the brain will have good blood also. If the body does not furnish good material, the brain will do, according to its capacity, poor work, or will not work at all. * * *

There are two kinds of brain-work,—one which we may very properly call body brain-work, and the other mind brain-work. Most people, including a great many educators of youth, consider mind brain-work to be the only kind of brain-work. But body brain-work is quite as essential to the healthy existence of the brain, and really comes first in the order of brain growth. The child, too young to know anything except its bodily wants, and conscious of them only when the denial of them causes pain, develops brain every time it makes a will-directed effort to grasp the thing it wants. The movement of its hand is as necessary to the development of its brain as the guidance and government of the brain are to the growth of the hand. What is true of the hand is true of the other bodily organs whose motion is under the control of the will. They and the brain are developed by reciprocal action. Interfere with this body brain-work in childhood, or at any period of growth, either by repressing it or by diverting from it too much vital energy to mind brain-work, such as is involved in the acquisition of knowledge, and you not only stunt the body, but also enfeeble the brain, by depriving both of their proper growth. * * *

Care to guard against this interference is all the more necessary in cases in which the brain is large or sensitive. Now, will any man say that at the time of life when young men come to our American colleges, when, in fact, all their bodily organs are approaching maturity, this body brain-work ought to cease, or can, without danger, be neglected? Is it not most essential that at this very period the reciprocal action between body and brain should be steadily maintained, in order that both should be able to endure the strain put upon them by the various stimulants of thought and feeling to be found in college life? The great pressure brought to bear upon them is toward conscious cerebration. Acquisitions of knowledge, scholarships, the ambitious desires of parents, and prizes, all incite them to neglect body brain-work, under the mistaken impression that time given to that is time lost to the other. Many a fine scholar has left college with great honors to experience in his subsequent career the serious results of the mistake made in college, and has discovered, often too late, that a vigorous body to carry his brain is more essential to success in life than a well-

---

[1] *College Athletics*, by Eugene L. Richards, Assistant Professor of Mathematics in Yale College.

trained brain full of knowledge but lacking a strong body from which to draw its nourishment and strength.

Again, exercise, to be beneficial, should be regular and systematic. To be most beneficial it should be in the open air. The oxygenation of the blood is not the least important effect of exercise. In consequence of the reciprocal action of mind and body, to be as beneficial as possible it should be accompanied by mental occupation. The mind should be interested in the exercise while the body is engaged. How shall all these requisites of the best kind of exercise be secured? First, a regularly set *time* for exercise; next, a fixed *amount* of time devoted to it; then, a *place* where the lungs should breathe fresh air; and, lastly, a *kind* of exercise which should engage the mind as well as the body. By the present system of college athletics these requisites are met, if not perfectly, at least as well as it is possible for them to be met. * * * They do furnish a mental stimulus. They set up an object to be striven for, and an ideal of strength or skill. The object is honor—honor of no great worth, perhaps, but still honor, to the student-mind. In boating, the object is a victory over a crew of a rival class or a rival college. In lacrosse, base ball, and foot ball, besides working for the ultimate object of the championship, the mind of the player has continual occupation in the game itself. To secure a victory in any of these sports, good brains in the players contribute quite as much as good muscles. In fact, it is the skilled muscles rightly directed by good brains which win, and not the players most skilled in the use of their muscles. Mind as well as body has to be considered by the successful captains in the selection of their men. Then there are minor considerations which keep students in steady training, and help to induce more men to work than finally appear in the great contests, such, for instance, as the ambition to secure an office or position in one of the university organizations, and thus an honorable standing as a college man. * * *

The following brief account of the exercise taken by the students is offered in order to insure a better understanding of the system of college athletics:

Almost as soon as the college opens in the fall, the various class nines begin their games for the college championship. At the same time the class crews, the foot-ball and lacrosse teams, put their men into training. This means regular exercise in the open air from four to six weeks for about 140 men. Quite as many more are benefited, some by actual participation in the games, in order to furnish opponents to the teams in practice, and others by training for the athletic association contests. After the class base-ball championship is decided, and the athletic association meetings have terminated, fewer men exercise. The interest of the college then centers in the foot-ball elevens, one selected from the whole university, and the other from the Freshman classes of the academic and scientific departments. To give these teams practice, all the college is urged to go to the field and play against them; and though, of course, the invitation is not accepted as extensively as it is given, yet it does induce quite a large number of men to exercise. But this is not the only good effect of the existence of these teams. Catching the enthusiasm of the sport, often the men of different dormitories and of different eating-clubs send out teams for matches. The foot-ball season terminates at the Thanksgiving recess. The two or three weeks intervening between this recess and the winter examinations see very little exercise taken by the students, except by the few who regularly use the gymnasium. Immediately on the opening of the winter term activity in athletics manifests itself again. The captain of the university crew, the captain of the university base-ball nine, the captains of the different class crews, and the captain of the Freshman base-ball nine, call for men who wish to try for positions on these organizations. The candidates are put into regular training in the gymnasium while the season prevents exercise out of doors. Nearly a hundred men come forward, who are actually in training for at least one hour a day. They are required to live rightly in all respects. Each man is bound to avoid excesses of all kinds. The force of a public opinion created by the sight of these men attending to their physical development, and living according to laws and rules, acts upon the college world to encourage regularity of life and obedience to authority. It is a moral power in the community. As soon as the season permits, the men are sent out of doors. The crews take their seats in the boats. The nines take their positions in the field. The spring regatta terminates the practice of the class crews, but, as that event occurs about three weeks before the June examinations, and five weeks before the close of the college year, it does not leave the young men a long time without exercise. The university, consolidated, and Freshman nines, the lacrosse team, and the university crew (with sometimes a second eight), continue their practice much longer, some of them stopping work only after the close of the college year.

Now, it may be said that the writer has only shown that regular exercise has been secured during a few weeks of the first term to 140 men at the most, and during the whole winter term to 100 men; and in the spring and summer to 100 men part of the term, and to half that number during the whole of the term. Granted. But there are other organizations which induce men to exercise. The athletic association has already been mentioned. This gives three exhibitions; one during the winter or early spring in the gymnasium, and two in the open air, one in the summer and one in the fall. The Dunham Rowing Club has a membership of 44 men. Then there are canoe clubs, tennis clubs, and gun clubs. It would be putting the estimate too low to say that at least half of the undergraduate members of the academic and scientific departments get quite a regular amount of systematic out-door exercise from, or in consequence of, the present system of college athletics. This activity, too, has been mainly the outgrowth of the attention given to boating and to base ball. They had the first regular organizations, and the others have taken pattern from them. It is no argument against the system that all the members of the university do not take advantage of it. The need of exercise is met, and opportunities for regular and systematic exercise are given, with inducements to take it, which do act upon at least half of the membership of the two departments most in need of it. The system might do more good if time were set apart by the various Faculties for the purpose of encouraging exercise, but in considering the system it must be borne in mind that it has grown up in a continual struggle for existence; and, until within a few years, without either help from graduates or favor from the college authorities.

* * * In addition to those already mentioned, we claim for it the following advantages:

(1) The college is sending out a better breed of men. College athletics send their healthy influence into the schools, and in them consequently increased attention is given to physical development. Thus the material coming from the schools is improved. In college this material is better preserved and better developed under the present system of athletics. More well-trained minds in more forceful bodies are graduated from college than in former years. What President Eliot says on this subject is as applicable to Yale as to Harvard:

It is agreed on all hands that the increased attention given to physical exercise and athletic sports within the past twenty-five years has been, on the whole, of great advantage to the university; that the average physique of the mass of students has been sensibly improved, the discipline of the college been made easier and more effective, the work of many zealous students been done with greater safety, and the ideal student been transformed from a stooping, weak, and sickly youth, into one well-formed, robust, and healthy.

(2) The system of college athletics gives opportunity for the development of certain qualities of mind and character not all provided for in the college curriculum, but qualities nevertheless quite as essential to true success in life as ripe scholarship or literary culture. Courage, resolution, and perseverance are required in all the men who excel in athletic sports. The faculty for organization, executive power, the qualities which enable men to control and lead other men, and again, those other qualities by which men yield faithful obedience to recognized authority, are all called into action in every boat race, in every ball contest, and through all the pre-

liminary training. In athletics the college world is a little republic of young men, with authority for government delegated to presidents, captains, and commodores, and loyally supported by the resources and bodies of the governed. Is the system not worth something as a means of preparation for the responsibilities of life in the larger republic outside the campus?

(3) The system is conducive to the good order of the college. It conduces to good order in furnishing occupation for the physically active. There are men in every class who seem to require some outlet for their superabundant animal life. Before the day of athletics, such men supplied the class bullies in fights between town and gown, and were busy at night in gate-stealing and in other pranks now gone out of fashion. * * * Any instructor who has kept track of the ways of college during the past fifteen years cannot fail to be struck by the decreasing number of the really great disorders, by the mildness of those which remain, and by the increasing regard on the part of the students for college authority, college property, and for the rights of fellow-students.

* * * * * * * * *

Again, the system conduces to good order in its effects upon class-feeling. It acts upon this class-feeling in two ways: first, in the contests between class organizations, furnishing a safety-valve for it; and second, in the university organizations, tending to moderate it. * * * Since these organizations are composed of men of all classes, it is impossible for a college to be enthusiastic for its crew, team, or nine, without a common sympathy binding all the classes together. Moreover, it is observable that the time of the year when the athletic contests are not absorbing the attention of the college is the very time when the disorders between classes and the persecutions of Freshmen are most prevalent. * * * Formerly it was the strong men who incited and took the chief part in disorders. Now all their interests and all their efforts are against them.

(4) The system furnishes to instructors an opportunity of meeting their pupils as men interested in a common good, without the chilling reserve of the recitation room. * * * The college officer who gives a little of his time even to the boys' play soon finds his sympathies widen, and, by learning from actual observation how young men feel and think, becomes able to deal more wisely with those under his charge, from a fuller knowledge of them.

(5) The power of the athletic contests to awaken enthusiasm ought not to be held of small account. The tendency of academic life is toward dry intellectualism. * * * It is not too much to say that in many a student, while passing from Freshman to the end of Senior year, this spirit would die for lack of culture were it not for athletics. There is training for it in every contest witnessed. * * *

(6) The system of athletics, by its intercollegiate contests, brings the students into a wider world. They are no longer "home-keeping youths" with "homely wits." They measure themselves by other standards than those they find in the limits of their own campus.

* * * * * * * * *

II. EVILS AND THEIR REMEDIES.

* * * That the present system has evils is no valid argument against it, unless it can be shown either that these outweigh the good, or that some other practical system can be devised which shall have all the good with less of the evil of the present system.

(1) One evil alleged against the present system is the excessive amount of time required for exercise under it. It is no doubt true that some students do give too much time to athletics. Some students also give too much time to study; yet that fact is not brought forward as a fatal argument against the college course of study. Of the two excesses—excess of study and excess of exercise—the dangerous pressure at present is toward excess of study. But, in point of fact, this evil of too much time given

to athletics has been greatly exaggerated. The winter term is not open to the charge of excessive athletics. The athletes then training do not devote an average of more than an hour a day to exercise. Perhaps a few give an hour and a half. It would be safe to say that, counting all the time consumed, including the time of exercise, the time used in going to and from the gymnasium, and the time used in dressing and undressing, it would not go beyond two hours per day, and in most cases would be less than that amount. So, to consider the question of excessive time, we must look at the fall and spring terms. In the fall, during days when afternoon recitations are held, the class nines do not spend more than two hours' time all together, including both practice in the field and the time of going to and from practice. The same may be said of the foot-ball and lacrosse teams. On Wednesday and Saturday afternoons the students give from two to three hours to practice. On these afternoons the match games occur. They are prohibited on other days, except during examinations, at which time they are allowed on any day, provided no player is thereby prevented from attending his examination. The crews, also, in practice on the water and in going to and from their boats, spend two hours daily. On Wednesdays and Saturdays they use more time, but the practice is so arranged as not to interfere with recitations.

In the summer the same amount of time daily is given to practice, except that when recitations cease and examinations begin the university and Freshman nines use more time. Even then that time will not average more than three hours per day. When match games are played out of town, to the time of the game must be added the time used in travel to and from the scene of the match. In the season of 1882, of the games played during the time when recitations or examinations were being held, only five were played out of town by the Yale University nine, though the men went out of town once or twice more but were prevented from playing by the rain. Of these five, three were played in New York City, which is only a little over two hours' ride from New Haven. Of the remaining two, neither needed more than thirty-six hours' absence from town.

The university crew row only one race a year. The foot-ball elevens and the lacrosse team play a few games out of New Haven, but do not use in this way as much time as the nine.

(2) It is said that the excitement attendant on these sports distracts from study. It is true that the contests do furnish excitement for the students, but it is excitement of a healthy kind. * * * Banish athletics, and you increase the attendance at the theaters and the saloons, where the temptations are greater, and the excitements less healthy, than those of the ball field and boat race.

(3) There is the evil of betting. This is not an evil peculiar to athletics. * * * Games and races in colleges do not create betting. They simply divert it from other channels.

(4) Then there are the disorders consequent upon victories. These disorders are sometimes quite serious, but are by no means so serious as they are often represented to be. On the campus such disorders have never been more serious than some disorders taking place after the conferring of degrees. They have always been easily controlled. * * *

It may be replied that disorders consequent upon victories are not confined to the college campus. Indeed, to the minds of many candid men, the great disorders which bring dangerous disgrace to the present system of college athletics, and reflect upon college government as well, occur at the intercollegiate contests, when the athletes meet on neutral ground. * * * For this evil a more general interest in the subject on the part of instructors and parents, and their more general attendance at the games, would easily suggest the remedies of a healthy and manifested public opinion, and a judicious personal influence.

(5) It is charged against athletics that they benefit the few, and that these few are those least requiring the exercise. One part of the charge can be appreciated—that few are benefited—these few being the members of the crew, nine, eleven, and la-

crosse teams of the university. These, with substitutes, amount to about fifty men. But it has been already shown that more men are induced to exercise than the actual membership of these organizations; and that the present system affects, in the matter of exercise, at least half of the undergraduate department.

The objection that the men under training in the university organizations are the men least requiring the training can be understood to be one of two propositions, viz., either that these men have naturally so much power or skill that they need not develop any more, or that they will cultivate their strength and nerve without being stimulated to do so by the workings of the present system. This would be like arguing that men of great mental gifts either do not need an education, or would get an education without any opportunities being provided for this purpose in a school or college system—a proposition which, however true in exceptional cases, taken as a general statement no argument is required to prove absurd. * * *

(6) It is said, again, that the system may develop men, but it only makes fine brutes of them, and sets before the college a false standard of excellence, viz., one entirely physical. It cannot be said with truth that the standard is false. * * * Other things being equal, the bright mind and good heart in a strong body are better than the same things in a weak body, because they can accomplish more in life.

* * * * * * *

(7) The evil of a general nature last to be considered is that of expense.

The expenses of the organizations which have special university representatives are only taken into account, since these are the organizations of which the evils have been so loudly proclaimed to the public. In the table given below (for Yale College) the "expenses" and "income" are the totals for both university and class clubs combined. For base ball, foot ball, and lacrosse, the amounts in the column headed "earned" are made up for the most part of gate-money taken at exhibition games. For the boat clubs, of the amount put in the same column, $1,045.36 was the net result of a dramatic entertainment given by the students for the benefit of the university club. The balance was obtained from entrance and carriage fees at regattas, renting of lockers, and sale of boat.

Clubs.	Expenses.	Income.			
		Total.	Balance from 1881.	Earned.	Subscribed.
Boat	$7,348 86	$7,426 52	$177 54	$1,322 11	$5,026 87
Base ball	6,863 38	7,254 15		5,457 15	1,797 00
Foot ball	2,689 80	2,792 36	1,080 71	1,329 65	382 00
Lacrosse	574 00	575 00		225 05	349 95
Total	17,476 04	18,048 03	1,258 25	8,333 96	8,455 82

It will be observed that the total amount subscribed is less than half the expenses. Two hundred and ninety dollars of this sum were given by graduates. Deducting this, and considering that, according to the catalogue of 1881-'82, there were, in the undergraduate, academical, and scientific departments, seven hundred and eighty-six students, the cost (above earnings) of the present system averages only a little over $10 per man. As all departments are benefited by the system, the average ought to be taken for the whole university. There being in the university over one thousand men, the average cost per man would be considerably less than $10. It will be said that part of the earnings come from the students, since they are the chief attendants at the game. This is true. Assuming that half the earnings come from the students (an amount probably in excess of the real amount), the average cost per man for the university will not be far from $12. Fifteen dollars per man would undoubtedly cover the whole cost of athletics throughout the year, counting not only the athletics represented in the table, but all other kinds as well. Certainly this does not seem an extravagant sum to pay for the benefits derived from the system. The writer believes that the expenses can be very much diminished. The tendency to unnecessary increase of expenses can certainly be diminished by measures hereafter noticed.

By the table, it will be seen that the subscriptions for base ball and foot ball were small in amount, as compared with their earnings. It is generally believed, among students, that the university organizations of both these sports can be made self-supporting.

The evils already commented on are general. There are other so-called evils which are special—some peculiar to one kind of athletics, but not belonging to the others. One of these, charged against base ball, is that the game brings the students into contact with "professionals." Whatever may be the extent of the evil in other colleges, at Yale it has not proved to be so great as to call for faculty interference, or even to excite apprehension. All the evils, real or imaginary, connected with ball-playing, are reduced to a minimum when the students meet "professionals." They meet them simply for practice. Betting is, as a rule, precluded by the fact that the result is generally a foregone conclusion, and men bet on only doubtful issues. Off the field there is no more intercourse between the students and the "professionals" than is necessary to transact the business attending the match. The professional nine are then generally represented by their business manager, and the students by the president or treasurer of their club. In the game one nine is in the field, while the members of the other are at the bases, or waiting for their turn at the bat. The "professionals" are under the strictest discipline, so that their presence does not invite or occasion dissipation in any form. Victories of college nines over "professionals" are not frequent, and are not attended by disorders on the campus.

But to some objectors the evils of "professionalism" in athletics includes more than playing with professional nines. The employment of professional "trainers" in preparing students for contests is, for some, the chief evil. Such trainers are looked upon as bad companions for our young men. It is contended that they undermine the morals of our students by their profanity and generally low talk. They are also supposed to give too high a standard of excellence for our amateur athletes, and thus to draw on too much of their time and strength in the effort to make them conform to this standard. All these things may happen in some cases, but they do not happen frequently.

* * * * * * *

An easy cure for possible evils in this direction would be for the Faculty of each college troubled by vicious trainers to forbid their students employing such men. An investigation, however, into the relations between such trainers and their pupils would show that the pupils despise the lowness of the men quite as much as do the Faculty themselves. Another and better remedy would be to select an amateur athlete from the graduates, educated as a physician, and give him a salaried office, with duties as general adviser and guardian of the athletic interests. Such a man, if properly qualified, would help the students to a safer and better physical development than they now get, and would, besides, soon drive away all trainers exercising improper influences among them.

* * * * * * *

What the condition of the college would be without a system of athletics is a question already partly answered by what has been said in meeting the charges against the system. We can understand, also, the effect of abolishing the present system by calling to mind the disorders reported in colleges in which no such system is allowed to exist. The revolts against authority and the great disorders between classes now occur with the most frequency, not at colleges which have the greatest number of students and the most extensive athletic organizations, but at the colleges in which the students either are not able or are not allowed to establish such organizations. The disorders which used to occur in New Haven thirty or even twenty-five years ago ought to convince any candid man that, however great the present evils of college life are *with* athletics, the past evils *without* athletics were worse.

* * * *

As to those evils which are capable of remedy, and of which the remedy has not been before expressed or implied, we will take up that of unnecessary expense. It has been before shown that the expense of the system is not enormous, considering the good done. But undoubtedly it is greater than it need be. Moreover, it will naturally tend to increase. * * * Each officer, as a rule, serves but a year, when he makes room for a new officer, who is as inexperienced as his predecessor. The experience gained each year might be made serviceable by associating with the incoming treasurer a permanent graduate treasurer. The vice-president might be elected to become president as soon as the year's service of the president expired, so that he would serve as vice-president one year and one year as president, his service thus extending over two years. * * * Besides the changes suggested, a general auditing committee for all the interests should be formed, consisting of graduates and undergraduates. * * * A committee of both graduates and undergraduates could audit the accounts, and would be able to make suggestions which would be sure of a hearing. By such changes in the system and the economies which ought to result from them, field sports, such as base ball, foot ball, and lacrosse, should be self-supporting. The income derived from gate-money should meet the expenses.

Since some very worthy people who believe in manly sports object to young men playing for money taken at the exhibition games, it is necessary to say a word of explanation with regard to this feature of all ball-games. If field athletics are to continue, the expense of them must be met in one of two ways, either by gate-money or by subscription. * * * It seems only just that, if the public desire to see a good game, they should pay for the exhibition. The men work hard in practice, and are entitled to have their expenses paid. More than that they do not ask. They do not play for gain, but for honor. By their rules, they do not allow any man to be a member of their organizations who has earned money as a professional.

The evil of liability to strains and injuries in athletics cannot be entirely obviated. * * * Yet, so far, according to the recollection of the writer, no regular member of a Yale crew, team, or nine, has been permanently injured by participating in a race or match. Still, it is possible that a slight injury, to a person having organic weakness, might result in a fatal difficulty. Such an issue might be avoided by the requirement that every candidate for trial should be examined by a competent physician, and, in default of procuring a certificate of physical soundness, should be excluded from participation in athletic contests. Besides this, every candidate for a place in a crew should be debarred from entering a race unless he had mastered the art of swimming.

If, moreover, the Faculty of every college having a system of athletics would exert a sympathetic as well as a judicious oversight of the students interested in the system, they would find the young men quite willing to listen to friendly suggestions. If, also, the times of recitation were so arranged that a proper amount of time could be devoted to exercise without interference with study, more brain-work, and of better quality, would be secured than by the policy prevailing in some colleges, according to which, not only no encouragement is given to athletic sports, but, on the contrary, every obstacle is thrown in their way.

The college which neglects or ignores physical culture may send out scholars, but it will not educate forceful men. It will not be the living power which it might be. Truth is not to prevail by the dry light of intellect alone, but through the agency of good, wise, and strong men.

The Yale authorities, we are assured, "take no official notice" in regard to athletics, and exercise no interference, except the negative one of granting no privileges. Individually two or three members of the Faculty take great interest and show sympathy by attendance and personal encouragement.

PROFESSIONALISM AND INTERCOLLEGIATE CONTESTS.

DEMORALIZING INFLUENCE OF PROFESSIONALISM.

Professionalism has done much within the last five years to bring discredit upon college sports; and by professionalism we mean the purpose to win a game by any means, fair or foul. Professionals make a business of contending for money, either as stakes or prizes or gate receipts, having little or no regard to the benefits which should accrue from the exercise of bodily force or skill. The enhancement of health and manliness by vigorous recreative action is the primary aim of athletics. This is frequently lost sight of in the pursuit of athletic honors. Honors obtained at the cost of physical strains or one-sided development are dearly bought and injurious. Not a few are stimulated to unduly exhausting and violent exertions by their ill-judged desire to win. Athletic honors are sometimes—not generally, but more and more frequently in recent years—sought by collegians through the use of dishonorable means. The intercourse between college teams smacks too often of the manners of professional pugilists and of roughs. Expedients to disable or outwit antagonists have come to be looked on with too great a degree of allowance. Questionable means are sometimes employed to enable professionals or semi-professionals to play in college teams. When college men are willing to travel with professional ball players, and especially under assumed names, it is time for college authorities to recognize and regulate college athletics.

THE REGULATION OF ATHLETICS AT HARVARD.

At Harvard the Committee on Athletics is one of the standing committees of the Faculty. The following regulations, promulgated by this committee October 7, 1882, serve to exemplify in a measure the ideas of the Harvard authorities with regard to the matter:

(1) No college club or athletic association shall play or compete with professionals.

(2) No person shall assume the functions of trainer or instructor in athletics, upon the grounds or within the buildings of the college, without authority in writing from the committee.

(3) No student shall enter as a competitor in any athletic sport, or join any college athletic club as an active member, including base ball, foot ball, cricket, lacrosse, and rowing associations, without a previous examination by the director of the gymnasium, and his permission so to do.

(4) From the beginning of the college year 1883–'84 no person shall be admitted as a member of any class or university crew unless he knows how to swim.

(5) All match games outside of Cambridge shall be played upon Saturday, unless permission to play on other days is first obtained from the committee.

It should be noted that certain remedies proposed last March by Professor Richards for admitted or " possible" evils in college athletics, were embodied, in 1882, by the Harvard Faculty in the above quoted Regulations 2, 3, and 4. They have also adopted by anticipatory action, we believe, another of his suggested remedies, viz., the appointment of an auditing or advisory committee in relation to expenditures for athletic purposes.

By some of their impatient critics it has even been proposed to abolish intercollegiate contests. To attempt such extreme measures would be unwise, if not futile. Those who propose them fail to appreciate how strongly rooted an institution athletics have become; how great is their educational value when rightly managed; and how far sympathy, tact, and reasonableness are demanded in governing undergraduates. We must think, however, that the endeavors of the Harvard authorities to eliminate the aims and methods of professionals from college athletics were called for and timely.

THE INTERCOLLEGIATE ATHLETIC CONFERENCE OF 1884.

Early in February, 1884, an Intercollegiate Athletic Conference was held in New York City, at which delegates from the Faculties of the following named colleges were reported to be present: Williams, Amherst, Dartmouth, Tufts, Harvard, Columbia, Trinity, Wesleyan University, Stevens Institute, Hobart, Rutgers, Lafayette, Bowdoin, Princeton, Union, Cornell, Lehigh, Brown, University of Pennsylvania, University of Vermont, and College of the City of New York. Harvard took the lead in calling the conference. Yale was not represented at it. The following circular letter was issued by the conference:

REGULATIONS FOR INTERCOLLEGIATE ATHLETIC SPORTS.

FEBRUARY 7, 1884.

The object of physical training is to confirm health, correct morbid tendencies, strengthen weak parts, give a symmetrical muscular development, and secure as far as possible a condition of perfect physical vigor. In order to accomplish these desirable ends, young men are encouraged to take exercise and to enter into the general practice of athletic sports and games. If, however, the object of physical training be lost sight of, and the desire to win the championship or to attain the highest degree of excellence in these sports be made the *paramount* aim, then the practice of athletics is likely to be attended with evils that demand consideration. Some of these evils have already begun to make themselves manifest in the practice of college sports. With a view to correcting them, and of making athletic exercises an aid instead of a hindrance to the cause of education, the Intercollegiate Athletic Conference recommend the adoption of the following resolutions:

It is deemed advisable that physical training should form an essential part of a collegiate course; that the person selected to superintend this branch of education should be a man of character and ability, and that the dignity of his position should be recognized by giving him the moral support of the appointing power of the college. Therefore,

(1) *Resolved*, That every director or instructor in physical exercises or athletic sports must be appointed by the college authorities, and announced as such in the catalogue.

The object for which young men come to college is to get an education. If this object is to be secured, it is impossible for them to make a serious business of anything else. Ball playing, boating, etc., are engaged in by students as recreations, and students ought not to be expected to compete on equal terms with those who make the practice of these recreative sports the business of their lives. Students who compete or practice with professionals undoubtedly gain in experience and skill, but this renders it necessary that their college opponents should have a similar advantage or the terms would be unequal. This would lead to the general employment of professional service in every branch of competitive sport. But it is known that the character of professionals, as a whole, is not high; that their aim is to win at all costs; that they are often ready to sacrifice honor and self-respect, and even to jeopardize health, for mercenary motives. It is believed that the general employment of this class and the infusion of the professional spirit into college athletics would lead to their speedy decline. Therefore,

(2) *Resolved*, That no professional athlete, oarsman, or ball player, shall be employed either for instruction or for practice in preparation for any intercollegiate contest.

Much of the expense and loss of time attending the practice of college sports is occasioned by playing games at a distance; yet for various reasons it seems advisable that intercollegiate contests in these sports should be continued. They develop strength and executive ability, as well as courage, presence of mind, and other important elements of character. They give students an opportunity to measure their physical powers with others, and, when conducted in the right spirit, tend to make friends of rivals and to subordinate class feeling to college unity. For these reasons, these games ought to be more generally played in college. Class nines and foot-ball teams should be formed as well as class crews; and the university teams should depend more largely upon these organizations for practice. If the base-ball nines of one college practice with expert amateur clubs, because such clubs exist in their vicinity, this compels the nines of other colleges, not so favorably situated, to practice with inferior amateur organizations, regular professionals, or, what is more to be regretted, with undisciplined semi-professionals. Therefore,

(3) *Resolved*, That no college organization shall row, or play base ball, foot ball, lacrosse, or cricket, except with similar organizations from their own or other institutions of learning.

During the past few years several disagreeable controversies have arisen and much ill-feeling has been occasioned by the manner in which intercollegiate contests have been conducted. Much of the consequent dissatisfaction may be attributed to want of proper preliminary arrangements, over-zealousness on the part of some of the officials to see their own men win, a neglect to make rules and regulations to prevent unfair play, and a failure to provide a referee willing to enforce the regulations prescribed. Students in their conventions represent no one but themselves, and often act without responsibility and without authority, committing their fellow students to a questionable policy and establishing precedents which are detrimental to the interest of college sports. Therefore,

(4) *Resolved*, That there shall be a standing committee, composed of one member from the Faculty of each of the colleges adopting these regulations, whose duty it shall be to supervise all contests in which students of their respective colleges may engage, and approve all rules and regulations under which such contests may be held.

The students who are selected to take part in college athletics are men of fine physique, who, in order to keep themselves in excellent condition, do not need the amount of training which they get. Not infrequently these men have built up their bodies on farms and in workshops, and are paying their way through college by tutoring and other means. Time is of great importance to them; but their physical powers are in demand, and they are forcibly urged to join the "crew" or "nine," and work for victory and athletic honors. This double draft upon their energies sometimes costs them their degree, and obliges them to spend another year in college. Men have even been induced to enter the professional schools after graduation that they might help retain the championship in certain sports.

The evil of such a course is twofold: It tends to raise the standard of the sport beyond the capacity of the undergraduate, and thus limits the number that can participate in it. It makes hard work of what was intended for a recreation, and sometimes obliges a young man to make serious changes in his plan of life. Therefore,

(5) *Resolved*, That no student shall be allowed to take part in any intercollegiate contest as a member of any club, team, or crew, for more than four years.

The practice of playing match games in large cities for the sake of gate money has crept into college sports within the past few years. The evils which result from this practice are many. It leads to the introduction or retention of such features in the games as tend to draw large crowds, independently of the merit of the game and the spirit of fair play. It induces college men to put themselves in the hands of speculators, who manipulate and manage them as they would any traveling combination for the money to be made by it. It cultivates a passion for excitement in both players and speculators, which makes the ordinary field sports and gymnastic exercises seem tame and uninteresting, thus depriving the great majority of college students of a motive for physical exertion. Therefore,

(6) *Resolved*, That all intercollegiate games of base ball, foot ball, lacrosse, and cricket shall take place upon the home grounds of one or other of the competing colleges.

Nearly every intercollegiate boat race in this country has been won at the end of the third mile. The result has been a "procession" for the fourth mile, or a desperate attempt on the part of the defeated crew to retrieve themselves. The consequent tendency has been to lessen the interest in college boating, or to endanger the health of the participants from over-exertion and heart-strain. The training of class crews is generally for two miles. The style of rowing for a four-mile race is essentially different from that of a two-mile race, and requires different qualifications. The work of the class crew should be preparatory to that of the university crew. This is the goal for which most of the members of the class crews are struggling, and they should not be discouraged by having the difference in style and requirements too marked at the outset. Therefore,

(7) *Resolved*, That no intercollegiate boat race shall be for a longer distance than three miles.

As long as intercollegiate contests are continued, the conditions under which the students of the different colleges compete should be as nearly equal as possible. It is manifest that the conditions could not be equal should any college which adopts these resolutions play with any college which does not adopt them. Therefore,

(8) *Resolved*, That the students of colleges in which these resolutions are in force shall not be allowed to engage in games or contests with the students of colleges in which they are not in force.

W. M. SLOANE (COLLEGE OF NEW JERSEY),
Chairman.
D. A. SARGENT (HARVARD COLLEGE),
Secretary.

The recommendations of this circular failed of adoption by the concurrent action of five colleges, and no subsequent attempt has been made to secure an intercollegiate athletic code. Of the code as proposed it may be said that, though many of the colleges taking part in the conference concurred as to its general principles, it was judged that its detailed working would entail hardships in many cases. The entire field of athletics can hardly be controlled in accordance with a single set of rules. It seems more feasible to have the rules under which intercollegiate contests shall take place enacted by special conferences touching each athletic interest, e. g., foot ball and base ball; care being taken to have the student organizations represented, as well as the different Faculties.

HARVARD'S ACTION REGARDING FOOT BALL.

Harvard, failing to secure the co-operation of other colleges for the regulation of intercollegiate sports, has very recently forbidden the foot-ball elevens of the university from engaging in any more intercollegiate matches. This action was due to the belief that foot ball had become a "brutal and dangerous" game. At Princeton, even more recently, i. e., in February, 1885, the Faculty have, it is reported, conditioned their consent to future participation by Princeton players in intercollegiate foot-ball matches on the revision and improvement of the present objectionable rules of the game. It is a curious fact that our imitative collegians, in adopting the Rugby game of foot ball, as has been so generally the case, have adopted one of the roughest of the English varieties of the game. The influence of "Tom Brown at Rugby" may be partly responsible for this. Foot-ball is played in such different fashions at the great English schools that interschool matches are less general in England than are intercollegiate matches in the United States.

We have given the Yale view of athletics as expounded by Professor Richards, because that exposition may stand as the best utterance of those who favor non-interference by college authorities in college athletics. The following report to the Faculty of Harvard University by its standing committee on athletics, is here given as an expression of the Harvard idea of regulating what is deemed by them the most objectionable of athletic games, viz., foot ball:

To the Faculty of Harvard College:

GENTLEMEN: On the 22d of November, 1883, the committee on athletics, believing that the game of foot ball had begun to degenerate into a brutal and dangerous contest, informed the captain of the Harvard eleven that the team could not be allowed to take part in any further intercollegiate match-game until substantial changes in the rules had been made. According to the rules then existing a player could hack, throttle, buff, trip up, tackle below the hips, or strike an opponent with closed fist three times, before he was sent from the field. Changes in the rules were made immediately, and they were subsequently adopted by the intercollegiate association. In June of the present year the committee said to the captain of the Harvard team for 1884 that the eleven would be allowed to play during the following season, on the understanding that the games should be regarded as a test whether or not the changes of rules had resulted in substantial changes of the character of the game.

At the beginning of this season your committee decided to attend the games of the intercollegiate series, and to observe them carefully. We have attended four games, the three of the Harvard-Yale-Princeton series, and one between Wesleyan and the University of Pennsylvania, played in New York on the morning of Thanksgiving day for the third place among the college teams. At each of the games we stationed ourselves in different parts of the field, and observed and carefully noted what seemed to us the objectionable feature of the play. Two of the games, those in which the Harvard team took part, were very one-sided contests. In the Yale-Princeton and Wesleyan-Pennsylvania games the opposing teams were very evenly matched. Of the four games, the Yale-Harvard game was the least objectionable, and the Wesleyan-Pennsylvania game was the worst.

In every one of these games there was brutal fighting with the fists, where the men had to be separated by other players, or by the judges and the referee, or by the bystanders and the police. We saw one such case in the Harvard-Princeton game, two in the Harvard-Yale game, three in the Yale-Princeton game, and three in the Wesleyan-Pennsylvania game.

In addition to these fights there were numerous instances where a single blow was struck, instances that occurred in every one of the games. A man was felled by a blow in the face in the Harvard-Princeton game, in the Harvard-Yale game, in the Yale-Princeton game. In the Wesleyan-Pennsylvania game a man was thrown unfairly, out of bounds, by an opposing player. Then, as he was rising, but before he was on his feet, his antagonist turned, struck him in the face and knocked him down, and returned in triumph with the ball.

In all the games the manifestation of gentlemanly spirit was lacking—the spirit that scorns to take an unfair advantage of an opponent. The teams *played to win* by fair means or by foul.

Unfair play, often premeditated and sometimes concerted, was a prominent feature in all of the games, and, although not always successful, was rarely punished. Intentional off-side play and unlawful interference with opponents who were not running with the ball were the rule rather than the exception. The game is demoralizing to the spectators mainly through its brutality; unfair play they usually fail to recognize. We often heard cries of "Kill him!" "Break his neck!" "Slug him!" "Hit him!" "Knock him down!" from those around us. That the game is dangerous needs no argument. The Rugby game of foot ball, under the present rules, might perhaps be played with advantage where public opinion was strong enough to make deliberate attempts at unfair or brutal play impossible. There is, unfortunately, no such controlling sentiment among college students. The nature of the game puts a premium on unfair play, inasmuch as such play is easy, is profitable if it succeeds, is unlikely to be detected by the referee, and if detected is very slightly punished. If two teams are at all evenly matched, and one plays a gentlemanly and the other an unfair game, the self-respecting team will always be beaten. The game is so complicated, so confused, and covers so much ground, that no referee, however honest and determined, can see half of what is going on, especially since the judges, who were originally intended to help him in securing fair play, have developed into captains of their teams, and purposely distract his attention and increase his difficulties.

After deliberate investigation we have become convinced that the game of foot ball, as at present played by college teams, is brutal, demoralizing to players and spectators, and extremely dangerous; and we do not believe that at the present time, and with the prevailing spirit, any revision of the rules made by the intercollegiate association could be effective in removing these objectionable features.

We therefore recommend that all games of foot ball be prohibited to students of the college, except those played by our own men on our own grounds, and that these shall be allowed only in case it shall prove possible to eliminate all objectionable features from the game. We believe that foot ball, played in the proper spirit, under proper conditions, may be made one of the most valuable of college sports, and we should deprecate its permanent loss. We have conferred with students interested in the game at a meeting where there was great unanimity of opinion concerning its present objectionable character, and have grounds for hope that means may be devised to make it a credit, in place of a disgrace, to the university.

JOHN WILLIAMS WHITE,
W. E. BYERLY,
D. A. SARGENT,
Committee on Athletics.

CAMBRIDGE, *December* 2, 1884.

The recommendation of this report, "that all games of foot ball be prohibited to students of the college," was adopted by the Faculty by a vote of twenty-four to five.

THE POLICY OF THE HARVARD COMMITTEE ON ATHLETICS.

Undoubtedly the firm stand taken at Harvard will have a stimulating and salutary effect upon the future action of other colleges. For the purpose of showing that good results have already been secured through the efforts of the committee on athletics, the following extract from the correspondence of the New York *Evening Post* is subjoined:

CAMBRIDGE, *Mass., February* 12, 1885.

Athletics at Harvard are slowly undergoing a great change—a change which, in the judgment of all who have without prejudice watched the movement, is for the better. In former days, when the Hemenway Gymnasium was as yet unbuilt, and the little octagonal building which is now the university carpenter-shop was the only place in which Harvard muscle could be cultivated, the college was overrun with ruffians—"professionals" in the worst sense of the term—who exhibited their feats to the students for hire. But this was not the worst. In many cases the object of the "professional" was not the earning of honest money by the teaching of his specialty, but the inducing of young men to go with him to the city under pretense of seeing some athletic exhibition, in order there to initiate them into all kinds of vice and to swindle them of their money.

This state of affairs has passed away. "Roughs" no longer have possession of the gymnasium, but instead there are honest instructors and a capable manager. But the war against professionalism still goes on. In this war the chief battlers are the three men who form the athletic committee.

The committee is not appreciated by the students; it is fashionable among them to joke about, oppose, and argue against all its acts. They say that Latin and Greek professors are not capable of managing athletics; that their actions are uncalled for and inefficient; that, finally, the committee has no reason for existence. The only thing that the students as a body will allow to the committee is "good intentions."

But this estimate is not supported by facts. The facts are that the members of the athletic committee are all trained athletes as well as cultured men; that they have the good practical knowledge necessary for the conduct of athletic affairs, and that they have a keen and friendly interest in all sports of the collegians. In fighting against a tangible evil their actions have been called for, and in a great measure efficient.

To those who are interested in Harvard athletics a clear statement of what this committee is, will be interesting. It is a committee of the Faculty, the special duty of which is the overseeing of all the athletic interests of the college. It may be said with truth that the athletic committee *is* the Faculty as far as athletics are concerned; for any suggestion which they may make to the Faculty is almost certain to be approved by that body.

To those who have watched the progress of affairs from the first forbidding of base-ball contests with professional players up to the late foot-ball manifesto and the dismissal of Colonel Bancroft as coach of the crews, the committee may seem to lack plan and to be often inconsistent. But this is not so, their policy in every case being "the greatest amount of exercise for the greatest number."

Under this policy foot ball, confined practically to eleven men, and base ball, also limited to a small number of men, have been discouraged, while all gymnastic work in which every member of the college can take part, all track athletics, which by their nature are open to an almost unlimited number of men, tennis, etc., have been encouraged.

To be convinced that this is so, one has only to look at the great prosperity of the Athletic Association, the success of the Harvard Mott Haven teams, and the great popularity and large entries in the fall, winter, and spring athletic contests. Wherever, in short, the scientific accuracy with which any game comes to be played debars from enjoyable exercise the general student, for whose benefit all sports ought to be, that scientific accuracy has to be given up.

All exercise at college is for the purpose of keeping body and mind in fit condition for study. When the means to this result become an end, then sport is abused and reform is necessary. In short, the present policy of Harvard is that there should be more sport and fewer "sports" about the college. The encouragement given to boating here is often advanced to show that the acts of the committee are inconsistent. The explanation is this: the real interest of the college in boating centers in the class races. Each class has its own crew, from which the 'varsity draws its material, and thus affords exercise to many men. But the class nines and the class elevens exist only in name. Everything centers in the 'varsity nine or eleven and in the contest with Yale. If the interest were centered in contests between evenly-matched nines or elevens from the different classes, brighter days would dawn for foot ball and base ball at Harvard.

Indeed, the dissatisfaction with the athletic committee, when examined closely, seems to arise wholly from the popular jealousy of Yale and the disappointment of men who hoped to win popularity among their fellows by helping to gain victories over a rival college. But the committee treats with supreme indifference the question whether Yale is to be beaten or not, and gives its attention wholly to making enjoyable exercise attainable by every student of the college, and it is more anxious to give this enjoyable exercise to the weak than to the strong.

One word about professionals. What is a professional? He is a man who depends upon the exercise of his specialty to make a living. Such a man has frequently associations which unfit him to come in contact with young men in college. A man who teaches only, and who is sober and honest, would not be ranked as a "professional." This is the general rule of employment of coaches and trainers of Harvard.

From the data here given it is easy to see what will be the future of Harvard athletics. If, as it is hoped, every man, no matter how small or weak, can have plenty of enjoyable exercise, then this future will be bright indeed.

We have now traced in outline the growth and development of gymnastics, military drill, and athletics, so far as the principal institutions of superior instruction in the United States are concerned. Very few of such institutions combine these three features in their course of physical training, as was the case in Fellenberg's schools, at Hofwyl, early in the century. At Cornell University, however, military and gymnastic drill are required of certain classes of male students, and calisthenics are obligatory on the female students.

PHYSICAL EDUCATION FOR SCHOLASTIC WOMEN.

ASSOCIATION OF COLLEGIATE ALUMNÆ.

The schools and colleges for women are, as a class, not so well organized on the side of physical training as are those for young men. That the physical education of women is likely to receive more intelligent attention than has been the case hitherto, may be inferred from the appended circular of the Association of Collegiate Alumnæ.

Physical education.—The members of the Association of Collegiate Alumnæ have had their attention drawn very forcibly to the present need for physical education among the women in our universities and colleges. They fully believe that college education *per se* is physically beneficial, and that college statistics show an average of health among women students higher than that among women at large; but they also realize that the physical status of American women of the educated class is painfully low, and they believe that the colleges ought to be among the first to take measures against this dangerous deterioration of physique. The following schedule, however, shows how fragmentary has been the work done hitherto in the nine institutions represented in the association:

Lectures on physiology.	Lectures on hygiene.	Gymnasium.	Calisthenics (under supervision).	Physician.	Hospital and nurse.	Voluntary boating, skating, &c. (Lake.)
Oberlin	Oberlin	Oberlin				
Vassar		Vassar	Vassar	Vassar	Vassar	Vassar
Cornell	Cornell	Cornell			Cornell	Cornell
Michigan						
Wisconsin		Wisconsin				Wisconsin
Boston						
Smith	Smith	Smith				
		Wellesley	Wellesley	Wellesley	Wellesley	Wellesley
Wesleyan		Wesleyan				

Vassar, Smith, and Wellesley are conducted on the dormitory system, Smith maintaining separate "cottage" dormitories, and Wellesley giving choice of large or small buildings.

Oberlin, Wisconsin, Cornell, and Wesleyan do not require students to board in college buildings.

Michigan and Boston do not provide boarding places.

One hour of physical exercise daily is required of students by Vassar and Wellesley.

A knowledge of elementary physiology is required for admission by Cornell.

The attainment of a certain standard of health is required for admission by Wellesley.

In view of these facts, the members of this association, as women college graduates, most earnestly and respectfully urge the following suggestions upon those interested in the higher education of women, and especially (1) upon parents, (2) upon the governing bodies of institutions which grant degrees to women, and (3) upon the women studying in these institutions.

I.

The members of the association are convinced that the low standard of health among women in and after college life is largely due to their common lack of physical training and disregard of the laws of health before they enter college. At sixteen it is often too late to undo all the mistakes made during the most important years of a girl's physical life. They therefore wish to call the careful attention of parents everywhere to the following evils among school-girls, which threaten every interest of educated women.

PHYSICAL TRAINING IN AMERICAN COLLEGES.

(1) Social dissipation and excitement, which is neither amusement nor recreation. Girls are too often stimulated to shine socially and intellectually at the same time. A mother proves her daughter's perfect health by saying, "She has been able to go to parties or entertainments four or five evenings a week all winter, and she stands at the head of her class!"

(2) Habitual loss of sufficient and healthy sleep.

In a New York Academy, a class of sixty girls, between the ages of twelve and eighteen, chanced to be asked by a recent visitor for the time they retired the night before. The average was found to be twenty minutes before midnight; but no surprise was manifested by teachers nor regret by pupils.

(3) Irregularity and haste in taking food, the use of confectionery in the evening, and the omission of breakfast.

The principal of a large girls' school in Philadelphia lately said that so many habitually came to school without having taken sufficient breakfast, and taking little or no lunch, that he had been compelled, in order to obtain good mental work, to have a warm lunch furnished, and to insist upon the scholars taking it in the middle of the morning.

(4) Tight, heavy, and insufficient clothing, which frightfully increases the tendencies to consumption and spinal diseases.

A physician of wide experience confidently states that this cause alone has incapacitated more women than over-study and over-work of all kinds.

(5) The lack of sufficient out-door exercise. When a proper amount of time is devoted to such exercise, no time will be left for over-study.

(6) The ambition of parents and daughters to accomplish much in little time, which sends students to college either hurriedly and imperfectly prepared, or with a thorough preparation gained at the expense of health.

(7) The usual postponement of instruction in the laws of physiology and hygiene to a college course. Thus, daughters go out from their mother's care wholly ignorant of the common laws by which they may increase and preserve the health upon which every hope and ambition depends.

II.

The members of this association believe that these faults in home and school training, as well as those found in college schemes, can be reached most effectually through the colleges. And, while recognizing the efforts already made in this direction, they respectfully recommend to the consideration of college-governing bodies the following remedies for existing evils:

(1) The introduction of a consistent, thorough, and scientific course of physical education for women.

(2) The appointment of a thoroughly competent woman as an instructor in this department, who shall superintend the gymnasium, give practical courses of lectures, and be, so far as possible, responsible for the general health of the women in her classes.

Where the dormitory system obtains, the appointment of a resident physician is also urged.

(3) The provision of an adequately equipped gymnasium.

(4) The provision of one or more courses of lectures by non-resident specialists on physiology, hygiene, sanitation, heredity, athletics, gymnastics, etc.

(5) The provision of special libraries on subjects pertaining to physical education.

(6) Careful study in the construction of buildings for recitation and dormitory purposes, with special reference to counteracting the acknowledged evils of the dormitory system.

(7) The requirement (whenever practicable) that candidates for admission shall reach a certain standard of attainment in physical education. Physical health is already required for admission by Wellesley College, and a knowledge of physiology by Cornell University.

III.

The women studying in our colleges are urged by the women graduates of these colleges—

(1) To bear constantly in mind in their own work the fact that the best intellectual results cannot be attained without perfect physical health.

(2) To maintain a constant and sensible watch over their own habits as regards sleep, exercise, food, dress, etc. Failure to take the requisite amount of sleep, food, or exercise, should be lamented as much as failure in recitation.

(3) To form athletic associations for the promotion of wholesome exercise and the stimulation of public opinion.

(4) To collect comparative statistics relating to the age, height, weight, size of waist, breadth of chest, weight of clothing, etc., of women college students. Such statistics should be taken at regular intervals throughout the college course. As taken by Dr. Sargent, of Harvard University, in his ladies' gymnasium at Cambridge, they have proved valuable as well as interesting.

The association hopes to publish a series of short, practical monographs on these and similar subjects at some future time. Meanwhile, information in regard to the practical working of these suggestions, many of which are already in operation, may be obtained on application to any of the officers of the association: President, Mrs. J. F. Bashford, University of Wisconsin, Auburndale, Mass.; vice-president, Miss F. M. Cushing, Vassar College, 8 Walnut street, Boston, Mass.; secretary, Miss Marion Talbot, Boston University, 66 Marlborough street, Boston; treasurer, Miss Margaret Hicks, Cornell University, Cambridge, Mass.; directors, Miss A. E. F. Morgan, Oberlin College, Wellesley, Mass.; Mrs. E. H. Richards, Vassar College, Jamaica Plain, Mass. Miss A. E. Freeman, University of Michigan, Wellesley, Mass.; Miss K. E. Morris, Smith College, Hartford, Vt.; Miss H. M. Peirce, Wellesley College, Newton Center, Mass.

PHYSICAL TRAINING AT WELLESLEY COLLEGE.

Wellesley College, in Massachusetts, has a more highly organized department of physical training than any other institution at present devoted to the education of women. The Sargent system is followed and out-of-door games are encouraged. Since 1880 all applicants for admission have been required to present a certificate from some reputable physician that they were physically fit to undertake the course of study prescribed in the institution. Out of 485 who presented such certificates in 1882–'83, 23 were found within nine months to be unable to continue their studies on account of ill health. During the same year 470 students underwent physical examination touching the condition of "spine, lungs, and heart," made by Miss E. H. Jones, M.D., the resident physician. Of these, 32 were found to have "narrow chests with poorly developed lungs;" 9 had valvular disease of the heart; 2 had hypertrophy of the heart; 16 had curvature of the spine; and 7 had spinal irritation.

No woman's college in America, however, has a gymnasium which approaches in costliness and completeness that of Bryn Mawr College, soon to be opened, to which allusion has been made already.

INSTRUCTION IN HYGIENE.

SUGGESTION OF THE APOSTLE ELIOT.

Lectures upon health topics were not uncommon in American colleges long before any systematic effort was made by any of them to provide its students with practical facilities for living in obedience to the laws therein enunciated. Even here American educators cannot lay claim to originality, for in Basedow's Philanthropinum at Dessau, in 1774, lectures were given by a physician on human anatomy and physiology. It is not possible for the writer to state when such lectures were first given to American students; but it is safe to surmise that their date is not earlier than the year 1647, when the following rather vague suggestion of a course of medical instruction for his Indian scholars was penned by the Apostle Eliot. "I have thought in my heart," he wrote to Thomas Shepard, the pious minister of Cambridge in Massachusetts, "that it were a singular good work if the Lord would stir up the hearts of some or other of his people in England to give some maintenance toward some schoole or collegiate exercise this way, wherein there should be anatomies and other instructions that way."

LECTURES AT HARVARD.

In 1781, Dr. J. Warren, father of Dr. J. C. Warren, alluded to in the early part of this paper as a lecturer on health to the students of Harvard College, at the request of the Boston Medical Society, "demonstrated a course of anatomical lectures at the hospital in Boston." This course was "quite public," and "some of the students of Harvard College were permitted to attend." In 1784 the Harvard Medical School was opened at Cambridge. Its first quarters proving unfit, the Holden Chapel was fitted up, and lectures in anatomy, surgery, and materia medica were delivered there. "The number of medical students who attended was small, but as the president permitted the two elder classes to attend the lectures the rooms were well filled."

It is not clearly shown in such statements as have come to our notice that instruction on the nature of the human body has regularly been provided for Harvard students since the time of those lectures alluded to as having been delivered in Holden Chapel; but it is stated in Quincy's "History of Harvard University" that in 1810, when the medical school was removed to Boston, "the medical professors were required to deliver an annual course at Cambridge, adapted to resident graduates and the Senior class of undergraduates." Dr. J. C. Warren, in 1825, and Dr. James Jackson, in 1830, were in the habit of giving such lectures. It is a part of Dr. Sargent's duty at the present day to deliver lectures on personal hygiene and physical training to the students of the university.

LECTURES AT DARTMOUTH.

The first published announcement of the course of instruction at Dartmouth College is contained in its catalogue for 1822. From it we learn that the members of the two upper classes were "permitted to attend all the lectures of the medical professors by paying a small fee." In 1825 this fee amounted to 67 cents a term for Juniors, and to twice that sum for Seniors. At present the Freshmen at Dartmouth are required to attend six lectures, and the Seniors twelve lectures, delivered by the professor of science and practice of medicine in the medical school.

INSTRUCTION IN HYGIENE AT OTHER COLLEGES.

Colleges of the present day very generally aim to give at least text-book instruction in "anatomy, physiology, and hygiene." At Amherst, Dr. Hitchcock instructs, both by lectures and recitations, the two lower classes in these subjects, especial stress being laid upon hygiene, and such has been his custom during almost all of his term of office, *i. e.*, since 1861. At Cornell University careful provision has been made ever since its foundation, in 1868, for the study of human anatomy, physiology, and hygiene. At Cornell, moreover, applicants for admission are required to pass an examination in physiology.

There is such a variety of usage in regard to the character and amount of instruction in hygiene in our principal colleges that the facts concerning it, so far as the inquiries made by the writer have elicited any information on this head, may best be set forth in tabular form.

PHYSICAL TRAINING IN AMERICAN COLLEGES. 137

TABLE No. 18, PART I.—*Amount and character of the instruction, practical and theoretical, in hygiene, in the principal colleges and universities of the United States.*

NOTE.—*r* stands for required; *o*, optional; *m*, males; *f*, females; *t*, times; *hr*, hour; *b*, building; *rm*, room.

	Name of institution.	Location.	Name and title of teacher.	Number of lectures given in 1882–'83.	Number of recitations conducted in 1882–'83.	Attendance upon lectures.
1	Amherst College	Amherst, Mass	E. Hitchcock, sr., M. D., M. A., prof. of hygiene and physical education.	40	40	70 1st yr. r; 88 2d yr. r.
2	Allegheny College	Meadville, Pa	Prof. of natural history	1 term r	1 term ? r	
3	Augustana College	Rockford, Ill	J. Lindahl, Ph. D., prof. of natural science.	Not given	1881–'82, 74 r.	
4	Beloit College	Beloit, Wis	None reported		Not given	
5	Boston University	Boston, Mass	do	do	do	
6	Bowdoin College	Brunswick, Me	I. A. Lee, B. A., prof. of geology and biology	10 pers. hyg	44	28 1st yr. r.
7	University of California	Berkeley, Cal				
8	Carleton College	Northfield, Minn	L. W. Sperry, M. D., prof. of geology, zoology, and physiology.	45	75	All of 3d yr. r; prep. and Eng. o.
9	Central Tennessee College	Nashville, Tenn	G. W. Hubbard, M. D., lecturer; R. F. Boyd, M. D., teacher of physiology.	24	100	354; 169 m, 185 f.
10	Central University	Richmond, Ky	A. W. Smith, D. D. S	25	25	15 r; 10 o.
11	Cornell University	Ithaca, N. Y	B. G. Wilder, M. D., prof. of physiology, comparative anatomy, and zoology.	{ 6 pers. hyg 36 phys		Nearly all Freshmen in university. All Sophomores.
12	Dartmouth College	Hanover, N. H	C. P. Frost, M. D., prof. of science and practice of medicine (Dart. Med. School).	18; 6 to 1st yr., 12 to 4th yr.		130; 86 1st yr., 64 4th yr.
13	De Pauw University	Greencastle, Ind	Prof. Baker, M. D			250 m in 1883.
14	Drury College	Springfield, Mo	Miss L. M. Saunderson (for 1882–'84), instructor	20	20	15 m and 20 f, r; 20 m and 25 f, o.
15	Fisk University	Nashville, Tenn	F. A. Chase, A. M., prof. of physical sciences		50	6 3d yr.; 5 m, 1 f, r.
16	Harvard University	Cambridge, Mass	D. A. Sargent, A. B., M. D., asst. prof. of physical training and director of gymnasium.	24		All students o.
17	Haverford College	Haverford, Pa	W. A. Ford, M. D., instructor in physical training. (†)			Examination, r; exercise, o.
18	Iowa College	Grinnell, Iowa	H. W. Parker, A. B., prof. of natural history		75	
19	Johns Hopkins University	Baltimore, Md	E. M. Hartwell, Ph. D., M. D., instructor in physical culture, 1882–'83.	12		30 o.
20	Kansas State Agric'l Coll	Manhattan, Kans	E. M. Shelton, B. Sc., professor	26	70	42 2d yr. o; mil. science

TABLE No. 18, PART I.—*Amount and character of the instruction, practical and theoretical, in hygiene, in the principal colleges and universities of the United States*—Continued.

	Name of institution.	Location.	Name and title of teacher.	Number of lectures given in 1882-'83.	Number of recitations conducted in 1882-'83.	Attendance upon lectures.
21	Lafayette College	Easton, Pa	Traill Green, M. D., prof. of chemistry; Charles McIntyre, A. M., M. D., lecturer on hygiene.	1 weekly 1st term.		82 m.
22	Lehigh University	South Bethlehem, Pa	J. Green, M. D., lecturer	20		106 1st yr. r.
23	Massachusetts State Agricultural College.	Amherst, Mass	J. M. Tyler, B. A., prof. biology (Am. College).	39	65	20 1st yr. r.
24	University of Michigan	Ann Arbor, Mich	V. C. Vaughan, Ph. D., M. D., professor of physiological and pathological chemistry.	30		100; 20 m, 20 f. o.
25	University of Minnesota	Minneapolis, Minn	C. N. Hewitt, M. D., prof. of public health, and Sec'y State Board of Health.			Attendance on instruction.
26	University of Nashville State Normal College.	Nashville, Tenn	Some one of instructors			Attendance required.
27	National Deaf-Mute College.	Washington, D. C				
28	College of New Jersey	Princeton, N. J	J. S. Schenck, M. D., LL. D., lecturer (?)			
29	Ohio Wesleyan University	Delaware, Ohio	E. T. Nelson, Ph. D., professor	13	30	122; 82 m, 40 f. r all years.
30	Pennsylvania College	Gettysburg, Pa	J. B. Scott, will lecture on anatomy, physiology, and hygiene, 1883-'84.			
31	Smith College	Northampton, Mass	Miss Ruth Hoppin, A. B., instructor	14		284 (?) r.
32	Syracuse University	Syracuse, N. Y	J. J. Brown, LL. D., prof. chemistry and physics	26		117 r; examined, too.
33	University of Tennessee	Knoxville, Tenn	H. Nicholson, B. A., prof. of natural history	30	30	21 2d yr. r.
34	Texas State Agric'l Coll	College Station, Tex	Chairman of Faculty			r in 1883-'84.
35	Tufts College	Medford, Mass				
36	U. S. Military Academy	West Point, N. Y	Hygiene not formally taught. The entire training is based on personal hygiene.			
37	U. S. Naval Academy	Annapolis, Md	do			
38	Vassar College	Poughkeepsie, N. Y	Mary E. Allen, M. D., professor and resident physician.	6	85	60 f, o.
39	Vanderbilt University	Nashville, Tenn	None reported			
40	Virginia State Agricultural College.	Blacksburg, Va		116		

41	Washington University	Saint Louis, Mo	J. H. Jenks, M. D	20		12 4th yr. r.
42	Wellesley College	Wellesley, Mass	Miss E. M. Mosher, M. D	10		250 f, o.
43	Wesleyan University	Middletown, Conn	W. N. Rice, Ph.D., prof. of natural history	20		28 41st yr. 5 2d yr., 33 3d yr., r.
44	University of Wooster	Wooster, Ohio	L. Firestone, M. D., prof. of anatomy, physiology and hygiene.	28	28 4th yr; none 2d yr.	38; 34 m, 4 f, 4th yr. r.
45	University of Wisconsin	Madison, Wis	E. A. Birge, Ph. D., prof. of zoology	75		15; 9 m, 6 f, o.
46	Yale College	New Haven, Conn	S. J. Sanford, M. D., professor	12		To Freshmen.

CIRCULARS OF INFORMATION FOR 1885.

TABLE No. 18, PART II.—*Amount and character of the instruction, etc., in hygiene, in the principal colleges and universities in the United States.*

NOTE.—r stands for required; o, optional; m, males; f, females; t, times; hr, hour; b, building; rm, room.

	Name of institution.	Attendance upon recitations.	Author of text-book used.	Date of adoption of teaching of hygiene.	Subjects taught.	Has a gymnasium or drill hall.
1	Amherst College	70 1st yr. r, 88 2d yr		1860	Human anatomy, physiology, and hygiene	b Pratt Gymnasium.
2	Allegheny College				Physiology and hygiene	None reported.
3	Augustana College	r R. A. and R. S. candidates.	Hutchinson	1876	Anatomy, physiology, and hygiene	Cheap frame, 1883, 24 x 96.
4	Beloit College					b 60 x 40.
5	Boston University		Martin	1874	Anatomy, physiology, and hygiene required	2 rm, each 35 x 20.
6	Bowdoin College	20 1st yr. r		1880	Anatomy, physiology, and personal hygiene	Gymnasium discontinued; now one contemplated.
7	University of California					b Harmon Gymnasium.
8	Carleton College	r All beginning, prep. and Eng. course.	Hutchinson	1875	Anatomy, physiology, and hygiene	rm 1883-'84, 40 x 40.
9	Central Tennessee College	354	Cutter	1872	Anatomy, phys., public and personal hygiene	Free gymnasium.
10	Central University	15 r, 10 o	Dalton	1880	Anatomy, physiology, and hygiene	"On the grounds."
11	Cornell University		Wilder; Martin	1868	Personal hygiene and physiology	b Armory and gymnasium, 150 x 60.
12	Dartmouth College			1867, 1822;	Public and personal hygiene	b Bissell Hall
13	De Pauw University			1876	Anatomy, physiology, and hygiene	rm Drill-room, 100 x 50.
14	Drury College			1874	Anatomy, physiology, and personal hygiene	None reported.
15	Fisk University	6 3d yr., 5 m, 1 f, r	Martindale	1871		School-rooms used.
16	Harvard University			1781		b Hemenway Gymnasium.
17	Haverford College			1880	Anatomy, physiology, and hygiene	rm 82 x 25.
18	Iowa College	3d yr. acad. students r. Some others o.	Cleland		do	rm 42 x 76, unfitted.
19	Johns Hopkins University			1882-'83 1884-'85	Anatomy, physiology, and hygiene, 1884-'85	b 1883.
20	Kansas State Agricultural College	30 r, 3d yr., 19 m, 11 f	Martin	1863	Anatomy, physiology, and hygiene	rm Armory, 40 x 90.
21	Lafayette College			1858	Anatomy and personal hygiene	b Gymnasium.

PHYSICAL TRAINING IN AMERICAN COLLEGES. 141

22	Lehigh University			Physiology and hygiene	b Lehigh University Gymnasium.
23	Massachusetts State Agricultural College.	2d 2d yr. r.	Martin	Anatomy, physiology, and personal hygiene	b Drill-hall, 120 x 60.
24	University of Michigan	(Undescribed) 25 o, 15 m, 10 f.	Dalton, 1860; required of all.	1867	Hygiene and sanitary science	Has none.
25	University of Minnesota			1869	Public and personal hygiene	b Military building, 120 x 140. Gymnasium to be built.
26	University of Nashville State Normal College.	28 1st yr. r.		1875	Physiology and hygiene, 1st year students	b Gymnasium, 80 x 30. Sept., 1884.
27	National Deaf-Mute College					b 62 x 48.
28	College of New Jersey				Personal hygiene by personal advice of Mr. Goldie; human anatomy taught.	b 78 x 52.
29	Ohio Wesleyan University	122, 82 m, 40 f.	Huxley; Foster	1872	Human anatomy and physiology	None.
30	Pennsylvania College					b McCreary Gymnasium, 5 j x 90.
31	Smith College			1875	Anatomy, physiology, o. Personal hygiene, r.	b Gymnasium.
32	Syracuse University			1871	Anatomy, physiology, and pub. and pers. hyg	None reported.
33	University of Tennessee	21 r, 2d yr.	Huxley and Youmans.		Comparative anatomy and physiology. Hygiene taught incidentally.	do.
34	Texas State Agricultural College			1883–'84	Human anatomy, physiology, and pers. hyg	do.
35	Tufts College			1855	Anatomy and physiology	b New, 90 x 45.
36	U.S. Military Academy			1802?	Personal hygiene inculcated	rm Gymnasium projected.
37	U.S. Naval Academy			1845	do	do.
38	Vassar College	7 f, o	Foster	1865	Anatomy and phys., o. Personal hygiene, r.	rm Improvem'ts projected.
39	Vanderbilt University				Not taught	b 90 x 60.
40	Virginia State Agricultural College				None reported, exercises in mil. sel. and tactics	b.
41	Washington University				Anatomy and physiology	rm.
42	Wellesley College			1875	Physiology and personal hygiene	
43	Wesleyan University	4 1st yr, 5 2d yr., 33 2d yr.; students.	Huxley	1839	Anatomy, physiology, and hygiene	b Gymnasium, 70 x 40.
44	University of Wooster			1883	Anatomy and physiology	b Gym. hall, 48 x 96, 1882–'83.
45	University of Wisconsin		Huxley and Youmans.		Anatomy, physiology, and hygiene	b 100 x 40.
46	Yale College			At an early date.	Hygiene	

142 CIRCULARS OF INFORMATION FOR 1885.

TABLE No. 18, PART III.—*Amount and character of the instruction, etc., in hygiene, in the principal colleges and universities of the United States.*

NOTE.—r stands for required; o, optional; m, males; f, females; t, times; hr, hour; b, building; rm, room.

	Name of institution.	Name and title of head of the department. (a=has assistant.)	Style of drill adopted. (Mil = military drill; S. G. = Sargent gymnastics; L G.=light gymnastics.)	Keeps vital statistics. (Y=yes; N=no.)	Attendance on drill in 1882–'83; required unless otherwise stated.	Remarks.
1	Amherst College	E. Hitchcock, sr., M. D., prof. of hygiene and physical education, a; and M. D.	L. G. r, S. G.	Y.	352 m, 4 t, ½ hr, 31 weeks	Has a medical adviser, head of department.
2	Allegheny College	G. O. Webster, 1st lieut. U. S. A.	Mil. o	N.	o 85 m, 3 t, 1¼ hr, weekly	Course changed, 1881–'82.
3	Augustana College	No head or organization, 1880		N.		
4	Beloit College	Department inorganized; drill-masters, upper-class men.	L. G. r of all	Y.[1]	All, 222 m !	
5	Boston University	A. H. Howard and Med. Pot?	L. G. o, S. G. o			Physiology may be elected in Junior year.
6	Bowdoin College			N.		Practical demonstrations in physiology given.
7	University of California	G. C. Edwards, Ph. B., instructor in mathematics and colonel of cadets.	Mil. r	N.	All able-bodied m, 143, 2 t, 1 hr, 37 weeks.	Hygiene Lot a required study.
8	Carleton College	No teacher of gymnastics	L. G. o, roller skating.	Y.[2]	o for ladies	
9	Central Tennessee College					Dr. Hubbard is medical adviser for colored pupils.
10	Central University	None reported				
11	Cornell University	E. Hitchcock, jr., M. D., M. A., acting prof. of physical culture and director of gymnasium, a, 1 male and 1 female. W. S. Schuyler, 1st lieut. U. S. A., professor of military science and tactics.	Mil. r, S. G. r	Y.	All unexcused males of two lower classes have Mil. r, 34, 1 hr. 36 weeks; Mil. o, for upper classes; S. G. r, for all males needing it, in director's opinion, 5 t, 1 hr. 36 weeks; L. G. r, 5 t, 1 hr, 36 weeks, for all unexcused female students	Since 1877, all entering the university have been required to pass an examination in elementary physiology.
12	Dartmouth College	T. W. D. Worthen, A. B., assoc. prof. of mathematics and instructor in gymnastics.	Lewis gymnastics r.	N.	1st year, 4 t, ½ hr, 11 weeks, 86 m; 2d year, 2 t, ½ hr. 11 weeks, 20 m.	2d 3d year elected gymnastics, 1882; since 1822, 3d and 4th year m allowed medical lectures.

PHYSICAL TRAINING IN AMERICAN COLLEGES.

13	De Pauw University	J. R. Gol, 2d lieut. U. S. A., 1883–'84	Mil. r for 3 y'rs, 1876	N.	250 m	Not detailed from the U. S. army.
14	Drury College	A. D. Brown, 1883–'84, instr. in mil. drill	Calisthenics	N.	All in 1883–'84, 10 minutes daily	
15	Fisk University					
16	Harvard University	D A. Sargent, A. B., M. D., asst. prof. of physical training and director of Hemenway Gymnasium.	S. G. o	Y.	o with all members of the university.	80 per cent elect gymnastics.
17	Haverford College	W. A. Ford, M. D., director of gymnasium	S. G. o	Y.	Examination r, exercise o	
18	Iowa College	None reported				
19	Johns Hopkins University	E. M. Hartwell, Ph.D., M. D., instructor in physical culture.	S. G. o for grad.; r for matric., 1884–'5.	Y.	Matriculates, 1884–'85; o for 240, 1883–'84.	
20	Kansas State Agricultural College.	A. Todd, B. A., 1st lieut. U. S. A	Mil. o	N.	o 100 m; 63 the 1st, 20 the 2d, 12 the 3d, 3 the 4th year.	3 t, 50 minutes, for 36 weeks.
21	Lafayette College	J. Updegrove, A. B., adjunct director; Chas. McIntyre, A. M., M.D., med. dir.	L. G. r, S. G	Y.	210 r, 10 5th year, o; 10 t, ¾ hr, all year.	
22	Lehigh University	W. H. Horrick, B. A., director of gymnasium.	S. G. r, L. G. r	Y.	108, 3 t, 1 hr, 39 weeks	
23	Massachusetts State Agricultural College.	V. H. Bridgman, 1st lieut. U. S. A	Mil. r	N.		
24	University of Michigan					
25	University of Minnesota	Place apparently vacant	Mil. r			Applicants for admission must have been vaccinated, and be examined in Dalton's text-book.
26	University of Nashville State Normal College.	Professor Hammerely	S. G. will be used	Y.	Probably all	Applicants for admission, also for scholarship, must present health certificate.
27	National Deaf-Mute College	J. J. Chickering, B. A	L. G. and S. G. r	Y.		
28	College of New Jersey	George Goldie, supt. of gymnasium	H. G. o and L. G. o	Y.	Drill, 11 t, ¾ hr, 28 weeks; L. G. 10 hours, weekly for 37 weeks; gymnastics.	Sept. 1884. Gymnastics req. 1st and 2d years, m, ½ hr, 4 t, weekly.
29	Ohio Wesleyan University	J. H. Grove, asst. prof. in Latin, tried to awaken an interest in military drill.	Mil. o	N.	Attendance o and occasional for 75 m.	
30	Pennsylvania College	None reported	None reported			
31	Smith College	Miss Luella Peck	L. G. and S. G. a little.	Y.	135 r, 140 o, 4 t, ½ hr, 18 weeks	
32	Syracuse University					
33	University of Tennessee	Col. S. B. Crawford, commandant	Mil	N.	All students daily	
34	Texas State Agricultural College.	C. T. Crane, 1st lieut U. S. A., a cadet officer assists.	Mil. r	N.	223 m, 3 t, 1 hr, 30 weeks	Has a college surgeon.
35	Tufts College	Department unorganized	S. G. probably			

¹ 1882–'83.   ² Somewhat.

TABLE No. 18, PART III.—*Amount and character of the instruction, etc., in hygiene, in the principal colleges and universities of the United States—Cont'd.*

	Name of institution.	Name and title of head of the department. (*a* = has assistant.)	Style of drill adopted. (Mil. = military drill; S. G. = Sargent gymnastics; L. G. = light gymnastics.)	Keeps vital statistics. (Y = yes; N = no.)	Attendance on drill in 1882-'83; required unless otherwise stated.	Remarks.
36	U. S. Military Academy	Lieut. E. S. Farrow, U. S. A., Instructor	Mil; mil. gym	Y.	G. required of all 1st-year men; mil'd. required of all cadets.	Swordsmanship and dancing are required exercises. Swimming is taught, too.
37	U. S. Naval Academy	M. Strohm, Instructor in boxing, swimming and gymnastics; A. J. Corbesier, sword-master, has 2 assistants.	Mil.; H. G.	Y.	G. required of all 1st-year cadets, and drill of all cadets.	Swimming, dancing, fencing, and boxing are required exercises.
38	Vassar College	Miss A. Thurston, B. A., instr. in gym	S. G. *r*	Y.	All able-bodied students	Improvements contemplated.
39	Vanderbilt University	E. H. Bowser, director of gymnasium and instructor in physical exercise.	L. G. *o*	N.	*o* for all, 6 hours weekly	
40	Virginia State Agricultural College.	Prof W. B. Preston	Mil. *r*		180 m, 6 *t*, 1 hr, 42 weeks	Has a college surgeon.
41	Washington University	A. H. Muggo	L. G. *r* and *o*	N.	20 1st year, 17 2d year, *r*; 10 3d year, 10 4th year, *o*.	2 *t*, ½ hr, 38 weeks.
42	Wellesley College	Miss L. E. Hill, director of gymnasium	L. G. *r*, S. G. *r*	Y.	350 *f, r,* 50 *o*, 2 *t,* ½ hr, 20 weeks.	Has several notable features.
43	Wesleyan University	Vacant	None	N.	All males, 4½ hours weekly	
44	University of Wooster	A. C. Sharpe, A. B., 1st lieut. U. S. A.	Mil. *r*, L. G, 1883	N.	All m, 145 in 1882-'83; since 1874.	
45	University of Wisconsin	G. W. Chase, 1st lieut. U. S. A., 1883-'84.	Mil. *r*, L. G. *o*	N.	Freshmen, 2d term	
46	Yale College	J. Seaver, B. A.	L. G. *o*	N.		Athletics in charge of a field director.

DR. BOWDITCH ON THE TEACHING OF HYGIENE.

In 1876 Dr. H. I. Bowditch, of Boston, Mass., delivered the Centennial Address before the International Medical Congress, in Philadelphia, on Public Hygiene in America. In the appendix to the volume in which the address is found, Dr. Bowditch gives summary statements setting forth the results of his correspondence with (*a*) sixty-two American universities and colleges, and with (*b*) twenty-three medical colleges, relative to the amount of instruction given by these institutions in public and private hygiene and physical culture. Under the first head Dr. Bowditch's conclusions are as follows:

(1) Instruction on public hygiene and state preventive medicine is wofully neglected.

(2) On private hygiene only about one-third of the colleges give any instruction.

(3) A full *special* course of instruction on either of the above themes is almost unknown.

(4) *Incidentally*, in connection with some other not necessarily allied subject, and therefore inefficiently, the topics are treated of by about three-fourths of the colleges, while one-fourth of them do not even perform this small duty in this most important matter. Meanwhile, although the instructors of the colleges thus neglect important duties, the youths, of their own free will, and at times lately with the aid and counsel of the college governments, have commenced athletic sports. This will gradually force the colleges to take, on their own parts, a higher position.

His conclusions under the second head, *i. e.*, as regards medical colleges, are—

(1) Only a little more than one-third of the colleges pay any attention to public or private hygiene.

(2) A still smaller proportion notice state preventive medicine.

(3) Only about one-fifth have special professors and special courses in hygiene.

(4) About one-half say they have subsidiary teaching given by various professors in other departments.

PRESENT TEACHING OF HYGIENE IN MEDICAL COLLEGES.

The Report of the Commissioner of Education for 1882–'83 enumerates eighty schools of medicine of the class known as "regular." About one-half of them, as shown in the following table, advertise to teach something of hygiene to candidates for their diplomas. An inspection of this and the preceding table affords evidence that there has been some slight improvement in the amount of attention given to hygiene in colleges and medical schools since Dr. Bowditch's investigation in 1876.

TABLE No. 19.—*Nature and amount of instruction in hygiene given in American medical schools for 1882–'83.*

Name of institution.	Location.	Name of teacher.	Title of teacher.
1. Medical Department, Arkansas Industrial University.	Little Rock, Ark.	John J. McAlmont, M. D.	Professor of materia medica, therapeutics, hygiene, and botany.
2. Medical Department, University of California.	San Francisco, Cal.	F. W. Hatch, A. M., M. D.	Professor of hygiene.
3. Denver Medical College	Denver, Colo	None given.	
4. Southern Medical College	Atlanta, Ga.	R. C. Wood, M. D	Professor of physiology and lecturer on hygiene.
5. Chicago Medical College	Chicago, Ill.	O. C. De Wolf, A. M., M. D.	Professor of State medicine and public hygiene.
6. College of Physicians and Surgeons	do	R. J. Curtis, M. D	Professor of State medicine and hygiene.
7. Rush Medical College	do	Norman Bridge, M. D.	Professor of hygiene, adjunct professor of practice.
8. Woman's Medical College	do	B. W. Griffin, M. D.	Lecturer on etiology and hygiene.
9. Quincy Medical College of Chicago	Quincy, Ill.	C. R. Ellis, M. D.	Professor of physiology and hygiene.
10. Medical College of Indiana	Indianapolis, Ind	W. B. Fletcher, M. D.	Professor of physiology, hygiene, and clinical medicine.
11. Iowa College of Physicians and Surgeons	Des Moines, Iowa	L. C. Swift, M. D.	Professor of physiology and clinical medicine, lecturer on hygiene.
12. College of Physicians and Surgeons	Keokuk, Iowa	A. G. Field, M. D	Professor of physiology, pathology, general therapeutics, and public hygiene.
13. Hospital College of Medicine	Louisville, Ky	J. J. Speed, M. D.	Professor of institutes of medicine and public hygiene, lecturer on insanity.
14. Medical Department, University of Louisville	do	T. S. Bell, M. D	Professor of State medicine and sanitary science.
15. Medical Department, University of Louisiana.	New Orleans, La	J. B. Elliott, M. D.	Professor of materia medica, therapeutics, and hygiene.
16. College of Physicians and Surgeons	Baltimore, Md	G. H. Rohé, M. D.	Professor of hygiene and clinical dermatology.
17. Woman's Medical College of Baltimore	do	J. C. Thomas, M. D.	Lecturer on hygiene.
18. College of Physicians and Surgeons	Boston, Mass	A. R. Morong, M. D.	Professor of physiology and hygiene.
19. Michigan College of Medicine	Detroit, Mich	None given.	
20. Medical Department, Minnesota College Hospital.	Minneapolis, Minn	H. J. Burnach, M. D.	Professor of clinical medicine and hygiene.
21. Fort Wayne College of Medicine	Fort Wayne, Ind	J. H. Kellogg, M. D.	Professor of sanitary science and hygiene.
22. Medical Department, University of Kansas City	Kansas City, Mo	C. W. Adams, M. D.	Professor of diseases of children and hygiene.
23. Northwestern Medical College of Saint Joseph.	Saint Joseph, Mo	F. A. Simmons, M. D	Professor of theory and practice of medicine and hygiene.
24. Saint Joseph Medical College	do	F. C. Hoyt, M. D	Demonstrator of anatomy and lecturer on hygiene.
25. Missouri Medical College	Saint Louis, Mo	J. S. Moore, M. D.	Professor of principles of medicine and hygiene, materia medica, and therapeutics.
26. Saint Louis Medical College	do	W. E. Fischel, M. D.	Professor of hygiene and forensic medicine.

PHYSICAL TRAINING IN AMERICAN COLLEGES.

27.	Albany Medical College	Albany, N. Y	J. S. Mosher, PH.D., M. D	Professor of pathological practice and clinical medicine and hygiene.
28.	Medical Department, University of Buffalo	Buffalo, N. Y	E. V. Stoddard, M. D	Professor of materia medica and hygiene.
29.	Medical Department, Niagara University	...do	None named.	
30.	Bellevue Hospital Medical College[1]	New York City, N. Y		
31.	College of Physicians and Surgeons	...do	J. C. Dalton, M. D	Professor of physiology and hygiene.
32.	Woman's Medical College of New York Infirmary	...do	E. H. James, M. D Elizabeth Blackwell, M. D	Professor of hygiene. Emeritus professor of hygiene.
33.	College of Medicine, Syracuse University	Syracuse, N. Y	N. Nivison, M. D	Professor of physiology, pathology, and hygiene.
34.	Medical Department, Willamette University	Portland, Oreg.	H. Carpenter, M. D	Professor of hygiene.
35.	Medical Department, Western Reserve University	Cleveland, Ohio	H. J. Herrick, A. M., M. D	Professor of pathology, State medicine, and hygiene.
36.	Columbus Medical College	Columbus, Ohio	None named.[2]	
37.	Medico-Chirurgical College of Philadelphia	Philadelphia, Pa	C. S. Mitchell, PH. D., M. D	Professor of chemistry and sanitary science.
38.	Woman's Medical College of Pennsylvania	...do	Frances Emily White, M. D	Professor of physiology and hygiene.
39.	Nashville Medical College	Nashville, Tenn	W. P. Jones, M. D	Professor of insanity and mental hygiene.
40.	Medical Department, Georgetown University	Georgetown, D. C	None named.[3]	
41.	Medical Department, Howard University	Washington, D. C	G. S. Palmer, M. D	Professor of physiology and hygiene.

[1] "The subject of public hygiene has been assigned to Professor Janeway, Associate Professor of Principles and Practice of Medicine."
[2] But it is stated that the professor of diseases of children will lecture on hygiene.
[3] Till 1884–'85 M. G. Ellzey was their professor of chemistry and State medicine.

TABLE No. 12.—*Nature and amount of instruction in hygiene given in American medical schools for 1882-'83*—Continued.

Name of institution.	Taught by means of—	Time devoted to hygiene.	Requirements.	Remarks.	Books recommended.
1. Medical Department, Arkansas Industrial University.	Lectures	Not specified	None		None.
2. Medical Department, University of California	do (?)	Third year of study	do	Hygiene and medical chemistry	do.
3. Denver Medical College	do (?)	Second year of study	do		do.
4. Southern Medical College	do		do	No other mention	do.
5. Chicago Medical College	do (?)	Second year of study	do		do.
6. College of Physicians and Surgeons	do (?)	Third year of study	do		do.
7. Rush Medical College	do	Spring term	do		Buck; Parkes.
8. Woman's Medical College	do (?)			do	None.
9. Quincy Medical College of Chicago	do (?)	Not specified	do		do.
10. Medical College of Indiana	do (?)	do	do		Parkes.
11. Iowa College of Physicians and Surgeons	do	do	do		None.
12. College of Physicians and Surgeons	do	do	do	General principles	do.
13. Hospital College of Medicine	do	do	do	No other mention	do.
14. Medical Department, University of Louisville	do	do	do		do.
15. Medical Department, University of Louisiana	do	One lecture weekly	Examination required (f)	Special attention called to it	Wilson; Parkes.
16. College of Physicians and Surgeons	do	Second year	Recommended in graduating course.		None.
17. Woman's Medical College of Baltimore	do	In spring course	Required in graduating course only.		do.
18. College of Physicians and Surgeons				No other mention	do.
19. Michigan College of Medicine	do (?)	Third year of study	Required for degree (?)		do.
20. Medical Department, Minnesota College Hospital.	do	Not specified			Parkes; Wilson; Rolen.
21. Fort Wayne College of Medicine		do		Rejected by American Medical College Association.	
22. Medical Department, University of Kansas City	do	do			Buck; Sanders.
23. Northwestern Medical College of Saint Joseph				No other mention	None.
24. Saint Joseph Medical College	do	do		do	do.
25. Missouri Medical College		do		"Hygiene and dietetics practically considered."	do.

PHYSICAL TRAINING IN AMERICAN COLLEGES. 149

26. Saint Louis Medical College	do	Two lectures weekly; one-half term.		Wilson.
27. Albany Medical College	do	Not specified		Bartholow.
28. Medical Department, University of Buffalo	do		Personal and municipal hygiene attended to.	None.
29. Medical Department, Niagara University		Therapeutics and hygiene, second year.	No other mention	do.
30. Bellevue Hospital Medical College	do			
31. College of Physicians and Surgeons	do		do.	Wilson; Parkes; Mapother.
32. Woman's Medical College of New York Infirmary	do	Second year of study	Required for final examination.	None.
33. College of Medicine, Syracuse University	do	Not specified	do.	Parkes; Bowditch.
34. Medical Department, Willamette University	do	do		Wilson; Buck.
35. Medical Department, Western Reserve University	do	Two lectures weekly		
37. Medico-Chirurgical College of Philadelphia	do	Third year of study	Personal hygiene in preliminary course.	
38. Woman's Medical College of Pennsylvania			1883–'84.	Wilson.
39. Nashville Medical College			Nothing mentioned, 1883–'84.	
40. Medical Department, Georgetown University		Second and third year studies.	Examination required second year.	Richardson's Preventive Medicine.
41. Medical Department, Howard University			In course	Parkes.

The foregoing table is compiled from as complete a set of catalogues of medical schools as was accessible to the compiler of this Report. It appears, however, from the conspectus of the medical schools of America, including those of Canada, published by the Illinois State Board of Health, received as we go to press, that in 1882–'83 there were 42 American medical schools having "chairs" of hygiene. Of these, 32 were regular, 7 homeopathic, and 3 eclectic. In 1883–'84 the number had increased to 80, of which 63 were regular, 8 homeopathic, 7 eclectic, and 2 physio-medical. So large an increase in "chairs of hygiene" is surprising. If they are indeed "chairs," and not stools, it is encouraging as well. We are inclined to suspect that many of them have been manufactured to order, on account of the action of the Illinois State Board of Health, whose schedule of minimum requirements, adopted in 1880 as its standard for determining the status of medical colleges under the Medical Practice Act of that State, took effect at the close of the lecture sessions of 1882–'83. Of the ten branches of medical science included in that schedule, hygiene is one, being placed ninth on the list.

THE STUDY OF HYGIENE IN SECONDARY SCHOOLS.

Elementary physiology, or, as it is usually entitled, "anatomy, physiology, and hygiene," is very generally given a place in the courses of study laid down for high schools, academies, and normal schools. If we were to base an opinion simply on the statements of catalogues and schedules, we might believe that hygiene, under the name of physiology, received ample attention in our secondary schools. But if any one who knows the difference between modern and mediæval notions regarding the nature and needs of the human body will glance at the text-books used, and inform himself as to the antiquated and unreal methods of instruction, he will cease to wonder at the unsatisfactory results thus far attained in attempting to teach the laws of health. It would be difficult to devise more unscientific and unnatural educational methods and practices than those which obtain in a very large proportion of the medical schools of the country. When medical men are so generally trained after vicious methods and amid unsanitary surroundings, it is too much to expect that the ordinary school committee-man and the average teacher will be anxious or able to work intelligently and successfully for the natural and healthy mental and bodily development of those intrusted to their charge. Of the 119 normal schools classed as public in the Report of the Commissioner of Education, at least 75, in 1882, specify physiology and hygiene in their courses of study. Less than one-quarter of them require gymnastics of their pupils.

REFORMS NEEDED.

The principles of hygiene—and hygiene is simply applied physiology—cannot be clearly and intelligently taught, much less authoritatively enforced, either in superior or secondary schools, so long as the main dependence of teachers is upon lesson cramming from text-books burdened with antiquated statements and exploded hypotheses. But much more is demanded in the domain of school and college hygiene, using the term broadly, than would be embraced in simply reforming methods of instruction. There is the additional need, not only of sanitary inspection and regulation of schools and scholars, but also of a thorough overhauling and general disinfection of the courses of instruction and of the rules and regulations for the conduct and control of teachers and taught. It is within the mark to say that the majority of our educational schemes and practices, especially in the field of female education, are not in harmony with the laws and facts of modern physiology and psychology. The need of such harmony is beginning to be apprehended. To bring about a clear and general recognition of its need, not to speak of its realization, will require a vast amount of patient and skilled labor on the part of the growing band of writers and workers who are concerning themselves alike about the physical and the mental well-being of the student class.

OPINION OF PROFESSOR HUXLEY ON ELEMENTARY INSTRUCTION IN PHYSIOLOGY.

The following opinion expressed by Professor Huxley, in an address on "Elementary Instruction in Physiology," seems pertinent and weighty in this connection:

It is, I think, eminently desirable that the hygienist and the physician should find something in the public mind to which they can appeal; some little stock of universally acknowledged truths, which may serve as a foundation for their warnings, and predispose toward an intelligent obedience to their recommendations.

Listening to ordinary talk about health, disease, and death, one is often led to entertain a doubt whether the speakers believe that the course of natural causation runs as smoothly in the human body as elsewhere.

Hence, I think, arises the want of heartiness of belief in the value of knowledge respecting the laws of health and disease, and of the foresight and care to which knowledge is the essential preliminary, which is so often noticeable, and a corresponding laxity and carelessness in practice, the results of which are too frequently lamentable.

I am not sure that the feeling expressed in the doctrine that all disease is brought about by the direct and special interference of the Deity does not lie at the bottom of the minds of a great many people who yet would vigorously object to give a verbal assent to the doctrine itself. However this may be, the main point is, that sufficient knowledge has now been acquired of vital phenomena to justify the assertion that the notion that there is anything exceptional about these phenomena receives not a particle of support from any known fact. On the contrary, there is a vast and increasing mass of evidence that birth and death, health and disease, are as much parts of the ordinary stream of events as the rising and setting of the sun, or the changes of the moon; and that the living body is a mechanism, the proper working of which we deem health; its disturbance, disease; its stoppage, death. The activity of this mechanism is dependent upon many and complicated conditions, some of which are hopelessly beyond our control, while others are readily accessible, and are capable of being indefinitely modified by our own actions. The business of the hygienist and of the physician is to know the range of these modifiable conditions, and how to influence them toward the maintenance of health and the prolongation of life; and the business of the general public is to give an intelligent assent and a ready obedience, based upon that assent, to the rules laid down for their guidance by such experts. But an intelligent assent is an assent based upon knowledge, and the knowledge here in question means an acquaintance with the elements of physiology.

From our point of view it is quite as necessary, though in a different degree, for the educator, as for the hygienist and the physician, "to know the range of these modifiable conditions" to which Professor Huxley alludes. Those who contemn or ignore the knowledge of such conditions and the means of influencing them, contemn or ignore that fundamental attribute of human nature which renders man capable of self-improvement and perfectibility through the exercise and training of his faculties. We may, and too often do, lose sight of the interdependence of the mind and body; but none the less is it impossible to separate the two and train either independently of the other; for, as was well said by Sterne, "The body and mind are like a jerkin and its lining. If you rumple the one you rumple the other."

CONCLUDING REMARKS AND SUGGESTIONS.

OUTLOOK FOR THE FUTURE.

We have now considered the peculiar features of the origin and development in American schools and colleges of physical training in its three principal branches, viz., gymnastics, military drill, and athletics, and have endeavored to indicate the nature and extent of the instruction undertaken in the science of personal hygiene. The present condition of affairs is such as to lead us to hope for even better results than those attained within the last twenty-five years. College authorities and patrons are very generally awake, or are awakening, to the necessity of providing better instruction and facilities for the physical training of the youth of either sex. With a very few, but very marked, exceptions, however, our colleges have not emerged from that stage of development in which the needs of physical training are supposed to be met by the construction and furnishing of a fine gymnasium building. Even in such institutions as have placed their gymnasia and their gymnastics under the charge of a medical director, only a beginning has been effected toward organizing the department on a broad, scientific, and thoroughly educational basis. It is a good thing to have taken the control of college gymnasia out of the hands of ignorant and low-toned trainers and athletes. Laudable results have already been brought to pass through putting the department of physical education into the hands of educated medical men. But a much more liberal outlay of imagination and money than has yet been expended in any of our colleges is indispensable to render such departments thoroughly and efficiently adequate to the demands that may fairly be made upon them.

QUALIFICATIONS OF A DIRECTOR OF A COLLEGE GYMNASIUM.

The director of a college gymnasium should possess sufficient academic and professional training to entitle him to a place in the Faculty, and to insure him the respect of his colleagues. The supply to meet even the present demand for such men is not large. The director's duties should be mainly those of a friendly medical, or rather hygienic, adviser of young men in regard to their habits of study, exercise, and recreation. He should be expected to make a close study of the bodily and mental peculiarities of those under his charge, not only for the purpose of diagnosis in individual cases, but also for the purpose of contributing the results of his observations toward the determination of the physical and mental constants of the student class. The director should have a sufficient staff of assistants subject to his orders to provide safe and graded instruction in the principal gymnastic and athletic specialties. It should be within the director's province to forbid men to take part in contests and exhibitions, when, in his judgment, on account of insufficient or improper training, or because of structural or functional weakness, such participation would be likely to prove injurious. He should also, by lectures or otherwise, give regular and genuine instruction in personal hygiene.

PROPOSED SCHEME FOR ORGANIZING A COLLEGE DEPARTMENT OF PERSONAL HYGIENE AND PHYSICAL TRAINING.

The following may serve to indicate what, in the opinion of the writer, should be the ends aimed at in the establishment and maintenance by a college or university, whether for men or women, of a department of personal hygiene and physical training.

Three special ends are to be subserved in such a department:

Firstly, The instruction of students in the laws of health, such instruction to be based upon an exposition of the modern doctrine of the human body.

Secondly, The guidance of students in a systematic attempt to attain sound bodies and vigorous normal functions by means of gymnastic exercise, the use of developing appliances, and the non-abuse of athletic sports and scholastic work, such guidance being based upon a careful examination into and study of the bodily endowments, constitutional peculiarities, and mental habits of the individuals under guidance. The counsel and direction of the director should be seconded by the instruction of special teachers in the principal branches of gymnastics and athletics, such teachers to be subject to his control and supervision.

Thirdly, The scientific study of the natural history of the student class. Toward the furtherance of these ends a well-equipped gymnasium and ample and conveniently-arranged play-grounds are indispensable, and the director should be expected to give—

(I) Instruction (a) by means of lectures; (b) by marking out a course of reading; (c) by anatomical and physical demonstrations; (d) by holding examinations. Undergraduate students should be required and other students allowed to attend such instruction.

The lectures might be grouped advantageously as follows: (1) on the nature and needs of the human body, in connection with demonstrations (a) on the skeleton, (b) with anatomical preparations, and (c) by means of physiological apparatus; (2) on the theory and practice of exercise and training; (3) on selected topics in public and personal hygiene; (4) on the aims and means of modern medicine, with hints as to the selection of medical advisers.

(II) Guidance, by means of personal suggestions, advice, and direction. Each undergraduate student should be required, and all others encouraged, to undergo a physical examination by the director, in order that he may be enabled to prescribe such exercises and the use of such developing appliances and measures as may be appropriate to the special needs of each individual. Each student should be examined at least twice a year, and the results of such examinations should be carefully recorded and tabulated.

(III) By making statistical and scientific reports of observations and experiments. The director should record, analyze, and discuss the results of his observations, measurements, and examinations; and be encouraged to investigate the problems appertaining to the development and maintenance of normal bodily and mental functions in members of the student class, to the end that physical education may be put upon a rational basis.

It is only through a wise combination of gymnastic training and athletic sports that the best results can be hoped for or attained. Athletic sports can, if wisely managed and supervised, be made most serviceable in securing manliness and self-control to those engaging in them. The abandonment of them as a general "elective course" to the unregulated control of unripe and inexperienced youth is, to say the least, unwise. He who shall consider intelligently and critically, in the light of our present knowledge of brain and nerve and muscle physiology, the various games and sports which are deservedly popular, and shall show wherein they are valuable as a means to manly and womanly development, cannot fail of contributing greatly to the advancement of pedagogical science.

So dense is the present ignorance, not only of the mass of the people, but also of a large section of the educated portion of the community, concerning the elementary truths of biological science in general and of psycho-physical science in particular, that it would be well-nigh hopeless to attempt to institute and administer any thorough-going system of physical training as a part of the system of public instruction in even the most enlightened States of the Union. Until the modern doctrine of bodily exercise is more generally apprehended, we can only look for sporadic efforts and fragmentary and discordant results in so much of the field of physical training as the richer and more advanced colleges and universities may occupy. The German, Swedish, and French systems of physical training and of educating teachers in gymnastics are well worth studying; but the greatest present need is to educate trustees, committee-men, teachers, and physicians in physiology and hygiene.

DU BOIS-REYMOND ON EXERCISE.

One of the pioneers and masters in modern physiology, Professor Du Bois-Reymond, of the University of Berlin, has given an admirable statement of the physiology of exercise. He says:

By exercise we commonly understand the frequent repetition of a more or less complicated action of the body with the co-operation of the mind, or of an action of the mind alone, for the purpose of being able to perform it better. We seek in vain in most physiological text-books for instruction respecting exercise; if it is given, only the so-called bodily exercises are generally considered, and they are represented as merely exercises of the muscular system; therefore, it is not strange that laymen in medicine, professors of gymnastics, and school teachers, generally believe that. Yet it is easy to show the error of this view and demonstrate that such bodily exercises as gymnastics, fencing, swimming, riding, dancing, and skating are much more exercises of the central nervous system,—of the brain and spinal marrow. It is true that these movements involve a certain degree of muscular power; but we can conceive of a man with muscles like those of the Farnesian Hercules, who would yet be incompetent to stand or walk, to say nothing of his exerting more complicated movements.

Thus it becomes clear, if proof were needed, that every action of our body as a motive apparatus depends not less, but more, upon the co-operation of the muscles than upon the force of their contraction. In order to execute a composite motion, like a leap, the muscles must begin to work in the proper order, and the energy of each one of them (in Helmholtz's sense) must increase, halt, and diminish according to a certain law, so that the result shall be the proper position of the limbs and the proper velocity of the center of gravity in the proper direction. Since the nerves only transmit the impulses coming from the motor-ganglion cells, it is evident that the peculiar mechanism of the composite movements resides in the central nervous system, and that consequently exercise in such movements is really nothing else than exercise of the central nerve-system. This possesses the invaluable property that the series of movements, if we may speak thus, which take place in it, frequently, after a definite law, are readily repeated in the same order, with the same swell and ebb and intricacy, whenever a singly felt impulse of the will demands it. Thus all the bodily exercises we have mentioned above are not merely muscle gymnastics, but also, and that pre-eminently, nerve gymnastics, if for brevity we may apply the term nerves to the whole nervous system.

Still, something else than the control of the muscles by the motor-nervous system comes into consideration in most composite movements. The sight, the sense of pressure, and the muscular sense, and finally the mind, must be prepared to take in the position of the body at each instant, so that the muscles may be in a proper state of adjustment; this is plainly shown in the exercises of fencing, playing billiards, rope-dancing, vaulting on horses in motion, or leaping down a mountain slope. Thus not only the motor, but the sensor nervous system also, and the mental functions, are capable of being exercised, and need it; and the muscles again appear to acquire a deeper importance in gymnastics. What is said here of the coarser bodily movements applies equally to all skilled work of the highest as well as of the lowest kind. Although a Liszt or a Rubinstein without an iron muscularity of arm cannot be thought of, and although, likewise, the movements of Joachim's bow during a symphony may correspond to many kilogram-meters, still their power as virtuosos resides in their central nerve-system. When Lessing asked whether Raphael would have been any the less a great painter if he had been born without hands, he perceived this truth. Is it necessary to add that the same principle applies to all the movements as well as to those of the hands? that, for example, vocal culture rests upon no other one?

The modern ideal of manly excellence is more nearly related to the Greek ideal than to the monkish or even the knightly. When modern methods for the realization of the modern ideal are perfected, they will doubtless as far surpass the methods of the Greeks as the physiology of Du Bois-Reymond surpasses that of Plato. Meanwhile, the true end and aim of physical training in America is the same that Plato enunciated, namely, that the bodies of the trained may, better than those of the untrained, minister to the virtuous mind.

And once more [to continue in Plato's words], when a body large and too strong for the soul is united to a small and weak intelligence, then, inasmuch as there are two desires natural to man, one of food for the sake of the body, and one of wisdom for the sake of the diviner part of us, then, I say, the motions of the stronger, getting the better and increasing their own power, but making the soul dull and stupid and forgetful, engender ignorance, which is the greatest of diseases. There is one protection against both kinds of disproportion,—that we should not move the body without the soul, or the soul without the body, and thus they will aid one another and be healthy and well balanced. And therefore the mathematician, or any one else who devotes himself to some intellectual pursuit, must allow his body to have motion also, and practice gymnastics; and he who would train the limbs of the body should impart to them the motions of the soul, and should practice music and all philosophy, if he would be called truly fair and truly good.

APPENDIX.

PHYSICAL TRAINING IN GERMANY.

Physical training has been accorded a considerable place in the educational systems of the principal countries of Europe, including Germany, Sweden and Norway, Switzerland, France, Austria, Belgium, and Denmark. It would be interesting and instructive to compare the systems of physical training now in vogue in these countries with what has been attempted and accomplished in Great Britain and the United States. The writer originally intended to embody such a comparison in this report, but found it impossible to gather, from the libraries to which he had access, sufficient data on which to base a comprehensive and accurate account of the actual working of physical education in any of the foreign countries named above.

Since the foregoing pages were prepared for publication, the writer has visited Germany, and, through personal observation and inquiry, made a tolerably comprehensive study of German methods of physical training, especially of those which obtain in Prussia. While he would not disparage the merits of the gymnastic training given in the schools of Sweden, Switzerland, and France, and of other countries which he was likewise unable to visit, the writer inclines to the opinion that the Prussian system is the most highly developed and the best organized of its kind, and is, therefore, more worthy than any other of close study on the part of those who desire to check the present tendency to brain-forcing in the education of American youth.

DEVELOPMENT OF GERMAN GYMNASTICS.

English and American writers on education have very generally either entirely neglected, or largely failed to apprehend, the lessons which German experience teaches in regard to physical education.

The German for gymnastics is *Turnkunst*, or *Turnen*, though the term *Gymnastik* occurs not infrequently, especially in the earlier writings. *Turnplatz* and *Turnhalle* correspond respectively to our terms out-door gymnasium and gymnasium, which latter ordinarily signifies a building for gymnastic exercises. A gymnasium, in the German sense, is the highest of the secondary schools, and leads directly to the university. The uniform use of this term to designate such schools dates, in Prussia, from the year 1812.

German gymnastics embrace three well-marked fields, or departments, viz: *Volksturnen*, or popular gymnastics; *Schulturnen*, or school gymnastics; and *Militärturnen*, or military gymnastics. The organization of the last two departments is maintained and controlled by the Government for strictly educational purposes; whereas the *Turnvereine*, as the societies of the turners are called, are voluntary associations of a social and semi-educational, but wholly popular and patriotic, nature. The fondness of the German people for gymnastic exercises is as marked a national trait as is the liking of the British for athletic sports. The germ of the turning system is to be found in the martial games and exercises of the ancient Teutons.

Considered from an educational point of view, British athletics are rude and primitive when compared with German gymnastics, which, in many of their features, are almost Grecian. The two systems are as widely different in their aims and methods as are the British school-boy and the German school-master, and for the same reasons.

GERMAN REFORMS AND REFORMERS.

The reform whereby mental and physical training have been made conjoint factors in the compulsory education of every German, has been worked out during the last hundred years. At every stage of its course the quickening and shaping influence of innovating educators has been felt. The three most eminent names in the list of men identified with the revival and upbuilding of German gymnastics are those of Guts Muths, Jahn, and Spiess. Each was a teacher and writer. Jahn was an agitator and popular leader in addition. Guts Muths lived from 1759 till 1839, Jahn from 1778 till 1852, and Spiess from 1810 till 1858.

GUTS MUTHS AND HIS WORK.

Guts Muths was teacher of gymnastics in Salzmann's Philanthropinum, at Schnepfenthal, from 1787 till his death, in 1839. His "*Gymnastik für die Jugend*," published in 1793, was the first German manual of gymnastics. He did much by his writings and labors to prepare the way for Jahn, the "Father of turning," and Spiess, the "Founder of German school gymnastics and the creator of gymnastics for girls." Guts Muths's success at Schnepfenthal led many private and a few public teachers to attempt to give their pupils some gymnastic training. The influence of Guts Muths is also traceable in the revival of gymnastics in Denmark, under the lead of Nachtigall, and in Sweden, where Ling, the founder of modern medical gymnastics, made gymnastics extremely popular. It should not be forgotten that Ling did much more than to develop the Swedish movement cure, on which his fame outside of his own country chiefly rests. He organized admirable systems of popular and school gymnastics, which are still extant and flourishing.

REFORMS IN PRUSSIA.

Prussia's commanding position in science and politics is due to the perfection of her educational and military systems. Their present excellence and efficiency are, in a large degree, the outcome of reforms begun by the sagacious and energetic ministers of the father of Kaiser Wilhelm, in the period of Prussia's deepest humiliation and distress, the period between the battle of Jena, in 1806, and the War of Liberation, in 1813. Bismarck and his coadjutors, Roon, Moltke, and Falk, have but cultivated the seed and reaped the fruits of the reforms instituted or marked out by Stein, and Scharnhorst, and Wilhelm von Humboldt.

Stein emancipated the peasants from serfdom, broke down the barriers between them and the middle classes, and gave enlarged freedom to trade. His name is also associated with radical and successful reforms in the constitution and administration of the State. Scharnhorst reorganized the army in accordance with the principle that all the inhabitants of a country should be trained to defend it. "In the field of educational reform the providential man," says Professor Seeley, "appeared in Humboldt, as great a master of the science and art of education as Scharnhorst was of war."

As early as 1804, Guts Muths urged upon the Prussian minister, Massow, the importance of introducing physical education into the schools as a means of promoting the military efficiency of the people. The minister replied that he proposed to make bodily training an essential part of his plan for national education. The war with Napoleon prevented this reform from being more than projected. In 1808 Scharnhorst's provisional scheme for the reorganization of the army was submitted to Stein for criticism and suggestions. Scharnhorst urged that fencing, swimming, leaping, etc., should be taught in the town and city schools. Stein approved the views of Scharnhorst in regard to bodily exercises, called attention to the success of Guts Muths at Schnepfenthal, and suggested the desirability of securing his co-operation in bringing about the general introduction of gymnastics into the schools. Humboldt likewise favored the scheme, but no efficient measures were taken, at this time, to carry it out. The first public gymnastic ground (*Turnplatz*) was established in the summer of 1809 at Braunsberg, in Prussia, under the auspices of a secret association formed under the name of "The Moral and Scientific Union," the so-called *Tugendbund*, for the purpose of arousing national feeling and throwing off the French yoke. The gymnastics adopted at Braunsberg seem to have been based on the principles of Guts Muths.

"FATHER JAHN" AND THE TURNERS.

That gymnastics under the name of *Turnen* became a popular institution and a potent factor in national development, was due to Jahn, a man of much more aggressive spirit than the quiet teacher of gymnastics at Schnepfenthal. In 1810 Jahn became a teacher in the *Köllnisches Gymnasium*, one of the city schools in Berlin, and in 1811–'12 he also taught in Plamann's Pestalozzian Institute in the same city. Prince Bismarck was a pupil in this institute from 1822 till 1827.

Jahn was an ardent patriot, and was filled with an enthusiastic admiration of the spirit, manners, and speech of the ancient Germans. His strong and rugged nature, and his eager, restless, passionate spirit, qualified him for popular leadership in the movement which he initiated. He seized the idea of making bodily training a force in national regeneration and education, and dreamed and wrote and labored for a free and united Germany. Before he had fairly entered upon his course as a teacher in Berlin, his book on "German Nationality" appeared in 1810. In the interval which elapsed between 1810 and 1816, the date of "*Die Deutsche Turnkunst*," he accomplished the main labor of his life. The nature of his work, the ideas by which he was animated, and the circumstances of the time which favored his success, are indicated in the following extracts from "*Die Deutsche Turnkunst*":

Like many other things in this world, the German turning system had a small and insignificant beginning. In the end of the year 1809 I went to Berlin to see the entry of the King. Love to my fatherland and my own inclinations now made me a teacher of youth, as I had often been before. During the beautiful spring of 1810 a few of my pupils began to go out with me into the woods and fields on the holiday afternoons of Wednesday and Saturday, and the habit became confirmed. Their number increased, and we had various youthful sports and exercises. Thus we went on until the dog-days, when the number was very large, but very soon fell off again. But there was left a select number, a nucleus, who held together even during the winter, with whom the first turning ground was opened in the spring of 1811, in the Hasenheide [*i. e.*, a pine forest on the outskirts of Berlin].

At the present time many exercises are practiced in company and before the eyes of all, under the name of turning. But then the names turning system, turning, turner, turning ground, and the like, came up all at once, and gave occasion for much excitement, scandal, and anthorship. The subject was discussed even in the French daily papers, and even here in our own country it was at first said that the ancient German ways have brought forth a new folly.

During the winter we studied whatever could be got on the subject, and we reflected with gratitude upon our predecessors, Vieth and Guts Muths. The stronger and more experienced of my pupils made a very skillful use of their writings, and were able, during the next summer, to labor as instructors in turning. In the summer of 1812 both the turning ground and system of exercises were enlarged. They became more varied from turning day to turning day, and were mutually developed by the pupils in their friendly contests of youthful emulation. It is impossible to say in detail who first discovered, tried, investigated, proved, and completed one or another exercise. From the very beginning the turning system has shown great community of spirit, patriotic feeling, perseverance, and self-denial. Every extension or development of it was used for the common good, and such is still the case.

Toward the end of the summer exercises of 1812, a sort of association of turners was formed for the purpose of the scientific investigation and artistic organization of the turning system in the most useful and generally applicable manner. On the King's proclamation of February 3, 1813, all the turners capable of bearing arms entered the field. After long persuasion I succeeded at Breslau in inducing Ernst Eiselen, one of my oldest pupils, to take charge of the turning institution during the war. I myself accompanied Eiselen from Breslau to Berlin, and introduced him to the authorities and to the principals of schools, who promised him all manner of co-operation, and who have ever since shown confidence in him. Since that time Eiselen has been at the head of the turning institution, during the summers of 1813 and 1814 and the intervening winter, and has conducted the exercises of those who were too young to carry arms.

At the end of July, 1814, I returned to Berlin. In the winter, when the volunteers returned, bringing many turners with them, the associated discussions were renewed. On the escape of Napoleon all the turners able to bear arms volunteered again for the field, only two who had fought during the campaigns of 1813 and 1814 remaining at home from the consequences of those campaigns.

The younger ones who remained behind now took hold of the work again with renewed zeal. During the spring and summer of 1815 the turning ground received still further improvements and enlargements. In the following autumn and early part of winter, the turning system was again made the object of associated investigation. After the subject had been ripely considered and investigated in the turning council, and opinions had been compared, experience cited and views corrected, a beginning was made in collecting into one whole all the results of earlier and later labors on the subject, and all the separate fragments and contributions relative to it, a labor which has lastly been revised by my own pen. Although it was only one architect who at first drew the plan, yet master, associates, pupils, and workmen have all labored faithfully and honestly upon the structure, and have all contributed their shares to it.

This is a brief account of my work, my words, and my book. Neither of the three is perfect; but the book may serve to promote a recognition of its ideal. It is put forth only by way of rendering an account to the fatherland of what we have done and endeavored.

The turning system would re-establish the lost symmetry of human development; would connect a proper bodily training with mere exclusive intellectual cultivation; would supply the proper counteracting influence to the prevailing over-refinement, and would comprehend and influence the whole man by means of a social mode of living for the young. Every turning institution is a place for exercising the bodily powers, a school of industry in manly activity, a place of chivalrous contest, an aid to education, a protection to the health, and a public benefit. It is constantly and interchangeably a place of teaching and of learning. In an unbroken circle follow constantly after each other, direction, exemplification, instruction, independent investigation, practice, emulation, and further instruction. Thus the turners do not learn their occupation from hearsay. They have lived in and with their work, investigated it, proved it, and perfected it. It awakens all the dormant powers and secures a self-confidence and readiness which are never found at a loss.

The director of a turning institution undertakes a high duty. He must cherish and protect the simplicity of the young, that it may not be injured by untimely precocity. He who is not thoroughly penetrated with a childlike spirit and national feelings, should never take charge of a turning institution. It is a holy work and life.

But all education is useless and idle which leaves the pupil to disappear, like a will-o'-the-wisp, in the waste folly of a fancied cosmopolitanism, and does not confirm him in patriotic feeling; and thus, even in the worst period of the French domination, love of king and fatherland were preached to and impressed upon the youth of the turning association. No one ought to enter a turning association who is knowingly a perverter of German nationality, and praises, loves, promotes, or defends foreign manners.

With such principles did the turning societies strengthen, train, arm, encourage, and man themselves for the fatherland, in the sultry times of the devil. Nor did faith, love, or hope desert them for a moment. "God deserts no German," has always been their motto. In war none of them staid at home, except those too young or too weak, and they were not idle.

The turning system [says Von Raumer] soon spread from Berlin throughout Germany, and a large part of Southern Germany. Next to Berlin, Breslau had the largest number of turners, some eight hundred. In that city students, Catholic and Protestant, seminary pupils, the pupils of four *Gymnasien*, officers, and professors frequented the turning ground. Singing flourished. On Wednesday and Saturday afternoons, after exercising from three to seven, the whole company returned singing to the city.

* * * * *

Together with this first natural development of the turning system, there came up also a reaction against many received and universal customs and manners. This necessarily aroused enemies, and the more because the turners frequently overpassed the bounds of moderation, and made turning identical with a warfare against all ancient errors. This was particularly the case after the war of freedom.

THE ATTITUDE OF THE STATE AUTHORITIES.

The state authorities, especially those at the head of the department of education, seem to have manifested a lively and, on the whole, friendly interest in Jahn and his work. In 1813, during Jahn's absence in the field, six hundred and seventy thalers were appropriated to enable Eiselen to conduct an eight weeks' normal course of instruction for teachers of turning, but it was impracticable to carry out the plan at that time. Several reports of a favorable nature were made to the Government on the pedagogical and hygienic worth of turning, and turning grounds were established in various parts of the Kingdom under governmental auspices. In 1814 the Prussian chancellor, Prince Hardenberg, bestowed a pension of five hundred thalers upon Jahn, in recognition of his services to the state. In September, 1815, Jahn's pension was increased to eight hundred thalers, and Eiselen was granted a salary of four hundred thalers. This was due to a report made to Hardenberg in April, 1815, by Minister Von Schuckmann, to whom Hardenberg had referred a plan of Jahn's for enlarging the turnplatz, purchasing certain buildings, and bringing the turning institution into close connection with the Berlin school-system. Von Schuckmann was averse, by reason of the low state of the treasury, to incurring the large expenditures suggested by Jahn, and deemed it unadvisable to introduce turning formally into the schools, lest it should lose its spontaneous popular character.

In 1818 Altenstein, the minister of education, caused an official investigation to be made into the nature, extent, and effects of turning throughout Prussia. During the period 1816–'19, the department of education elaborated a provisional scheme for a general education law, which, however, was never enacted in its entirety. In this scheme a place was assigned to gymnastics, and it was proposed to introduce them into the rural schools as well as into the middle schools, normal schools, and Gymnasien.

At last, in 1819, a plan was perfected by the educational authorities for the establishment of turning grounds thoughout Prussia in connection with the schools. On March 23, 1819, the very day that this plan was laid before the King for his approval and signature, the news of Kotzebue's murder by Sand, who was a student and a turner, reached Berlin, and the King refused his approval. Sand's deed of crazy violence had, as it appears now, no political significance; but the Prussian Government feared revolution, and looked upon the spread of liberal ideas among the rising generation with alarm. The *Burschenschaften*, or students' societies, and the *Turnvereine* were put under the ban as being hotbeds of liberalism. Jahn was arrested in July, 1819, on the charge of engaging in revolutionary practices and conspiring to assassinate a privy councilor, Von Kamptz by name. Francis Lieber, then a youth of nineteen, one of Jahn's oldest and favorite pupils, was also arrested on suspicion. Lieber regained his freedom in a few months, but was forbidden to study at a Prussian university. Jahn was acquitted and set free in 1825, but was banished from Berlin, and forbidden to reside in any town where there was a university or Gymnasium. Francis Lieber came to the United States in 1827 for the express purpose of taking charge of the then recently founded Tremont Gymnasium, in Boston, Mass., where he established a swimming school on his own account.

In January, 1820, the Government abolished turning in Prussia by closing the turning grounds, some ninety in number. Volkstnrnen was not again allowed until 1842. Gradually gymnastics found a place in the instruction of a few schools. In 1836, Dr. Lorinser, of Oppeln, published in a medical journal an article entitled "The Protection of Health in Schools." Dr. Lorinser was very severe in his strictures on the management of the schools, especially of the Gymnasien. He declared that bodily and mental weakness were on the increase among school children, and especially the Gymnasium pupils, by reason of the overburdening due to multiplicity of studies, too many school hours, and an undue amount of home work. This paper gave rise to a wide and somewhat heated discussion, and indirectly brought about a renewed interest in school gymnastics.

In 1840 the department of education recommended the introduction of bodily training into all the higher schools for boys. In April, 1842, the ministers of war, the interior, and education, united in recommending to the King the reintroduction of turning. In June following, the King gave his sanction to the proposal of his ministers that "bodily exercises should be acknowledged formally as a necessary and indispensable integral part of male education, and should be adopted as an agency in the education of the people." The King also authorized the establishment of "gymnastic institutes," in connection with "the Gymnasien, the higher middle schools, the training schools for teachers, and the division and brigade schools in the army."

THE REVIVAL OF TURNING.

Volksturnen revived, after the promulgation of the above cited cabinet order of King Frederick William IV; but its aims and usages were too strongly colored by political views for the turning societies to pass unscathed through the troublous years 1848–'50. It was not until 1860 that the turning movement began to regain its lost momentum. Great enthusiasm for turning was awakened by the first German turning festival, held at Coburg, in 1860, in which some thousand or more turners took part in celebrating the victory of Waterloo. In August, 1861, came the second general *Turnfest*, when the turners celebrated, at Berlin, the fiftieth anniversary of the establishment, by Jahn, of the original turnplatz in the Hasenheide. Nearly six thousand turners, representing more than two hundred and sixty districts, took part in this festival, which is also notable for the laying of the corner-stone of the national monument to Jahn. The completed monument, consisting of a bronze statue of Jahn upon a pedestal of stones contributed by turning societies in every quarter of the world, was dedicated in August, 1872.

Between 1859 and 1862 the number of German turnvereine increased from 241 to 1,279. In 1863, 20,000 turners took part at Leipzig in the celebration of the fiftieth anniversary of Napoleon's defeat near that city by the allies. A year later the societies numbered nearly 2,000, and their members nearly 168,000. The great majority of German turnvereine have, since 1860, belonged to the organization known as the *Deutsche Turnerschaft*.

THE "DEUTSCHE TURNERSCHAFT."

The Turnerschaft comprises fifteen circuits, or geographical divisions, within the German Empire and Austria. Each circuit (*Kreis*) is subdivided into districts (*Gaue*), and each district into societies (*Vereine*). On January 1, 1885, there were 220 *Turngaue* within the Turnerschaft. In 1880, out of 2,226 turnvereine in 1,741 municipalities and villages, 1,971, with a total membership of 170,315, belonged to the Turnerschaft. On January 1, 1885, the number of vereine within the Turnerschaft had risen to 2,878, an increase of 223 over 1884; while the number of vereine outside the Turnerschaft had decreased from 343 to 329. The membership in 1885 was 267,854, of whom 114,134 were active turners; or, to express it differently, in 2,413 localities there was an *active* member of the Turnerschaft for every 134 of the population. During 1882, 1,915 vereine practiced turning in the winter; 294 owned a turnplatz, and 153 a turnhalle; while in 1884, 2,409 societies practiced winter turning, 353 owned a turnplatz, and 182 owned a turnhalle.

It is almost as common to find turnvereine among Germans in foreign lands as to find cricket and foot-ball clubs among British colonists. Turning societies flourish in the United States, Brazil, Chili, and Australia, as well as in every country in Europe. In the United States the principal association of the turners is the North American Turnerbund, which embraces more than two hundred vereine with a membership of more than twenty thousand.

The nature and working of the spirit which animates the German folk are disclosed to a highly interesting degree in the organization and the management of the *Deutsche Turnerschaft*, which is, in a sense, the most genuinely popular of German institutions. In their Volksturnen we find the people acting with more freedom and spontaneity than in almost any other field. It is one of the few fields in which the folk has been left comparatively untrammeled by the Government. While its aims are broadly national and social, and tinged with sentimental idealism, the Turnerschaft reflects in its democratic organization and government, its systematic methods, and its economical administration, the severely practical German spirit, with all its love of order, discipline, and minute division of labor. The turnvereine are in their way as much center points of the popular life of Germany as the gymnasia were center points in Greek life. It is to be noted, however, that the Turnerschaft is largely recruited from such classes as were enslaved by the Greeks.

Volksturnen of the present day differs somewhat from that which flourished in the time of Jahn and Eiselen. Individualism is less rampant for one thing, and certain styles of exercise first made prominent by Spiess, whose method and work we shall consider under Schulturnen, have been adopted by the turners. Then, too, the turnvereine have ceased to resemble political clubs. The committee of the turnvereine declared at Gotha in 1861 that turning could only yield abundant fruit when it should be considered a means for training strong men for the entire fatherland. The turnvereine should hold themselves entirely aloof from the consideration of party questions as such. The formation of definite political opinions was the affair and duty of the individual turners. The general adoption of military exercises by the turners was deprecated. A genuine normal training to render the body equal to the performance of all manly exercises should remain the principal concern and business of the turnvereine.

The hand-book of the *Deutsche Turnerschaft* very clearly sets forth the distinctive features of the Volksturnen of the present day. What follows in relation to the aims, organization, and practices of the Turnerschaft is based upon statements made in that work, and in the organ of the Turnerschaft, the *Deutsche Turn-Zeitung*, a weekly paper published at Leipzig, and also upon personal observations made in various German cities, particularly in Dresden, during the continuance of the Sixth General German Turning Festival, held there in July, 1885.

The aim of the Turnerschaft is to promote the interests of turning, as a means to bodily and moral strength. Its members (any German of good moral character who is fourteen years old, may join it) are urged to render turning attractive to boys and apprentices who have passed the school age; to cultivate simple German customs and manners; to cultivate national exercises and games, such as free and class exercises, running, leaping, climbing, casting the weight, hurling the spear, wrestling, fencing, and sword play; to promote sociability through the singing of folk songs, and those having freedom and the fatherland for their themes—such songs should be thoroughly known by every turner, and not merely their first lines; to participate in all popular festivals, especially those commemorative of national events, such as the Kaiser's birthday, Sedan day, and the like; to manifest an active interest in useful public enterprises and associations, such as fire and salvage companies, and sanitary corps for the care and transportation of the sick and injured.

The turners are divided into two main sections, viz, boys from fourteen to seventeen years of age, and men. These divisions are subdivided according to their gymnastic ability into squads, or classes (*Riegen*), each class being under the lead and guidance of a "foreturner" (*Vorturner*), chosen on account of fitness. The chief foreturner is the turnwarden (*Turnwart*). Strength alone is not enough. It is the foreturner's business to make his squad as expert as possible, and above all to secure to each of its members an erect, firm, and graceful carriage of the body.

The times most favored for turning are Sundays, holidays, and certain appointed evenings during the week. The order recommended for the ordinary evening turning is as follows: A brief *Kürturnen*, i. e., gymnastic exercise in which each individual follows his own taste and inclination as to apparatus and movement. Then comes the formation of the classes, which fall into line at a signal from the turnwart, and at a second signal march to the machines, the bars, horse, horizontal bar, etc., to which each has been assigned. The exercise on each piece of apparatus is set by the fore-turner at the head of the class. Usually after exercising for a quarter of an hour the lines are reformed and each class marches to a machine of a different character. After this second period of fifteen minutes of heavy gymnastic exercise (*Gerätturnen*) the ranks are reformed, and "free movements" are made by the assembled classes. No apparatus is used in the free movements, which are made in unison and according to commands given by the turnwart. The evening closes with a second Kürturnen. The affairs of the verein are regulated by officers elected by its members. The programme of exercises, i. e., the amount and nature of the Gerätturnen, or heavy gymnastics, is determined by the officers and is duly bulletined. The foreturners are bound to practice together at appointed times. The order of exercises on the gymnastic machines is changed from evening to evening, and variety and interest are further secured, when the weather is favorable, by engaging in out-of-door games (*Turnspiele*) in the turnplatz. The cultivation of gymnastic specialties and of one-sided dexterity is discouraged.

From time to time the societies comprised in a district, and the districts included in a circuit, hold festivals, when both individuals and squads compete for prizes. The intervals between these festivals vary greatly in the different circuits and districts. The General German Turning Festival (*Das Allgemeine Deutsche Turnfest*), as the grand festival of the entire Turnerschaft is termed, occurs at intervals of at least four years. It continues for at least three days, one of which must be Sunday. Six such festivals have been held in different German cities since the first was celebrated at Coburg in 1860.

THE DRESDEN TURNFEST IN 1885.

The programme carried out at the sixth *Deutsche Turnfest* in Dresden, July 18–23, 1885, was in the main as follows:

Saturday, July 18.

Reception during the day at the railroad station and steamer wharves on the Elbe of the visiting turners. At 8 P.M. reception at the festival hall. Transfer of the standard of the Turnerschaft from the Frankfort-on-the-Main color guard to the Dresden color guard. Celebration of the twenty-fifth anniversary of the founding of the Turnerschaft. Music and singing in the festival hall.

Sunday, July 19.

6 to 7 A.M. Reveille (*Weckruf*).
7 to 9 A.M. Bathing in the Elbe.
11.30 A.M. Formation of festival procession.
11.45 A.M. to 2.30 P.M. March to the festival grounds.
3.30 P.M. Assembly of turners and general free gymnastics in the festival grounds.
5 to 7 P.M. Class exercise (*Musterriegenturnen*) of the most proficient squads, representing single circuits, districts, and societies.
7 to 8 P.M. General Kürturnen and gymnastic games.
From 8 P.M., in the hall, concert by the united singing societies of Dresden.
From 5 P.M., on the grounds, music and dancing.

Monday, July 20.

7 A.M. to 12 M. Prize turning (*Wettturnen*) and class turning.
12 to 3 P.M. Banquet in the hall.
3 to 5 P.M. Free gymnastics by the Saxon turners, including the pupils of the higher boys' schools of Dresden.
5 to 7 P.M. Class turning; exhibition sword play (*Schaufechten*).
7 to 8 P.M. Kürturnen by the most expert turners. Games.
8 P.M. Convention of the German teachers of gymnastics.
8 P.M. Reunions of fellow-countrymen.
From 5 P.M. Music and dancing on the grounds and in the hall.

Tuesday, July 21.

7 A.M. to 12 M. Prize turning and conclusion of class turning.
2 to 3 P.M. Prize sword play (*Preisfechten*).
3 to 7 P.M. Prize turning.
7 to 8 P.M. Games.
9 P.M. Torch dance.
From 5 P.M. Music and dancing.

Wednesday, July 22.

7 to 10 A.M. Conclusion of prize turning.
10 A.M. to 12 M. Gymnastic games by the boys and girls of the public schools (*Volksschulen*) of Dresden.
2 P.M. Wrestling.
8 P.M. Announcement of the victors.
10 P.M. Illumination and official close of the festival.
From 5 P.M. Music and dancing.

Thursday, July 23.

Turner excursions (*Turnfahrten*) to the Saxon Switzerland, and other points of interest.
From 3 P.M. Social reunions on the grounds; music and dancing.

The festival was characteristically German in its object, arrangements, and detailed workings. It afforded an admirable opportunity for studying national traits and peculiar folk customs, and furnished abundant evidence of the sturdiness, good humor, and order-loving disposition of the common people, as well as of their genuine liking for and ability in gymnastic drill and gymnastic games. In the opinion of competent judges, moreover, a very considerable increase in gymnastic proficiency over that exhibited at any former festival was noticeable.

It concerns us here to note only the more striking of the turning exercises and regulations, without attempting to describe the festival as a whole, or venturing to enlarge upon its many attractions for the lover of the picturesque or the student of men, manners, and institutions.

More than 20,000 turners, including delegations from England, France, Russia, Holland, Switzerland, Austria, Hungary, Sweden, and the United States, took part in the street parade, which was reviewed by the King of Saxony from a balcony of his palace on Sunday. The grounds set apart for the use of the turners were something more than ten acres in extent, and were situated in the outskirts of the city, adjoining the Grosser Garten, the principal park of the King. Chief among the temporary buildings erected on the Festplatz was the festival hall, with an estimated capacity for 10,000 people. The main part of this hall was left unfloored, so that in case of unfavorable weather all the heavy gymnastics might take place under cover.

As the weather was fine during the entire continuance of the festival, the hall was used chiefly for speech-making and merry-making, and the turning of every description was carried on out of doors on the Turnplatz, which had an area of more than three-quarters of an acre.

The most noteworthy gymnastic features of the festival were as follows: The free gymnastics (*allgemeine Freiübungen*) on Sunday; the class turning of the most proficient turners (*Musterriegenturnen*) on Sunday, Monday, and Tuesday; the Kürturnen, or exhibition gymnastics, on Sunday and Monday; the prize turning (*Wettturnen*) on the last three days, and the gymnastic games of the Dresden school children on Wednesday.

The Free Gymnastics.

The free gymnastics resemble somewhat the "setting-up drill" employed in the United States Army, inasmuch as they are bodily movements arranged in groups of related exercises, which are executed at command and in unison. In them no apparatus of any kind is made use of. They may be characterized as calisthenics raised to their highest power. The free gymnastics on this occasion included sixteen different movements, and required nearly three-quarters of an hour for their completion. The order and character of the movements had been determined and ordained by the proper committee of the Turnerschaft months before, and the movements had been practiced by the different vereine at home, but only there. The turners who took part in the free movements numbered 4,544, and were formed in seventy-one "open ranks" of sixty-four men each, facing toward the front, the distance between the "files" being a full arm's-length. Facing the huge class was a high platform, on which two marvelously expert foreturners first executed each movement in sight of the class, and then, at signals given with a flag by the turnwart in command of the class, and re-enforced by strokes given on gongs in the middle of the field, the foreturners repeated the movement, the entire body of 4,500 men following in unison. The sight of 4,500 bareheaded, white-shirted men, many of them grayheaded, executing complicated movements, which involved tossing of the arms, bowing and bending of the trunk, facing now this way and now that, and all with military precision, in nearly perfect time, was a novel and inspiring one. The free movements, on Monday, of the Saxon turners and the Dresden school-boys, in all 2,300 persons, were even more complicated, difficult, and picturesque than those above spoken of. The King and Queen of Saxony, with a numerous retinue of courtiers, were among the interested spectators of the free movements on Sunday.

The Class Turning, or "Musterriegenturnen."

Class turning under the lead of a foreturner has been a peculiar feature of Volksturnen since the days of Jahn, and many of the machines used in this class of exercises were devised by Jahn and his early followers. Such are the parallel bars, the horizontal bar, the horse, and the buck. Only the most proficient members of a verein are allowed to represent it in the *Musterriegenturnen*. At Frankfort, in 1880, sixty-one classes, or squads, were entered under this head. At Dresden the number of classes entered was two hundred and seventy-six. Of these, one was from the United States, one from Belgium, one from Denmark, one from Hungary, and four were from Holland; the remaining 268 were from within the Turnerschaft. Of the 276 classes entered, 244, comprising 2,517 turners, turned and were reported upon by the judges. The number of turners in a class varied from four to sixty-four; the mean number was, however, nine. The extremes of age were sixteen and seventy-one years. An unusual number of men past middle life took part in the heavy gymnastics. There were fully a dozen classes composed of men over forty years old, and nearly three hundred men over thirty-five years of age appeared in the ranks of the "proficients." The class of the "Eldest turners," numbering eleven men between the ages of sixty and seventy-one, engaged in free movements, putting the stone, and high leaping; while several squads of younger veterans, ranging in age from forty to sixty, exercised on the parallel bars, the horse, and the inclined ladder. Yet there are those who would have us believe that agility and bodily force in adults are the almost sole possession of the modern Englishman! If they would take the trouble to inform themselves in regard to the national games of the Germans, the Norsemen, and the Swiss, they would learn that the athletic vesture of the ancient Greeks has not all fallen to the lot of the British.

Each class was allowed twenty minutes for exercise, and machines enough were provided for twenty classes to exercise at a time. It was the duty of the judges to note and report upon the number, age, and general appearance of the class members; upon their carriage, marching, and clothing, as well as upon the worth and character of the exercises chosen by them and the degree of their proficiency in the exercises. The ability of the foreturner and his use of technical terms (*Turnsprache*; this has attained the proportion of a special dialect) were also items for note and comment.

The scale of marks for the actual turning ranged from 5, extremely good, through 3, barely good, to 0, bad. Of the 244 classes reported on, the rating of the judges was as follows:

18 classes were marked 5.
10 classes were marked 4 to 5.
70 classes were marked 4.
23 classes were marked 3 to 4.
87 classes were marked 3.
18 classes were marked 2 to 3.
13 classes were marked 2.
1 class was marked 1.

In the case of four classes the report was incomplete.

Some notion of the kind of exercises chosen may be gained from the following statement:

115 classes turned with the parallel bars.
51 classes turned with the horizontal bar.
51 classes turned with the horse.
1 class turned with the buck.
3 classes turned with the buck and horse.
2 classes turned with the buck and horizontal bar.
6 classes turned with the flying rings.
2 classes turned with the jumping table.
1 class turned with the ladder.
5 classes engaged in wand exercises.
1 class engaged in free exercises.
2 classes engaged in wrestling.
1 class engaged in club swinging.
1 class engaged in disk throwing.
1 class engaged in casting weights.
1 class engaged in marching figures.

Outside of the class of professional acrobats and of the ranks of the Turnerbund it would be difficult, if not impossible, to find in the United States more than a handful of men who could compare in strength, agility, grace, and bodily self-control, with even the average member of the Musterriegen of the Turnerschaft. The reason for this is not far to seek. Those who affect gymnastics in America, whether for recreation or training, are, as a rule, ill-taught or not taught at all; while in Germany good teaching is general and highly appreciated.

The Prize Turning, or "Wettturnen."

The prizes for individual excellence in heavy gymnastics consisted simply of wreaths of artificial oak leaves and diplomas. Out of six hundred persons whose names were entered in the lists of competitors, only three hundred and seventy-eight put in an appearance. In 1880, at Frankfort, only one hundred and thirty out of a list of one thousand entries actually competed for the prizes. Of the three hundred and seventy-eight above mentioned, sixty-four withdrew before the completion of the competition, mostly on account of blistered hands or some other slight ailment. Of the three hundred and fourteen turners who made a complete record, thirty-six were adjudged victors, having scored at least fifty points out of a possible total of seventy-five points. Two of the victors were from the United States. All the victors received wreaths and diplomas. Under the rules, only the first eighteen were entitled to wreaths, but on account of the exceptional difficulty of the exercises the judges awarded wreaths to the second eighteen also. The best record made was sixty-one and one-eighth points. Each of the prize turners was required to execute three exercises on the horizontal bar, three on the parallel bars, and three on the horse. Two exercises on each of these machines had previously been ordained by the committee of the Turnerschaft; the third in each was left to the individual choice of the competitors. Each competitor was also required to try his skill in three selected "national games." Those selected by the committee for this occasion were high jumping, long jumping, and weight lifting.

The highest attainable mark in each of the nine "machine exercises" was five, and in each of the national games ten. Two of the victors scored five on the horizontal bar; seven scored five on the parallel bars; but none scored more than four and seven-eighths on the horse. One of the victors scored ten in high jumping, three scored the same number for long jumping, and ten scored ten in the weight lifting.

The victors did not seem to be men of phenomenal muscular development, though it should be said that the turner costume of loose jacket and trousers is not calculated to set off the figure to the best advantage. They did, however, exhibit an astonishing power of executing difficult and pleasing feats—feats which called for a combination of strength, dexterous agility, prolonged endurance, close attention, purposeful daring, and cool judgment. They illustrated most admirably the truth of the poet's lines:—

> It is not growing like a tree
> In bulk, doth make man better be.

The qualities which make "the better man" among athletes and gymnasts are moral and mental, rather than muscular, in their nature. Muscular action, unless it be altogether abnormal, cannot be dissociated from mental and nervous action. Precise and purposeful movements of the trunk and limbs involve the possession of an intelligent and educated nervous system. From the failure of parents and teachers to apprehend this fact, it has come to pass that the average man can control and use only fractional parts of his muscular system. The German turner's aim is to make his entire body the ready servant of his will, and every Turnfest demonstrates the fact that he has achieved an encouraging measure of success.

Sword play and wrestling were minor attractions of the festival. Under the former head were included contests with the foils, the *Schläger*, or straight sword, such as is used in the ordinary students' duel, and the saber. Such contests were included in the programme of a general festival of the Turnerschaft for the first time at Dresden. Twenty-eight men fought with the foils, fourteen men with the schläger, and twenty men with the saber. Only thirty-two men engaged in the contests in wrestling. Only such turners as had completed the twelve exercises ordained for the prize turning were eligible to take part in the wrestling.

On Wednesday the Festplatz, from 10 A.M. till noon, was given up to the games of the Dresden school children. There exists a general but erroneous opinion among foreigners that German children do not play, though the history of the kindergarten system and of school turning affords abundant evidence to the contrary. Not only have the Germans a great variety of national games for children and youth, but in many cases they have made vigorous efforts to introduce and acclimatize foreign games, like cricket and foot ball. Base ball and lacrosse are apparently unknown to them. In some cities, and notably in Berlin, Dresden, and Frankfort, special efforts

PHYSICAL TRAINING IN AMERICAN COLLEGES. 169

are made by the school authorities and various private associations to secure public play-grounds for the children of all classes, and much has been accomplished in this direction. No one could witness the play of 1,600 school girls and 1,200 school boys, under the lead of their teachers, on the Dresden Festplatz, and deny that German children are gamesome as well as tractable. The girls played at catch, running races, ball, skipping rope, etc., and the boys engaged in foot ball, bat and ball, tug of war, and the like. As a rule, the German school and city authorities provide more generously and intelligently for the recreation of the children under their charge than is the case in Great Britain or America.

SCHOOL GYMNASTICS.

We pass to a consideration of the salient facts regarding the development and present organization of school gymnastics (*Schulturnen*) in Germany, particularly in Prussia. The essential differences between Volksturnen and Schulturnen are based on the fact that the former is a free art, originating with and maintained by the common people, and the latter is a discipline imposed by authority upon persons in a state of pupilage. The ends of training and education are not lost sight of in Volksturnen, but in Schulturnen they occupy the foreground.

Although Volksturnen has lost many of the extravagant and marked peculiarities of its assertive and aggressive youth, and has become better regulated and systematized with the lapse of years, it still bears the impress set upon it by Jahn and the times which produced him. The democratic organization of the turnvereine; the voluntary submission of the turners to taxation, drill, and discipline, for common and patriotic ends, and the predilection for heavy gymnastics under foreturners, all survive. The turners are men and youths who devote a portion of their spare time, particularly during the evening hours and on holidays, to the exercises of the turnplatz and the turnhalle, for the sake of social entertainment and the promotion of health. Schulturnen, on the other hand, is a department of instruction in the educational system ordained by the state. As such, it is administered by officers of the state, who aim, by means of a graded, progressive series of bodily exercises, to bring about the symmetrical and normal development of pupils of both sexes, ranging between the ages of six and twenty.

School turning works in the interest of folk turning by preparing promising recruits for the turnvereine, and the turners have ever been its zealous friends, doing much to secure its spread and to enhance its usefulness.

The Work and Influence of Spiess.

It is chiefly to Adolf Spiess and his followers that German Schulturnen owes its most distinctive and valuable peculiarities. Spiess was a Hessian, born in 1810. Like Jahn, he was a pastor's son and a teacher. In his father's private school, which was conducted according to the principles of Pestalozzi, he was trained in gymnastics, partly after the methods of Guts Muths and partly after those of Jahn. While a student of theology at the universities of Giessen and Halle, he was an active turner and duelist. In 1829 he became acquainted with Jahn. In the following year, while still a student, he formed a class of boys at Giessen, and made a beginning in teaching what came to be known as "common exercises" (*Gemeinübungen*), or class drill "in standing, walking, running, and jumping." "Class turning," consisting in the simultaneous performance by a number of persons, either with or without the aid of apparatus, of a given exercise at the word of command, was introduced by Spiess, and lies at the foundation of his system of physical training; whereas in the Jahn-Eiselen system the members of the class followed in succession the example set them by their foreturner.

In 1833 Spiess became a teacher of history, singing, drawing, and turning, in the public schools of Burgdorf, a town in the canton of Bern, in Switzerland, where he became intimate with Froebel. Spiess is sometimes called the "creator of gymnasties for girls" (*Mädchenturnen*). The exercises for girls which he introduced at Burgdorf were chiefly of his own devising. They included free gymnastics, dumb-bell exercises, and exercises on the suspended ladder and the see-saw, besides a variety of exercises in running, jumping, and swinging. In 1844 he removed to Basel to take charge of the gymnastic instruction in the higher schools of that city.

In 1848 Spiess returned to Germany, having been appointed to a high office in the department of education of the Grand Duchy of Hesse, and took up his residence in the city of Darmstadt. It devolved upon Spiess to organize and supervise school turning throughout that state. In 1849 and 1850 he conducted special normal classes for the purpose of preparing trained assistants for his work. At Darmstadt, as at Basel and Burgdorf, Spiess was highly successful in introducing gymnastics into schools for girls. He died in 1858.

Spiess based his theory of bodily training on the laws of anatomy and physiology, and grouped and ordered his exercises in compliance with those laws. He applied his principle of common exercises to the Jahn heavy gymnastics as well as to the free movements, which latter were often made to music. It was his distinctive work to render German gymnastics systematic and scientific, and to adapt them to pedagogical purposes and methods. As a teacher, organizer, and writer, his influence has been wide and **weighty**. His principal books were "*Lehre der Turnkunst*," Basel, 1840–'46, and "*Turnbuch für Schulen*," Basel, 1846–'51.

The Rise of School Gymnastics in Prussia.

Allusion has already been made to the cabinet order of June, 1842, in which Frederick William IV formally recommended the adoption of "bodily exercise as an indispensable integral part of male education" throughout the Kingdom of Prussia. Eichorn, the minister of education, by an ordinance issued in February, 1844, undertook to carry the King's recommendations into effect. This ordinance directed that a sufficient number of turnplätze and turnhallen should be established to furnish all the Gymnasien, higher burgher schools, and normal schools for males, with accommodations for winter and summer turning. Those in charge of school affairs were charged to do their utmost for the promotion of the new department of instruction. When it was feasible, pupils were to exercise daily for an hour after school. At least the afternoons of Wednesdays and Saturdays should be devoted to gymnastics, on which days no home study was to be exacted. In the "certificate of ripeness," given at the "leaving examination," the examiner must indicate the degree of gymnastic ability attained by the candidate.

Spiess had an interview with Eichorn in Berlin, in the summer of 1842, in relation to the proper mode of organizing school gymnastics, and there seems to have been a somewhat general expectation that he would be called from Burgdorf to Berlin. Spiess was, however, passed by, and Massmann, who had since 1827 been engaged in teaching gymnastics in Munich, where the sons of Ludwig I, King of Bavaria, and the royal corps of cadets were numbered among his pupils, was in 1843 called to Berlin to aid Eichorn's department in carrying into effect the views expressed in the King's cabinet order.

Massmann had been a Berlin turner in the palmy days of 1811–'13, and was strongly wedded to the methods of Jahn and Eiselen. He looked with disfavor upon the new methods of Spiess, and, not being endowed with sufficient skill or energy to adapt Volksturnen to school needs, his administration, which lasted until 1850, was, on the whole, a failure.

A serious obstacle to the success of gymnastics in the schools was the lack of competent teachers. To meet this want the Central Normal School for Training Teachers of Bodily Exercises was opened in Berlin, under Massmann's direction, in 1848. The school died in 1849. In 1851 the Royal Central Gymnastic Institute, with particular courses of instruction for officers of the army and school teachers, was established in Berlin under the conjoint control of the ministers of war and education, and Capt.

H. Rothstein, of the Prussian army, was placed at its head. This institute has exercised a powerful influence upon the rise of military and school turning in Prussia. Its dual constitution remained unchanged until the year 1877; since then two separate training schools have been in operation; the one for army officers is entitled the *Königliche Militärturnanstalt;* the other, for teachers of turning in the schools, is termed the *Königliche Turnlehrerbildungsanstalt.*

Rothstein was a firm partisan of the Swedish system of gymnastics as developed by Ling and his followers, while the civilian teachers of the Central Institute either favored the Jahn-Eiselen system or a compromise between it and that of Spiess. Rothstein banished the horizontal and parallel bars from the institute, thereby giving rise to a long and bitter controversy. The turners and their champions attacked the Swedish gymnastics on the ground that they were too formal, one-sided, and uninteresting, as well as un-German and outlandish. Medical men and university professors took an active part in the discussion over the merits and faults of the "bar exercises." Professors Virchow and Du Bois-Reymond, of the Berlin University, stood up for German gymnastics and the "bars." Finally, in December, 1862, a commission, composed of the most eminent medical men in Prussia, declared that "the bar exercises might, from a medical point of view, be improved, but ought not to be done away with." The triumph of the "bar exercises" involved the defeat of the Ling-Rothstein system of school turning. In 1863 Rothstein left the Central Institute; in 1865 he died.

In 1860 Lehnert, then minister of education, issued an order for the gradual introduction of gymnastic instruction into the elementary schools (*Volksschulen*) for boys. In 1862 attendance upon such instruction was made obligatory. In recent years turning has become quite general in girls' schools of all grades. It is obligatory in female normal schools, and also in all the girls' schools of some cities, for example, those of Berlin, Frankfort-on-the-Main, and Hanover.

THE ORGANIZATION SCHOOLS AND ARMY.

Popular education in the German sense involves compulsory attendance upon school instruction and compulsory military service.[1] Speaking broadly, the state requires every Prussian child to go to school for eight years, and every Prussian man to serve twelve years in the army. In order to render clear the relation which physical training bears to school training on the one hand, and to military training on the other, in the Prussian system of education, we must first give some account of the organization of the Prussian schools and army, and of the character of the instruction imparted in each.

The population of Prussia may be divided, for convenience, into three classes: (1) The *Volk*, which includes 90 per cent. of the whole, and embraces the peasant class and unskilled laborers of every sort; (2) the middle class, embracing the burgher class, the farmers, the smaller tradesmen and manufacturers, skilled mechanics, and a great variety of petty officials; (3) the scientifically educated or upper class. To this class belong the officers of the army, professors in the universities, teachers in the schools of superior instruction, literary men, the members of the learned professions, the great landowners, manufacturers and merchants, and officials in the higher grades of the civil service.

There are three grades of schools corresponding to the social classes above mentioned: (1) The elementary schools (*Volksschulen*); (2) the intermediate schools (*Mittelschulen*), including the so-called "burgher schools" and the lower *Realschulen*; (3) the higher schools, including the *Gymnasien*, *Realgymnasien*, the normal training schools, the technical schools, and the universities.

In the army the rank and file (*Soldaten*) are drawn from the *Volk*; the under-officers corresponding to our non-commissioned officers come mostly from the middle classes;

---

[1] Prussia pays annually not far from $37,000,000 for her schools and $50,000,000 for her army.

and the officers, who constitute the only professional military class, belong to the upper class, and are to a large degree of noble birth. Regimental schools are provided for the soldiers; schools of a higher sort for the under-officers; while the scientific training of the officer class is carried on in the cadet institutes, the war schools, and the War Academy.

The Schools.

The elementary schools in the larger cities and towns consist usually of eight classes, in which instruction is provided for children between the ages of six and fourteen. The complete course, which is not always enforced in the remoter country districts, embraces the following subjects: Religion, reading, writing, the common rules of arithmetic, the rudiments of algebra, the elements of geometry, history, drawing, geography, elementary physics and natural history, German composition and grammar, singing, and gymnastics. Girls are, in addition, taught sewing and knitting.

The intermediate schools have only a five or six years' course. They aim at giving a practical education, supplementary to that of the elementary schools, for pupils intending to follow technical, industrial, or mercantile pursuits, or who look forward to subordinate positions in the civil service. French and English are taught in these schools, but the ancient languages are not.

Both the Gymnasien and the Realgymnasien have a nine years' course, in classes designated in descending order: I. A., or *Oberprima;* I. B., or *Unterprima;* II. A., or *Obersecunda;* II. B., or *Untersecunda;* III. A., or *Obertertia;* III. B., or *Untertertia;* IV., or *Quarta;* V., or *Quinta;* and VI., or *Sexta.*

In the Gymnasien much attention is given to Greek and Latin, while French and English are less thoroughly taught. The Gymnasium graduates usually enter the university for the sake of preparing themselves to enter upon a career in one of the learned professions, or in one of the higher grades of the civil service.

The course of the Realgymnasien differs from that of the Gymnasien in that Greek is omitted, and that more stress is laid upon mathematics, natural sciences, and the modern languages. The graduates of a Realgymnasium are admitted to one only of the university faculties, that of philosophy, with its departments of natural science and modern languages. As a rule they pass to one of the higher technical schools instead of to the university.

The normal schools for teachers are of the nature of special technical schools having a three years' course. Preparatory schools (*Vorschulen*) with a three years' course have been organized in connection with many Gymnasien, Realgymnasien, and higher girls' schools, so that children of the upper classes need not mingle with the children of the Volk in the elementary schools.

The Army.

With few exceptions, the able-bodied men of all classes are liable to be called on for military service as soon as they reach the age of twenty and until they have attained the age of forty-two. The term of active service "with the colors" is three years, during which period the soldier is continuously subjected to military discipline, and is liable to be sent to the field in case of war. Then follow five years of service in the reserve, during which one is occasionally, and for some weeks at a time, called out for drill, or to take part in mobilization or the annual field maneuvers. Men in the reserve are liable to field duty, either at home or abroad, in case of war.

In the *Landwehr* the term of service is four years. Service with the colors for three years and in the reserve for five is considered sufficient to make a trained soldier of a man, so that members of the Landwehr in time of peace are released from active military duty of any kind. They are, however, organized into regiments, and must keep their arms and accouterments in readiness for instant service. The Landwehr is officered mostly by men from the middle classes. In time of war the Landwehr garrisons the forts, guards the frontier and the prisoners captured from the enemy, and covers the lines of communication between the base of supplies and the field army. The *Landsturm*, composed of men between thirty-two and forty-two years of age, is only called out for purposes of defense and in case of great need.

The German Empire can muster 1,300,000 trained soldiers, excluding the Landsturm, of the different states. The Prussian army, on a peace footing, numbers more than 330,000 men and under-officers, and 14,000 officers. It can be mobilized for field service in a week.

A soldier who becomes incapacitated after eight years' service for further active service, or who has been for eighteen years in active service, may demand a certificate recommending him for such a place in the civil service as his education may fit him for. Accordingly schools for the further instruction of soldiers in reading, writing, grammar, geography, arithmetic, history, and drawing, are organized in every regiment. Six special schools for the higher training of under-officers are also maintained by the War Department. The same studies as those pursued in the regimental schools, and certain other special subjects, are taught in the under-officer schools; but the subjects are pursued farther. A soldier with a good record, if he is intelligent enough to pass the examination for promotion to the grade of under-officer at the end of twelve years' service, *i. e.*, at the expiration of his service in the Landwehr, becomes eligible, is, indeed, a sort of preferred aspirant, for a subordinate post in the civil service. Such positions are those of janitor, messenger, clerk, etc., in various governmental bureaus which pertain to postal, customs, telegraph, and railroad affairs. If an under-officer possess the necessary qualifications, after nine years' service in the army and at least five years' service as an under-officer, he may be appointed a gendarme or become a policeman. Almost all the offices with which in America "the boys" are rewarded for yeoman service in "politics," are in Prussia given as rewards of merit and intelligence to old soldiers.

The Training of Officers.

The ordinary course of procedure by which a civil aspirant attains to the lowest grade in the corps of Prussian officers, that of second lieutenant, is as follows: (1) He is nominated an *avantageur* by the colonel of some regiment; (2) he serves for six months in the ranks; (3) he passes the examination for promotion to the grade of "sword-knot ensign," the requirements of which examination are practically the same as those of the "leaving examination" at the completion of the course in a Gymnasium or Realgymnasium; (4) then, after ten months of professional study in a war school (*Kriegsschule*), he passes the "officers' examination"; (5) and in case the officers of the regiment to which he has been nominated vote favorably upon him, he is commissioned a second lieutenant by the King.

Perhaps a third of those who enter the corps of officers receive their preliminary education as members of the corps of cadets. Since 1877 the course of study in the cadet institutes has been the same as that followed in the Realgymnasien. There are six lower cadet institutes in Prussia, having five classes, viz: VI., V., IV., III. B., and III. A.; and one chief cadet institute, that at Lichterfelde, near Berlin, having classes which correspond to II. B., II. A., I. B., I. A., of a Realgymnasium, and an advanced class, the "*Selecta.*" For each class a year's work is laid out. Boys from ten to fifteen years are received in the lower cadet-schools. The corps of cadets is largely composed of the sons of officers. It numbers 2,088 members, 880 of whom are at Lichterfelde. All of the cadet institutes are organized with two boards of instructors, an academic board of civilians, and a military board of officers, and are subject to military regulations. The discipline is strictest in the chief institute.

A premium is put by the state on mental training, by allowing all who hold certificates of fitness to enter Obersecunda (II. A.) of a Gymnasium or Realgymnasium, to absolve their service with the colors by one year's volunteer and unpaid service. Fitness to enter Unterprima (I. B.) entitles one to stand the "sword-knot-ensign" examination on completing six months' service as "avantageur" in the ranks. The "certificate of ripeness," *i. e.*, of having completed satisfactorily the studies of Oberprima (I. A.), admits its possessor to the University or to the higher civil service positions, and exempts "avantageurs" from the "sword-knot-ensign" examination.

In the chief cadet institute, at Lichterfelde, when a boy is seventeen years of age and his bodily development is up to a certain standard, if he has passed II. A., *i. e.*, is ready to enter Unterprima, he may try the "sword-knot-ensign" examination. If he pass this examination he may (*a*) begin his service in the ranks and aspire to the officers' examination at the end of the required course of study in a war school; or (*b*) he may, if a very promising youth, be admitted to the Selecta; or (*c*), should he not aspire to an officer's career, he may enter the ranks as a volunteer for one year (*Einjährig-Freiwilliger*). Many cadets complete the course laid out for Unterprima (I. B.) in order to be eligible, should they ever leave the army, to positions in the higher grades of the civil service, which would otherwise be closed to them on the ground of insufficient education. Should he complete the year I. A. satisfactorily, a cadet may enter a war school at once, being then exempt from serving as an "avantageur," and from passing the "sword-knot-ensign" examination. If he pass the officers' examination, he may receive his commission from the King as second lieutenant without being voted on by the officers of a regiment. The cadet who goes successfully through the Selecta is not required to enter the ranks, or even to attend a war school, but is promoted directly from the corps of cadets to that of officers.

There were formerly nine war schools for the special preparation of civil aspirants for the officers' examination. Within recent years they have been consolidated to three. The ten-months' course of study in the war schools is of a strictly professional nature, such subjects as tactics, fortification, siege practice, and the like, being included in it. Concerning the physical training in the cadet and war schools we shall speak under the head of Military Turning.

The War Academy (*Kriegsakademie*) in Berlin is the central scientific school of the German army. At the most, only three hundred officers may attend its classes, each class in the three years' course being limited to one hundred members. Only officers who have served three full years with the troops, and are recommended by their colonels as men of exceptional energy, character, and intelligence, are allowed to attempt the severe entrance examination in mathematics, history, geography, military science, and the French language. Nine months of each year of the course are devoted to scientific instruction, which consists of lectures of the most advanced character given by civilian and military professors, while the remaining three months are yearly given up to practical studies in topographical engineering and general staff duty, and in familiarizing the student with other arms of the service than his own. The course at the War Academy is so severe, its examinations and practical tests so minute and searching, that only a very few, the "best of the best," are able to pass into the charmed circle of the general staff, under Field Marshal Von Moltke. The men composing the general staff of the Prussian army are the consummate flower of Prussian education. As a corps they are unrivaled, and the individuals are few anywhere who possess trained powers of mind and body in anything like so high a degree.

SCHOOL GYMNASTICS.

As regards physical training in the schools of Prussia, the case stands thus: Attendance upon instruction in turning is exacted of all unexcused pupils for two hours weekly in all schools for boys, and also, in some cities, in all schools for girls. As a rule, each school has its own turnhalle, and in very many cases its own turnplatz, furnished with appropriate gymnastic machines. Some cities, for instance, Frankfort-on-the-Main, provide special playgrounds and swimming baths for the use of school children.

While gymnastic drill is not universal in the public schools, it is very general. As might be expected, it is more common and better provided for in the cities than in the country. In 1882 only ten per cent. of the pupils in the higher schools for boys were excused from turning, and they were excused on the certificates of physicians that the exercise would be prejudicial to their health; only eighteen per cent. of this class of schools were obliged to discontinue turning in winter through having no proper turnhalle, and sixty per cent. of them possessed a turnhalle.

In the course of study each class has its special time for gymnastics, just as it has special hours set for arithmetic and reading, and in the majority of cases the instruction is given by one of the ordinary class teachers, and not by a special teacher of turning. The amount of time devoted to turning, singing, and drawing, is usually the same, viz, two hours weekly.

The exercises are carefully adapted to the age and sex of the pupils. The youngest pupils, from six to ten years old, engage in a great variety of simple games, easy, free movements, marching, jumping, and climbing exercises, and the fundamental exercises on the easier gymnastic machines. In free, light, and heavy gymnastics the exercises grow more complicated and difficult with the advancing age of the pupil. The expertness of the boys in the upper classes is often quite astonishing. In the Gymnasien and Realgymnasien fencing is taught in the upper classes. Pedestrian tours, skating parties, and excursions into the woods are frequently made under the lead of those who teach turning. The gymnastic course for girls comprises the ordinary free gymnastics; class gymnastics with "hand apparatus," such as dumbbells, wands, and skipping ropes; marching, dancing, and balancing exercises; various games of ball, easy jumping, swinging, and climbing; and a few of the simplest exercises on the parallel and horizontal bars. Singing, especially during the march and the minuet, is frequently engaged in during the hour given to gymnastic instruction.

In nearly every university, voluntary associations of students are formed to practice turning. The university masters of sword-play and riding are survivals from feudal times.

SCHOOL GYMNASTICS IN BERLIN.

In 1881 there were 4,815,974 children of school age in a total population of 27,250,000 in the Kingdom of Prussia. The number of teachers was over 61,000. The population of Berlin in 1880 was 1,122,330. The total number of pupils in schools of every kind in the city was more than 149,000, of whom not more than 25,000 were in private schools. In schools wholly maintained at the city's expense, there were 104,726 pupils. Of 70 turnanstalten, 9 were under royal patronage, including the *Militär-turnanstalt*, the *Turnlehrerbildungsanstalt*, and the gymnasia belonging to the Royal Asylum for the Blind and the Royal Institution for the Deaf and Dumb. Of the 62 turnhallen belonging to the city, 41 had turnplätze adjoining or near to them; 2 belonged to higher schools for girls; 11 belonged to higher schools for boys; and 48 belonged to schools of the grade of Volksschulen (termed in Berlin *Gemeindeschulen*); and 1 belonged to the Berlin Orphan Asylum. The city paid nearly $50,000 in 1880–'81 for the instruction given its school children in gymnastics, which sum is equal to about one twenty-third of its total expenditure for schools in that year.

In June, 1885, Berlin provided free-school instruction for some 143,000 children, which shows an increase of 10,000 over the corresponding class in 1884. On the same date the city had 148 Gemeindeschulen in operation, and buildings for 8 more in process of construction. The new school-houses are provided with turnhallen.

The present number of city turnhallen used for educational purposes in Berlin is 98. The largest of them is the *Städtische Turnhalle*, in the Prinzenstrasse. This was established in 1864; its cost was as follows: for land, including a turnplatz, 99,000 marks; building, 254,000 marks; apparatus, 18,000 marks; total, 371,000 marks, or $92,750. The building is of brick, and consists of two three-story wings and a one-story main hall. The wings contain residence flats for the use of the officials charged with the oversight and direction of school gymnastics. The main hall is 150 feet long, 75 feet wide, and 48 feet high, and easily accommodates 400 turners at a time. Adjoining it is a well-appointed turnplatz, with an area of more than half an acre, which is planted with shade trees. The City Turnhalle is open every day and evening, and is used at appointed times by several of the Berlin turnvereine, also by the association of Berlin teachers, the royal firemen, the normal classes for teachers of turning, and by eight of the city schools for school turning. In all, more than 13,000 persons exercise here weekly. The annual appropriation for its maintenance, exclusive of salaries, is between $2,500 and $3,000.

As a rule, the school gymnasia in Germany are separate and specially designed buildings, and not refitted rooms. As a class, the German gymnasia are not so luxuriously fitted or so architecturally imposing as many of the newer American college gymnasia, but they are admirably adapted to the teaching of free and class gymnastics of every description. As much as possible the apparatus is adjustable and portable. A plain, one-story, brick turnhalle, 60 by 33 feet and 15 to 20 feet high, can be built in Germany at a cost of $5,000, and well furnished with apparatus for $1,000.

The city of Frankfort-on-the-Main, which is about the size of Washington, D. C., spends yearly about $27,000 for the gymnastic instruction of its school children, some 18,000 in number. About one-third of this sum goes toward the furtherance of turnspiele. Boys and girls, unless excused on a physician's certificate, have two hours' weekly instruction in turning, and two hours weekly of compulsory play besides. The majority of the school children in Frankfort are also taught and practiced in swimming under the auspices of the city.

In this connection the following facts regarding the Volksschulen of Vienna may be of interest: In 1882-'83 Vienna, whose population in 1880 was 704,756, had 72,912 pupils in its 135 Volksschulen. Of this number 44,614 (20,047 of whom were girls) practiced turning under the guidance of 658 teachers. The city paid for the teaching of turning and the care of the turnhallen, in 1882-'83, a sum equal to $34,860, or one-twenty-ninth as much as its total ordinary expenditure for the Volksschulen.

THE TRAINING OF TEACHERS OF TURNING.

The teachers of gymnastics in Prussia, indeed throughout Germany, are specially trained for their duties. They are not, as is too often the case in England and America, retired drill sergeants, broken down athletes, or merely enthusiastic gymnasts. There are, it is said, more than 1,000 teachers in Berlin alone who are competent to give instruction in turning. According to the regulations now in force, in order to be installed as a teacher of turning in a Prussian school, one must first pass a satisfactory examination and secure a certificate of fitness; such certificates must be obtained at Berlin, and from one of two sources, viz., the *Königliche Turnlehrerbildungsanstalt*, or the *Turnlehrer Prüfungs Kommission*. The latter is simply an examining board, originally established in 1867, which holds examinations for male candidates annually in February, and for female candidates in the spring and autumn of each year.

The Turnlehrerbildungsanstalt holds two examinations yearly, one at the end of its winter course of instruction for male teachers, the other at the end of its spring and summer course for female teachers. Those who take the examinations set by the Kommission are mostly teachers who have attended courses in turning at a normal school, or have received special training in classes formed for the purpose by the educational authorities of one of the provincial cities; some are university students who look forward to a teacher's career.

At the examination held by the Kommission in November, 1884, 43 women passed; at that held in February, 1885, 39 men passed, 8 of whom were pronounced fit to teach swimming as well as turning; 83 women were passed at the examination in May, 1885. The number of males who completed the winter course of instruction at the Turnlehrerbildungsanstalt and secured the certificate of fitness to teach turning was 71, of whom 42 were passed also in swimming; while the number of women who were passed at the close of the course given in April, May, and June, 1885, was 82, of which number 28 took the course of instruction in swimming.

The examinations of the board of examiners of teachers of turning (*Turnlehrer Prüfungs Kommission*) are conducted by a board consisting of the principal teachers belonging to the Turnlehrerbildungsanstalt and other teachers of turning named by the Minister of Education. The board seldom exceeds five in the number of its members. The teacher of anatomy in the Bildungsanstalt takes part in the examination of male candidates, and a female teacher of turning is always a member of the board when women are examined. The candidates are of three classes: (*a*) Those who have already been found competent to be installed as teachers in the schools; (*b*) students who have completed five semesters at a university; (*c*) persons of sufficient age (twenty years in the case of men, eighteen years in that of women), not teachers, who have had a good school education.

The examinations are both theoretical and practical. The theoretical examinations are both written and oral. The written examination consists in the preparation, within a limited time and without the assistance of books or persons, of a thesis on such questions relating to school gymnastics as the examiners may select. The candidate is examined orally on his knowledge in relation to the most important points in the history of turning, particularly of school turning; in the literature and technical language of turning; on the kinds of exercise adapted to pupils of different ages and states of proficiency; on the principles involved in the construction and use of the various gymnastic appliances; on human anatomy, physiology, and hygiene, and their relation to gymnastics; and on the means of rendering first aid to the injured. In the practical examination the candidate is required to show what degree of expertness he possesses in the exercises made use of in school turning.

THE ROYAL INSTITUTE FOR TRAINING TEACHERS OF TURNING.

As has already been stated, this institution, known as the civil section of the Centralturnanstalt till 1877, dates from 1851. Since the separation of the military and civil sections in 1877, the latter has been known as the *Königliche Turnlehrerbildungsanstalt*. Prof. Dr. Carl Euler, who, though not the titular "director" of the Bildungsanstalt, actually directs its daily affairs, is a highly accomplished teacher, and one of the best known German writers on turning. He has occupied his present position as the chief normal teacher of turning in Prussia since the year 1860, when he was called from Schulpforta to take charge of the civil section of the Centralturnanstalt, of which Rothstein was then the head. The writer is deeply indebted to Professor Euler and his assistant, Oberlehrer Eckler, for many kindnesses and much valuable information concerning gymnastics in Berlin and Prussia. Messrs. Euler and Eckler not only conduct most of the theoretical courses in the Bildungsanstalt (with the exception of the course in anatomy and physiology, which is given by Dr. Hoffmann), but they are also charged with the inspection, as regards turning, of the schools in all the provinces of Prussia. The number of assistant teachers in the Bildungsanstalt varies with the number of pupils from year to year. In the winter course of 1883–'84, five male assistants were connected with the institute, and an equal number of female assistants gave practical instruction in the summer course of 1884. The winter course for men begins in October of each year, and lasts six months; the course for women begins at the close of the Easter vacation, and continues for three months.

Since 1879 the institute has occupied a building of its own at 229 Friedrichsstrasse. This building is a model one of its kind. It consists of a main building two stories high, with an L one story high. On the first floor there are, besides several reception rooms and the living rooms of the janitor, three rooms appropriately fitted for gymnastic exercises. One in the main building is for the use of girls and women, and is 65 feet long, 32.5 feet wide, and 17.8 feet high; another, for the use of school children belonging to the model classes, is 81.25 feet by 40.6 feet; and the third, for the use of males, is 91 feet by 47.7 feet. The principal rooms on the second floor in the main building are the waiting and cloak rooms, a large office, two lecture rooms, a museum containing a collection of models of a great variety of gymnastic appliances, and a library.

The examinations of the Turnlehrer Prüfungs Kommission are held in the rooms of the Bildungsanstalt.

Courses of lectures are given in anatomy, physiology, and dietetics; on first aid to the injured; on the history of bodily exercises and the science and methods of turning; and on the construction and use of apparatus. The practical instruction comprises lessons and practice in free gymnastics; exercises with "hand apparatus"—dumb bells, wands, and the like; exercises on the heavy gymnastic appliances; fencing and sword-play, and swimming. The pupils of the institute are required to conduct classes in gymnastics, under the supervision of their instructors, in several of the city schools. As might be expected, numerous systematic works in the form of handbooks and manuals on all branches of turning have been published.

The systems of school turning in the other states of the German Empire do not differ very widely or essentially from that in vogue in Prussia. Each of the principal states, too, maintains a Turnlehrerbildungsanstalt. There is one at Dresden, for the Kingdom of Saxony, which dates from 1850; that at Stuttgart, for the Kingdom of Würtemberg, was founded in 1862; that for the Grand Duchy of Baden, at Carlsruhe, was established in 1869; and the one at Munich, for the Kingdom of Bavaria, was opened in 1872.

MILITARY TURNING.

Gymnastic exercises constitute a considerable and important part of the preliminary training of officers in the cadet and war schools, and of the drill to which recruits and soldiers in the army are subjected. Military drill of the technical and special sort is not a prominent feature in the course of the six preparatory schools for cadets (*Voranstalten des Cadetten Corps*), whose pupils, from ten to fifteeen years of age, are arranged in five classes, corresponding to the classes Sexta to Tertia, inclusive, of a Realgymnasium. The boys of the lower classes have gymnastic instruction adapted to their age and strength, and are encouraged to engage in out-of-door sports, such as foot ball, tug of war, and snowballing, during their play hours. Only the boys in Unter- and Obertertia are allowed to drill with muskets. At Lichterfelde the eight hundred and eighty youths are organized as four battalions of infantry, and much attention is given to infantry drill and evolutions, target practice, gymnastics, fencing, and riding. The pupils in the war schools are also thoroughly drilled in the above-mentioned branches of physical training. Two hundred lieutenants are annually trained as leaders of military turning at the *Königliche Militärturnanstalt* in Berlin.

Gymnastics are also taught in the *Militärreitinstitut* at Hanover. This institute includes a riding school for officers and a riding school for under-officers. The pupils in the former are lieutenants, and in the latter under-officers, who are mostly detailed from the Prussian cavalry, though a few are drawn from the field artillery. The number detailed annually to each school is eighty-three. The majority of these return to their regiments after a year's instruction, while the remainder, twenty-nine officers and twenty-eight under-officers, stay a second year at the institute.

The Militärturnanstalt.

The system of gymnastic instruction originally adopted as an essential factor in the training of the Prussian soldier was that of Ling. In 1845 General Von Boyen, the Minister of War, who had three years before joined his colleagues, Von Rochow, Minister of the Interior, and Eichorn, Minister of Education, in urging upon the King the views expressed in the epoch-making cabinet order, sent two officers, one of whom was Rothstein, to investigate the nature and working of the Swedish system of gymnastics, especially as regarded its military side. Rothstein and his companion repaired to Stockholm, went through the regular ten months' course of instruction in the Royal Central Gymnastic Institute, which had been in operation since 1814, and graduated as teachers of Ling's gymnastics. They then spent three months at Copenhagen in the Danish Royal Central Institute, whose date of establishment is 1806. They returned to Berlin in June, 1846, and early in 1847 the War Department adopted the main recommendations of their report by ordering the establishment of a Prussian central institute for the gymnastic instruction of the army. This institute was opened in Berlin October 1, 1847, with eighteen officers as pupils. The revolutionary outbreak of 1848 caused the suspension of the institute for three years. In 1851 the Königliche Centralturnanstalt, to which allusion has already been made, was opened in Berlin with Rothstein at its head.

Although Rothstein's opponents were able to defeat his efforts to supersede the Jahn-Eiselen and Spiess gymnastics, as regarded school gymnastics, the system of military gymnastics introduced by Rothstein was never fully abandoned by the War Department. In the Militärturnanstalt of to-day one does not find the horizontal bar or the parallel bars in use; and various pieces of gymnastic apparatus are still used there and throughout the army, which are seldom, if ever, used in Volksturnen or Schulturnen.

Two five-months' courses are annually given at the Militärturnanstalt. The number of officers enrolled at one time as pupils is usually one hundred. Lieutenaut-Colonel Von Dresky is at present the director of the institution. His assistants, including a medical officer who lectures on anatomy and physiology, are all army officers. Practical instruction is given in free gymnastics, heavy gymnastics, jumping, sword-play, bayonet exercise, and in what may be termed "applied military gymnastics" (*Hindernissturnen*), in which squad exercises in clearing ditches and scaling intrenchments, walls, and spiked fences, occupy a prominent place. The training given at the Militärturnanstalt is such that those officers who complete its course are thoroughly fitted, on returning to their regiments, to give practical instruction to their subordinates.

In the gymnastic drill of the troops, the under-officers play an important part; but they learn and perform their duties as teachers of gymnastics under officers who have had the benefit of the Berlin course. All officers of infantry are required to be familiar with the principles of military gymnastics, and the younger officers must be able to teach and practice them.

* *Peculiarities of Military Turning.*

The following statements, derived from the latest "*Vorschriften über das Turnen der Infanterie,*" may serve to indicate the salient features of military turning, at least so far as the infantry arm of the service, which includes more than 230,000 men and officers, is concerned:

Gymnastic exercises constitute an essential factor in the military training of the individual man. They should not only increase the strength, agility, and endurance of his body, but should strengthen his will power, resolution, self-confidence, and courage, and call forth a healthy spirit of emulation. In order to attain these ends, the soldier must be taught the natural, sure, and energetic use of his limbs by means of properly devised exercises. These exercises are divided into (*a*) free and weapon exercises, (*b*) exercises with gymnastic machines (*Rustübungen*), and (*c*) exercises in applied turning, by which are understood exercises to render soldiers able to surmount artificial or natural obstructions in the field.

Turning should be practiced by all the men from the beginning of their term of service, due regard being had to individual peculiarities and circumstances. During the entire term of service the free and weapon exercises are to be pursued as exercises for the promotion of the soldier's health. In the course of every hour devoted to gymnastics, all parts of the body are, so far as possible, to be brought equally into play. In judging of the excellence of the exercise, strength, dexterity, and the carriage and control of the body are to be considered, rather than the difficulty of the exercise. The performance of gymnastic tricks and feats is never to be considered the aim of the exercises.

The free movements are those which are performed without the aid of any apparatus. They lie at the foundation of the bodily training of the soldier, both as regards drill and gymnastics. They are the especial means for suppling the stiff joints of the raw recruit. The free movements are to be arranged in groups, so that head, arms, back, legs, and feet shall be exercised in equal measure. Exercise in the quick-step, 165 to 175 steps in the minute, are included in the free movements.

Weapon exercises (*Gewehrübungen*) are defined as exercises in which the musket is used for the further development of the soldier's strength. In these exercises the musket is used in something the same way that the staff or wand is used in light gymnastics. The exercises are of two sorts—with both hands and with one hand. In the one-hand exercises the left and the right hands must be equally taught.

The principal machines employed in the *Rustübungen* (which is a Ling-Rothstein word for the Geratübungen of the turners) are the horizontal beam; the spring-board; the cross-tree, or beam, which resembles the horizontal bar; the ladder-plank; the inclined ladder; the leaping-table; the vertical ropes and poles, for climbing.

In the applied military gymnastics the soldiers are taught to leap ditches and barriers, and to scale walls, fences, and stockades of various kinds. In these exercises the men carry their muskets and side arms, and are divided into larger and smaller squads, which are, of course, required to keep step and time as much as possible. These exercises are very useful, and by no means easy in some of their branches, yet it is astonishing to a civilian to witness the celerity, precision, and certainty, with which a squad of a dozen men will surmount a wall or a high, spiked fence, or cross a wide, deep ditch on a narrow, shaky bridge.

Rothstein, in his account of the Centralturnanstalt published in 1861, describes the "obstructed running track" (*Laufbahn mit Hindernissen*) in which the pupils of the institute were exercised in "applied gymnastics." The track was U-shaped, 195 paces long, and 18 feet broad. The obstructions were arranged in the following order: (1) A ditch 6 feet wide, for the running leap; (2) a mound of earth 3 feet high and 4 feet wide at the base, for the high jump; (3) a ditch 12 feet wide, for the long leap; (4) a mound 6 feet high and 10 feet wide at the base, on the edge of a ditch 12 feet wide, for the "deep leap"; (5) a board fence 5 feet high, to be vaulted over; (6) an "escalading stage," 12 feet high and 6 feet wide at the top, to be climbed by ladders, ropes, or poles, and jumped or dropped from; (7) a ditch 10 feet deep and 9 feet wide, with an escarpment wall rising 4 feet above the hither edge of the ditch, and bridged by a shaky beam; (8) a palisade 7 feet high, of sharpened planks; and (9) a glacis. A section of twelve men in three ranks of four files each, the men having muskets, side-arms, and knapsacks, usually made the entire course from end to end in three to three and a third minutes. Without weapons or knapsacks, four men, each doing his best to outstrip his fellows, usually covered the course in sixty to seventy seconds; while a few individuals were able to cover the course in forty-three to forty-five seconds.

The following extract from a circular on the teaching of gymnastics in the elementary schools, addressed to the superintendents and inspectors of schools in the district of Liegnitz, province of Silesia, in 1871, by the section for church and school affairs, may serve as an indication of the esteem in which turning is held by those most concerned with educational affairs:

It is acknowledged everywhere by soldiers and civilians that the astonishing accomplishments of our armies in the late war, especially their thorough discipline, exhibited in the most cheerful and self-sacrificing manner, their skill in overcoming natural and artificial obstacles in the enemy's country, their courage and calmness in battle, the resolution with which they bore pain and privation, must, in a large measure, be attributed to the gymnastic training of the rank and file.

As has been well said, "Hardly any army deserves better than the Prussian-German the name *Exercitus*." Prussia, in the interval between Jena and Sedan, demonstrated most clearly and strikingly the power and worth of comprehensive and scientific "training." Even the English are beginning to doubt the infallibility of the notion of which they have been so fond, "that you come to do a thing right by doing it, and not by first learning to do it right and then doing it." It is a conspicuous merit of the Prussian scheme of national education, that both in mental and physical training little or nothing is left to the rule of thumb.

It may fairly be doubted if any modern nation can vie with Prussia in ability to mobilize its strength; nor can it be doubted that her system of physical training has proven a very considerable factor in developing her power to transform her potential energy into work.

It is impossible that Prussian turning, reaching, as it does, nearly a fifth of the entire population of the kingdom, through the instrumentalities of the school, the army, and the Turnerschaft, should not exercise a powerful influence upon the national life and development.

A belief in the validity of Prussian methods has led to a more or less general and close imitation of them throughout Germany. And France has, since 1870, introduced gymnastic training into the plan of work ordained for its system of public schools.

If physical training should ever be pursued intelligently and systematically in the schools of any American State or city, many of the same problems with which the educational authorities in Germany, Switzerland, Sweden, and France, have been so deeply engaged, will inevitably present themselves. The writer is far from thinking that such problems can be satisfactorily solved by the attempted introduction of any unmodified foreign system of gymnastics or athletics. But he is firmly convinced that whoever may be impelled or called upon to attempt to provide an adequate remedy for the present lamentable neglect of physical training in American schools and colleges, can readily save money, time, and trouble, if they will but study the German system of turning; "for there can be no doubt," to borrow the words of Prof. Du Bois-Reymond, "that German turning, in its wise mingling of theory and practice, exhibits the happiest, yes, the most adequate solution of the great problem with which pedagogics has been busy since Rousseau, a truth which, after a short obscurity, is now hardly contested, but the physiological principle of which a few are beginning to understand."

THE NORTH AMERICAN TURNERBUND.

The largest association of turners in the world, outside of the Deutsche Turnerschaft, is that formed by the German gymnastic societies of the United States, under the name of the North American Gymnastic Union, or Turnerbund. The aims of the Turnerbund are most gloriously broad and general. The sole and simple end of its members is "to aid each other in rearing a people strong in both body and mind." As a means to the furtherance of this end, the framers of the platform and statutes of the Turnerbund, which were adopted at its national convention held at Davenport, Iowa, in 1884, pronounce in favor of "a thorough reform of social, religious, and political life."

The maxims and demands expressed in the declaration of principles of the Turnerbund are held "to form the programme for the realization of a system of pure popular sovereignty," under which "not only everything should be done for the people, but also by the people." This programme seems to us so fantastic, so impracticable, so entirely irrelevant to the legitimate purposes of a "gymnastic union," that we shall content ourselves with the bare mention of a very few of its main features, and confine our attention chiefly to the field of practical endeavor, in which the Turnerbund has achieved substantial and really commendable results.

The officers and members of the gymnastic union are "earnestly admonished" to make such propositions as follow, the subject "of special and thorough discussion"; "Senate and Presidency are but copies of monarchical institutions, being undemocratic and unrepublican, and should be abolished." The general convention of the gymnastic union recommends, "as proper means of relieving public distress and of ameliorating social conditions, the protection of labor against spoliation, and securing to it the real product thereof; sanitary protection of citizens; a prohibition of the abuse of employing the labor of children for industrial purposes; a cessation of all further land grants or sales to individuals and corporations; free instruction to everybody; a progressive income tax, and a legacy or succession duty or tax; abolition of all monopolies; a thorough reform of our judicial system; the abolition of all indirect taxation."

The practical aims of the Turnerbund are well set forth in sections 21 to 23, inclusive, of its statutes. They read as follows:

21. It is one of the chief aims of the gymnastic societies, and of the gymnastic union, to labor for the introduction of systematic gymnastic training into the existing schools, since such training is indispensable to the thorough education of the young.

22. It is therefore obligatory upon the gymnastic societies to see that their gymnastic exercises are conducted according to rational principles, and to take special care to employ only such persons as teachers of gymnastics, supervisors of exercises (Turnwarte), and leaders of practice sections (Vorturner) as are thoroughly qualified to understand and teach gymnastics in harmony with those principles.

It is furthermore the duty of the societies to labor in their own sphere for the establishment and perfection of good German-English schools, in which music, singing, drawing, and gymnastics receive full attention, and to work in favor of compulsory school attendance; and lastly to take pains to have the German language taught in the public schools.

23. It is obligatory upon the societies to provide for the further education of their members by arranging for instructive addresses, lectures, or discussions once a month; and such topics chiefly shall be selected for this purpose as relate to the resolutions or principles of the gymnastic union.

In January, 1885, the North American Turnerbund consisted of 213 vereine, with a total membership of 21,800, an increase of 2,096 over the previous year. In the Turnschulen of the Bund, 12,223 boys and 4,005 girls received instruction in gymnastics during the year 1884–'85. The Turnschulen, which are maintained by the turnvereine, have come very generally into vogue within the last ten years. They have been established for the purpose of securing to the children of German and German-American parents instruction in the German language and literature, as well as in the ordinary branches of a common school education and gymnastics. Very frequently the children attend a public school and a Turnschule at the same time, the session of the latter being held after the completion of the daily session of the public school. The gymnastic societies in many of the larger cities, like New York, Chicago, Saint Louis, Milwaukee, and San Francisco, have dramatic, musical, and art sections. The New York Turnverein, for instance, supports an evening art school, with classes in drawing and modeling.

The Turnerbund owned property worth $2,409,375 in 1885. This represented a total indebtedness of only $840,427. Its Turnhallen (gymnasia) numbered 140, an increase of 13 over the previous year. Its trained and salaried teachers of gymnastics numbered 98.

The teachers of gymnastics receive their special professional training in the *Turnlehrer Seminar*. The gymnastic aims and methods of the Turnerbund and its teachers are closely modeled after those which obtain in Germany. The Turnlehrer Seminar is, in the writer's opinion, the best normal school for teachers of gymnastics in the United States. It has for some years had its headquarters at Milwaukee, Wis., and been under the charge of Director G. Brosius. It was formerly located in Chicago, and still earlier in New York.

It is interesting to note that a grandson of "Father Jahn" is one of the eighteen pupils who constitute this year's class at the Milwaukee Seminar. Jahn's son has lived in poverty and obscurity for many years in Baltimore, Md. He receives an annual stipend from the Turnerbund, which has adopted his son, the youth above referred to, as its foster child.

The course of instruction given in Milwaukee approximates, on the whole, so nearly in character to that of the Turnlehrerbildungsanstalt in Berlin that it is unnecessary to characterize it further. Graduates of the Seminar are now required to speak and read English.

Thus far the Turnerbund has made but little progress toward bringing about the introduction of gymnastic instruction into the public schools. Meager results, not worth mentioning in comparison with what may be observed in almost any German city, have been attained in the cities of Milwaukee, Saint Louis, and Cleveland, where feeble experiments in giving instruction in calisthenics have been made.

It is nearly a year since the committee on course of study and school books of the board of education of the city of New York voted in favor of testing a plan, which emanated from the Turnerbund, for the introduction of gymnastic training into the public schools of that city. It was voted to furnish three schools with gymnastic appliances at a cost not exceeding $94 for each school, and that "an instructor be employed, at a salary of not more than $50 per month, to take charge of these schools for one year, under the direction of the city superintendent as to time, etc." As it was found that the committee had no right to vote an appropriation, physical training in the New York public schools remains in the same unsatisfactory condition in which it was before the vote was passed.

No city or town can secure physical training to its school children unless it provide gymnasia and specially trained and well-paid teachers. A salary of $50 per month, we need hardly add, will not secure competent teachers of gymnastics; and without competent teachers gymnasia are useless, or worse than useless.

The Turnerbund owns more gymnasia than do all the colleges of the country taken together, and its corps of teachers of gymnastics is made up of the best the country affords; yet the aims, methods, and achievements of the Turnerbund are almost unknown to the mass of men and women engaged in the education of American children. One would think from the utterances of some of the prophets and disciples of "physical culture" that the field of bodily education was white for the harvest. Such facts as those above cited seem to us to indicate that the field is only here and there ready for the sowing of seed.

711

www.ingramcontent.com/pod-product-compliance
Lightning Source LLC
Chambersburg PA
CBHW020909230426
43666CB00008B/1382